Palgrave Series in Contemporary Korean Studies

Series Editors
Hyeong-ki Kwon
Department of Political Science
Seoul National University
Seoul, Korea (Republic of)

Song Chong Lee
Department of Religious Studies
Seoul National University
Seoul, Korea (Republic of)

Building on the current cultural momentum of interest in contemporary Korea and growing scholarly interest, this book series aims to refresh, update, and, where necessary, redirect the discourse in Korean Studies. The focus is on contemporary issues and concerns, organized around seven major thematic areas, with more to be added later: 1) Value and Identity (religion and society), 2) Politics and Economy, 3) K-Future (philosophy), 4) K-Narratives (literature), 5) Modernity and Development, 6) Contemporary K-Music, and 7) Hallyu (Korean Wave). This project is initiated by Seoul National University to help shape global discussions about Korea. The goal is to advance contemporary Korean studies with global networks of scholars.

Hyeong-ki Kwon
Editor

Korean Political Economy from a Comparative-Historical Perspective

palgrave
macmillan

Editor
Hyeong-ki Kwon
Seoul National University
Seoul, Korea

ISSN 3059-3549 ISSN 3059-3557 (electronic)
Palgrave Series in Contemporary Korean Studies
ISBN 978-981-95-9784-0 ISBN 978-981-95-9785-7 (eBook)
https://doi.org/10.1007/978-981-95-9785-7

This Palgrave Macmillan imprint is published by the registered company Springer Nature Singapore Pte Ltd.
The registered company address is: 152 Beach Road, #21-01/04 Gateway East, Singapore 189721, Singapore

Contents

Notes on Contributors

Sea-Jin Chang is a Lim Kim San Chair Professor of Business Administration at the National University of Singapore. He received his BA and MA in Economics from Seoul National University and Ph.D. in Strategic Management from the Wharton School, University of Pennsylvania. He was previously a faculty member at the Stern School, New York University and Korea University, Korea Advanced Institute of Science and Technology (KAIST), and also had visiting appointments at Stanford, INSEAD, London Business School, and Hitotsubashi University. He is a Fellow of the Strategic Management Society and of the Academy of International Business.

Professor Chang is primarily interested in the management of diversified multinational firms. His book *Sony vs. Samsung: The Inside Story of the Electronics' Giants Battle for Global Supremacy* (Wiley, 2008) compares and contrasts these two firms' global strategy. His other books include *The Rise and Fall of Chaebols: Financial Crisis and Transformation of Korean Business Groups* (Cambridge, 2003) and *Business Groups in East Asia: Crisis, Restructuring and New Growth* (Oxford, 2006), and *Multinationals in China: Entry Strategies, Competition, and Performance* (Oxford, 2013). He previously served as an Area Editor of the *Journal of International Business Studies* and an Associate Editor of the *Strategic Management Journal.*

Yin-wah Chu was Professor of Sociology, teaching at the Hong Kong Baptist University before her retirement. Her research interests include the political economy of development in China, South Korea, and Taiwan, social and political movements, as well as socio-economic inequalities in these societies. Her research articles have been published with *Asian Perspective*, *Asian Survey*, *Cities*, *Critique Internationale*, *Economy & Society*, *International Journal of Urban and Regional Research*, *Japanese Journal of Political Science*, *Journal of Contemporary Asia*, *Review of International Political Economy*, *Urban Studies*, among others. She is the editor of *Chinese Capitalisms* (Palgrave Macmillan, 2010), *The Asian Developmental State* (Palgrave Macmillan, 2016), co-editor of *East Asia's New Democracies* (Routledge, 2010, co-edited with Siu-lun Wong), and co-author of *The Global Rise of China* (Polity, 2016, co-authored with Alvin Y. So). She is currently completing an RGC-funded research on inequality and precarity in four East Asian societies. Email: ywchu@hkbu.associate.edu.hk; yinw.chu@gmail.com.

Stephan Haggard is a Distinguished Research Professor at the School of Global Policy and Strategy in the University of California San Diego, and Research Director for Democracy and Global Governance at the Institute on Global Conflict and Cooperation. He has written widely on the political economy and international relations of East Asia including *Pathways from the Periphery: The Newly Industrializing Countries in the International System* (1990); *The Political Economy of the Asian Financial Crisis* (2000); *From Silicon Valley to Singapore* (with David McKendrick and Richard Doner, 2000); and *Developmental States* (2018). His work on North Korea with Marcus Noland includes *Famine in North Korea* (2007), *Witness to Transformation: Refugee Insights into North Korea* (2011), and *Hard Target: Sanctions, Engagement and the Case of North Korea* (2017). His current research centers on reversion from democratic rule (with Robert Kaufman, *Dictators and Democrats: Masses, Elites and Regime Change*, 2017, and *Backsliding: Democratic Regress in the Contemporary World*, 2021) and the consequences of the rise of illiberal regimes for global governance.

Yong-Chool Ha is Korea Foundation Professor at the Jackson School of International Studies, University of Washington and received his Ph.D. from the University of California, Berkeley. Before he moved to University of Washington in January 2008, professor Ha taught at the Department of International Relations, Seoul National University, where he served as chairman of the department, associate dean of the College of Social Sciences and chairman of the Unification Forum. He also served as president of Korean Association of International Studies. He has written and published extensively on Korean domestic and international relations, North Korean politics, and Soviet and Russian politics in English, Russian and Korean journals such as *Comparative Political Studies*, *Asian Survey* and *Cambridge Review of International Relations.* He led the trans-Siberian railroad research trip for the first time in Korea in 2000. He also visited Pyongyang, Kagesong and Keumgan Mountain in recent years and met with a number of North Korean "Saeteomin" (defectors) people. Recently, he initiated an international consortium for Northeast Asian community building with a particular focus on linking Siberia and the Far East to Northeast Asian economies. His research interests are community building and international relations theories, late industrialization and IR. Changing elite-mass relations in late industrializing countries. Currently, he is finishing a book on "Late Industrialization, the State and Social Change in a Comparative Perspective".

His recent publications include: *The Dynamics of Strong State* (SNU Press, 2006), *Late Industrialization, the State and Tradition: the Emergence of Neofamilism in Korea* (2007, CPS), *Colonial Social Change* (ed.) (U. of Washington Press, 2013), *The International Impact of the Colonial Rule in Korea* (UW Press, 2019), *Late Industrialization, Tradition and Social Change in South Korea* (UW Press, 2024).

Djun Kil Kim was a visiting research fellow at the Institute of Economic Research, Seoul National University from 2017 to 2025. He is the author of the 2005 book *The History of Korea*, which was published as a part of the Greenwood Histories of the Modern Nations series. A second edition was published in 2014. In October 2011, he was awarded the "Global Korea Award" by the Council on Korean Studies at Michigan State University. He taught and conducted research on Korean studies for more than a decade at Yonsei University, Sejong Institute, Chongju University, and Myongji University in Korea. He has also taught at Brigham Young University in the United States, Stockholm University in Sweden, and the University of Asia and the Pacific in the Philippines. Professor Kim also served in several key government positions within the Ministry of Culture and Information between 1977 and 1999. Prior to working in government, Professor Kim had an extensive journalistic career. From 1962 to 1977, he worked as a Seoul-based journalist for several major Korean newspapers, including *Chosun Ilbo*, *Seoul Shinmun*, and *Hankook Ilbo*. His assignments during that period included domestic politics, foreign affairs, urban issues, and culture. Professor Kim earned his bachelor's and master's degrees in Sociology from Seoul National University in 1962 and 1964, respectively

Kyung Mi Kim is a tenure-track researcher at the Italian Institute of Oriental Studies (ISO), Sapienza University of Rome. Dr. Kim's research areas include Korean political economy and history. After receiving a Ph.D. in Political Science at Seoul National University (SNU) in 2017, she worked for the Department of Political Science and International Relations at Ewha Womans University from 2017 to 2019 and the Philosophy, Politics, and Economics in Seoul National University from 2019 to 2024, and then joined to the ISO in Sapienza University of Rome from November 2024. Her main research interest is to trace the characteristics of the Korean political and economic system and its changes historically and comparatively. Dr. Kim's main work is the book, *The Korean Developmental State*, which was published in Palgrave Macmillan in 2020. She has also published several articles in international journals, including "The State's Role in Globalization: Korea's Experience from a Comparative Perspective" published in *Politics & Society* in 2017, and "Varieties of Globalisation and National Economy: Korea's Experience from a Comparative Perspective" published in *Journal of International Relations and Development* in 2021 with Professor Hyeong-ki Kwon.

Hyeong-ki Kwon is Professor of Political Science at Seoul National University. Since graduating from the University of Chicago in 2002, he has studied the changes in various governing regimes of advanced economies under globalization, including the U.S., Germany, Ireland, and Korea. His publications in comparative politics include *Openness and Coordination: National Economies of the U.S., Japan, and Germany in a Globalized World* (Palgrave Macmillan, 2024), *Changes by Competition: The Evolution of the South Korean Developmental State* (Oxford University Press, 2021), *Fairness and Division of Labor in Market Societies* (Berghahn Books, 2004) and articles in major journals including *Politics & Society*, *Theory and Society*, *Comparative Political Studies*, *Comparative European Politics*, *Contemporary Politics*, and *Economic and Industrial Democracy*.

Keun Lee is a Distinguished Professor of Chung-Ang Univerisity and Seoul National University (emeritus), a Fellow of the CIFAR (Canada), the Honorary President of the Korean Economic Association, and the chairman of the Center for Economic Catch-up. He is also an editor of *Research Policy* and an associate editor of *Industrial and Corporate China*.

He is the winner of the 2014 Schumpeter Prize for his monograph on *Schumpeterian Analysis of Economic Catch-up* (2013, Cambridge Univ. Press) and also the 2019 Kapp Prize by European Association of Evolutionary Political Economy (EAEPE). He is also awarded the title of Eurasian Business and Economics Society (EBES) Fellow of the Year 2023 by the EBES. He write regularly for Project Syndicate. Previously, he served as the Vice-chairman of the National Economic Advisory Council for the chair and President of Korea, also as the President of the International Schumpeter Society (2016–18), as a member of the Committee for Development Policy of UN (2013–18), and as a Global Future Council (GFC) member of the World Economic Forum (2016–19). He obtained Ph.D. in Economics from the University of California, Berkeley. His total citations received is about 20,000 with H-index of 63 and I-10 index of 175 (Google Scholar).

Jaeyong Song is AMOREPACIFIC Professor of Strategy and International Management at Seoul National University. He was elected as a Fellow of the Academy of International Business. He served as the Chair of the International Management Division, Academy of Management and an editor of *Journal of International Business Studies* (JIBS). He received his Ph.D. at Wharton and was a professor at Columbia. His papers were published in *Management Science*, *Harvard Business Review*, *Strategic Management Journal*, *Organization Science*, *JIBS*, *Research Policy*, *Journal of Management* and *California Management Review*.

Elizabeth Thurbon is Professor of International Political Economy and Deputy Head of School and Director of Research in the School of Social Sciences, Faculty of Arts, Design and Architecture (ADA) at UNSW Sydney. She is also the Director of the Green Energy Statecraft Project. She has previously held an Asia Society Australia-Korea Fellowship (2021–2022) and a UNSW Scientia Fellowship (2019–2022), as well as Visiting Fellowships at Seoul National University (as a Korea Foundation Fellow) and China Foreign Affairs University. Elizabeth's research examines the state and its strategic role in the process of national techno-industrial development, adaptation, and transformation. Her most significant contributions to the field examine varieties of economic statecraft, the rise and transformation of East Asia's developmental states, the state's strategic role in the clean energy shift, and the political economy of international trade and investment agreements, with a particular focus on the impact of these agreements on states' policy 'room to move'. She has written widely on these topics for academic and popular audiences.

List of Figures

List of Tables

CHAPTER 1

Introduction to South Korean Political Economy

Hyeong-ki Kwon

South Korea's successful political-economic development, from one of the poorest countries to one of the most advanced democracies, has attracted international attention from both policy-makers and political economists. In the early 1960s, when Korea began industrialization in earnest, it was an underdeveloped and authoritarian country. But in the 2020s, Korea has entered the ranks of the world's strongest economies. It has become one of the world's most digitalized societies, and has developed a stable democracy.

The Korean economy has grown more rapidly than any other nation-states, as seen in Fig. 1.1. To measure how well the Korean economy performed, we use percentile ranks of GDP per capita as noted in Fig. 1.1, rather than absolute ranking of GDP per capita, which does not indicate

H.-k. Kwon (✉)
Seoul National University, Seoul, South Korea
e-mail: kwonhk@snu.ac.kr

H.-k. Kwon (ed.), *Korean Political Economy from a Comparative-Historical Perspective*, Palgrave Series in Contemporary Korean Studies, https://doi.org/10.1007/978-981-95-9785-7_1

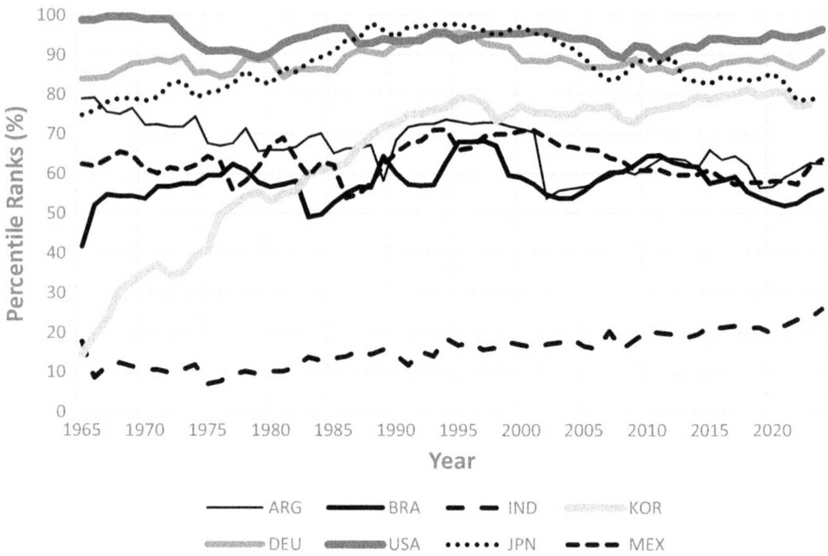

Fig. 1.1 Trends of percentile ranks of GDP per capita

its relative performance.[1] In Fig. 1.1 the percentile growth of the Korean economy in GDP per capita is striking, from one of the lowest ranking

[1] GDP per capita is normally used to measure how well a country has performed economically, especially to measure a country's relative performance in comparison to other countries. But absolute ranking of GDP per capita does not capture relative performance. For example, the 5th highest score among 10 examinees is different from 5th highest score among 100 examinees. To remedy this problem we use percentile rankings. The percentile rank of a raw score is interpreted as the percentage of examinees in the norm group who scored at or below the score of interest. The mathematical formula is

$$\frac{Fb + 0.5 * Fa}{N} * 100\%$$

where *Fb* (frequency below) is the frequency of all scores below the score of interest, *Fa* (frequency at) is the frequency of the score of interest, and *N* is the number of examinees in the sample. For example, when there is only one 5th highest score, 5th highest score among 10 examinees is calculated as 55 percent, and 5th highest score among 100 examinees as 95.5 percent. Now that percentile ranks can be a consistent measure irrespective of examinees' size (total number of countries), percentile ranks can keep track of relative economic performances of a country over a span of years. For a detailed account of the relative performance, see Kwon (2021), pp. 41–43. I gratefully acknowledge my friend Jaehong Yi for this idea.

worldwide, at 14.4 percent in 1965, to one of the highest, around 80.6 percent in 2021. In contrast to other countries' performance: India remained among the lower ranking groups, from 8.6 percent in 1966 to 21.7 percent in 2021, while Argentina and Mexico each declined, from 78.9 percent in 1965 to 59.0 percent in 2021, and from 62.3 percent in 1965 to 58.1 percent in 2021, respectively. Although Japan and Taiwan performed well, their growth is not as large as Korea's: Japan rose from 74.8 percent in 1965 to 78.6 percent in 2022. Germany and the United States stayed relatively in the highest-ranking group: Germany rising from 83.8 percent in 1965 to 86.7 percent in 2022; the U.S. moving from 98.7 percent in 1965 to 94.4 percent in 2022.

Korea attracts international attention not just for its rapid and successful political-economic development, but more importantly, for the way Korea has successfully developed its political economic system. Korean development has sparked significant theoretical debates among political economists. Scholars differ in accounting for why Korea has achieved such sustained economic success, from the 1960s to the 2020s.[2] Neoliberals and neoclassical economists emphasize Korea's liberalization and free market system for its economic success, while developmental statists underline the state's leading roles in developing its political economy. In accounting for Korea's economic success, neoclassical economic approaches gained ascendancy initially in the 1970s and 1980s.[3]

However, in the late 1980s and first half of the 1990s, developmental state (DS) theories proved more persuasive, mostly based on their empirical studies of the heyday 1970s. In contrast to neoclassical economists who emphasize free market policies as the cause of East Asian economic success, DS theorists emphasize the strong state's institutional capabilities, such as meritocracy and the cohesiveness and rationality of bureaucracy, which enable the state not only to extract, mobilize, and target resources to a particular purpose, but also to sanction private firms for not making productive use of state resources.[4] For example, in accounting for why Japan, Korea, and Taiwan could succeed in economic development while

[2] This section is mainly based on a revision of Kwon (2021, Chapter 1).

[3] For neoclassical economic approaches regarding East Asian economic success, see Cole and Lyman (1971), Chen (1979), Balassa (1981), Balassa and Williams (1987), and World Bank (1993). They emphasize free market policies for the causes of East Asian economic success, including open trade, comparative advantage, and limited state intervention.

[4] For an overview of developmental state theory, see Haggard (2015, 2018), Fine (2013), Routley (2012); Stubbs (2009), Woo-Cumings (1999). For classical developmental theory,

Latin American countries and India failed, DS theorists emphasize the state's institutional capability to impose its development policy on business.

However, since the late 1990s, particularly with the Asian financial crisis of 1997, the neoliberal view has prevailed, based on the universal relevancy of the free market. Not only Korea but also many countries reformed under the pressure of globalization, particularly with neoliberal reforms as a condition of the IMF bailout. Most DS demise theorists believe that following the Asian financial crisis, Korea changed from a developmental state to a neoliberal free-market system.[5] Not only was the financial crisis of 1997 believed to signify most clearly the effects of globalization and financialization, but also that *state failure*, due to overregulation, state-controlled finance, crony capitalism, and moral hazard, was a key cause for the crisis. Neoliberals hold that developmental policies should be limited under globalization in order to optimize comparative advantages.[6] Neoliberal globalists hold that industrial policies, whether new or old, are irrelevant in the course of globalization because they hinder optimal use of the advantages of "international supply chains" by the free market (Yeung, 2016; Pack & Saggi, 2006).

In actuality, the Korean developmental state has significantly changed from an extreme version of its 1970s authoritarian developmentalism toward more inclusive and democratic forms of capitalism, based on private sector initiatives. However, the Korean state did not simply retreat in facing the 1997 Asian financial crisis, but revised its existing developmental policy while disciplining large corporations and creating a new version of industrial policies, shifting from input-oriented to a knowledge-based economy, creating venture companies and an innovative industrial ecosystem. Korea no longer uses old-style subsidies directly given to large corporations, in order to avoid violating the World Trade Organization rules. However, it uses more R&D support as a developmental policy to strategically target industrial development. As many empirical studies show, the

see Johnson (1982), Amsden (1989, 2001), Chang (1994), Evans (1995), Haggard (1990), and Wade (1990).

[5] For the argument that Korea has transformed to neoliberalism since the 1997 crisis and subsequent reforms, see Kim (2014), Kim (2005), Kirk (2000), Kong (2000), Kwon (2010), Lim (2010), Lim and Jang (2006). For the debate on the developmental state 10 years after the 1997 crisis, see articles in *Asian Survey* vol. 47, no. 6 (2007).

[6] For neoliberal globalism, see Friedman (2007), McKinsey and Company (2003), Sirkin et al. (2011), Bhagwati (2010), and Yeung (2016).

Korean government has maintained its initiatives in technology development through agenda setting and industrial targeting.[7]

For example, Korea has been much more involved in setting strategic priorities and coordinating R&D programs in the Information and Communication Technology sector than even France. Korea no longer uses old developmental methods, such as mobilizing massive capital and funneling it exclusively to a few large corporations, to achieve economy of scale. Instead, it focuses on improving innovative capability by collaborative relations among large and small firms. Unlike the global value chain theorist expectation, the Korean state focuses on building industrial commons and an industrial ecosystem at home to avoid the hollowing-out of national industries, and continuously upgrades its innovative capabilities.

Recently, against the backdrop of the U.S.-China rivalry, in which even advanced economies, including the U.S. and Germany, adopt statist industrial policies, proponents of statist coordination development gain ascendancy, pointing out Korea's statist development method.[8]

How can we understand the Korean model's political-economic development? Does neoliberalism based on neoclassical economics or the development state sufficiently account for Korea's political economic success? What are the particular features of Korean development, compared with other countries' methods of development? Can the statist coordination model, represented by Korea, be effective even in a digitalized and globalized world? What does the Korean model mean for the future?

To answer these questions, the Korean political economy team of SNU Contemporary Korean Studies explores the evolution of Korean political economy from comparative and historical perspectives. Our project explores what the Korean model of political economic evolution means in the context of theoretical debate on political-economic development, as seen in Haggard's and Lee's works. Then, we empirically compare Korea not only to the Western models, but more importantly to other East-Asian countries including Japan and Taiwan, as seen in Kim and Kwon's chapter and Yin-wah Chu's chapter. We examine the recent performance of Korean political economy in terms of technology strategies at the firm level (see

[7] For the literature on the recomposition of Korean state-led developmentalism to a new model of statist-coordination, see Kwon (2021), Kim (2020), Kim and Kwon (2017), Chu (2009), Kim, S.-Y. (2012, 2019), Larson and Park (2014), Kang (2002), and Thurbon (2016).

[8] For the recent changes in which even the liberal U.S., as well as the social coordination model Germany, also adopted the industrial policy, giving up the existing neoliberal policy, see Kwon (2024) and Haggard's article in this book.

Song's chapter) and Korean chaebols' transformation and adaptation (Chang's chapter). We also historically trace the evolution of Korean political, social and economic system (Ha's chapter). Finally, we explore lessons embedded in South Korea's experience for both developed and developing countries (see Thurbon's chapter).

Detailed summaries of each chapter are as follows.

In Chap. 2, Stephan Haggard examines South Korea as a key case in "the securitization of international political economy." Korea played an important role in the field of comparative development and international political economy, particularly in its apparently successful use of industrial policy. While issues of industrial policy continue to have importance, a new turn has occurred in international relations and political economy toward the role of security calculations in foreign policy making, motivated in large party by changes in China's development strategy in a more statist direction. This chapter reviews five questions raised in this new literature: the relationship between grand strategy and trade openness; the "weaponization of interdependence" and responses to it; the new emphasis on strategies of denial of critical technologies to adversaries; the role that industrial policy should play; and how these new efforts at securitization affect global and regional governance, including the nature of alliances relationships.

In Chap. 3, Lee and Kim locate Korean capitalism's changes in the context of *Verities of Capitalism*. They characterize the evolution of South Korea's capitalism from an economic perspective with the distinctive concept of "from compressed development to compressed convergence." South Korea has achieved compressed growth and convergence of its income level to that of typical advanced economies. The authors adopt a narrow definition of compressed development as a form of late development that lacks political democracy and open markets, and then define decompression as the process of democratization and economic liberalization. The chapter applies this framework of "compressed development, decompression, and diverging convergence" to analyze the dynamics of Korean capitalism since the 1980s after the death of the modernizer-dictator, President Park. First, Korea's middle class emerged in the 1980s due to compressed growth since the 1960s, linking economic growth to democratization. Second, an ill-managed first wave of economic decompression (liberalization) led to a financial crisis, and post-crisis reforms (the second, more radical decompression) imposed by the IMF planted the institutional seeds for convergence with Anglo-American capitalism.

Third, Korea is experiencing the end of the East Asian miracle, as evidenced by slowing growth and rising inequality, and is undergoing a multifaceted convergence toward different varieties of capitalism. Korea seems to be realizing "divergent convergence" as it remains distinct from any form of Western capitalism.

Chapters 4 and 5 explore the characteristics of Korean capitalism by comparing it with other East Asian developmental states, including Japan and Taiwan. In Chap. 4, Kim and Kwon demonstrate the divergent evolution of statist coordination models through a comparative analysis of Japan and South Korea.

By examining the different patterns of policy-making, this chapter investigates the divergent evolution of statist coordination capitalism in Japan and South Korea. Since the 2008 global financial crisis, along with the escalation of U.S.–China rivalry and intensifying technological competition, the traditional state-led industrial policies of both countries have attracted renewed scholarly attention. For institutionalists and culturalists, Japan and South Korea represent critical cases that challenge neoliberal convergence arguments in the era of globalization and the digital revolution, demonstrating the persistence of national diversity. Yet existing approaches still fall short in explaining the diverging trajectories of the two economies in terms of economic performance and reform politics since the 1990s.

Despite sharing a broadly similar statist coordination model—distinguished from both the U.S. free-market model and Germany's social coordination model—the recent evolution of Japan and South Korea reveals significant differences: Japan has experienced prolonged stagnation and institutional inertia, whereas South Korea has shown comparatively greater flexibility in adapting to globalization and digitalization. Focusing on these two countries' differing policy regimes, this chapter highlights that although the two countries maintain similar institutional frameworks and policy practices, the way these systems operate in practice diverges: Japan relies on a consensus-based regime of state–bureaucracy–business, while South Korea employs a presidentially driven hierarchical model. This comparative perspective both clarifies the backgrounds of their different developmental paths and offers insights into the respective strengths and weaknesses of the two statist coordination models.

In Chap. 5, Yin-wah Chu compares the developmental states of South Korea and Taiwan by analysing their core characteristics and divergent trajectories. This paper makes two arguments concerning current developmental state literature in general, and the cases of South Korea and Taiwan in particular. First, it contends that current efforts to advance the developmental state literature have often ignored the geopolitical and social structural contexts of its emergence, and one-sidedly analyzed its institutional features and applied it as an abstract model. This study re-examines the cases of the pre- mid-1980s South Korea and Taiwan and argues that not only have their geopolitical contexts facilitated the pursuit of developmental strategies, but divergencies in social structural conditions have led them to mobilize different policy tools with dissimilar distributive outcomes. Second, this chapter contends that developmental state institutions should not be examined as static entities. They may reconfigure and navigate new policy instruments or dissolve in the face of global and national changes, which in South Korea and Taiwan include the deepening of globalization, China's rise, and democratization. Again, how they adapt depends in part on geopolitical contexts and social structural conditions. That Taiwan has faced more complex challenges from China's rise and South Korea has a more vigorous labor movement have triggered divergent trajectories. This point will be demonstrated in part through an examination of the changes in the state institutions themselves and in part through two case studies. In so doing, this chapter also contributes to the debates on the demise of East Asian developmental state.

In Chap. 6, Jaeyong Song explores the evolution of Korean capitalism and its strength at the micro level, by focusing on Samsung Electronics. He traces the evolution of technology sourcing strategies in Korean electronics companies through an empirical case study of Samsung Electronics.

Empirical research has demonstrated that the majority of technological and industrial domains are persistently dominated by firms from a limited number of countries over extended periods. Endogenous growth theory offers an explanation for this persistence, positing that technological catch-up is challenging due to increasing returns to scale of physical and human resources and the geographical localization of technological knowledge. Despite the ominous implications of these new growth theories for developing nations, Korea is a notable exemplar of countries that have indeed "caught up" and are now leaders in a number of technological domains, including electronics and semiconductors. Song explores how Korean electronics firms such as Samsung Electronics acquired and developed technologies so rapidly, and what kind of knowledge sourcing modes such as in-house R&D, licensing, alliances, and learning-by-hiring, the Korean electronics firms used to acquire knowledge and build their innovative capacities.

In Chap. 7, Sea-Jin Chang examines the post-crisis restructuring and subsequent development of South Korea's chaebols. Korean business groups, commonly referred to as chaebols, are collections of legally independent companies that operate under shared family ownership. Between 2000 and 2024, following the Asian Financial Crisis, chaebols underwent significant structural transformations. Many engaged in spinoffs of non-core or subsidiary businesses, driven by generational succession and regulatory pressures. Additionally, numerous chaebols transitioned to holding company structures, enhancing governance transparency and accountability. These changes reflect chaebols' ongoing adaptation to Korea's complex regulatory and market environments.

In Chap. 8, Yong-Chool Ha focuses on the emergence of neofamilism within Korean society during the process of late industrialization. Ha's presentation focuses on a paradox in Korea's economic development: an ultra-modern industrial economy has been achieved, yet traditional networks of obligation and solidarity, such as blood relations, school, and regional ties have persisted, and even become more deeply reinforced, profoundly affecting fundamental aspects of Korean politics and socio-economic relations. Ha contends that this paradox is not accidental, and that the course of Korea's late economic development shaped and entrenched these "primordial" ties into Korea's politics, society, and economy. Thus, the persistence and predominance of these ties, what he calls "neofamilism," requires an explanation as to when, why, and how it arose. Analysis of the paradox reveals distinct social phenomena which arose through interactions between the developmental state, traditional institutions, and economic tasks.

Finally, in Chap. 9, Elizabeth Thurbon addresses what advanced economies can learn from Korea, offering discussion from an Australian perspective. South Korea stands as one of the most remarkable cases of latecomer industrialization, long admired as a model for developing nations seeking rapid catch-up. Yet far less attention has been given to the lessons which Korea's transformative trajectory might hold for advanced economies. This chapter reorients the lens, distilling ten lessons from Korea's experience over the past two decades for policymakers in "developed" countries like her own, Thurbon writes, who grapple with a complex range of challenges, from deindustrialization to geostrategic rivalry and the climate crisis. At the same time, the chapter identifies major obstacles to lesson-learning in advanced liberal market economies, including ideological constraints, institutional fragmentation, entrenched path dependencies, and political capture. It concludes by advancing some practical strategies to overcome these barriers. Korea should not be treated as a blueprint, but as a mirror through which policymakers in "developed" countries can challenge prevailing assumptions, expand their strategic repertoire, and re-imagine the role of the state in navigating today's complex economic and geopolitical terrain.

References

Amsden, A. H. (1989). *Asia's Next Giant: South Korea and Late Industrialization.* Oxford University Press.

Amsden, A. H. (2001). *The Rise of "the Rest": Challenges to the West From Late-Industrializing Economies.* Oxford University Press.

Balassa, B. (1981). *The Newly Industrializing Countries in the World Economy.* Pergamon Press.

Balassa, B., & Williams, J. (1987). *Adjusting to Success: Balance of Payments Policy in the East Asian NICs.* Institute for International Economics.

Bhagwati, J. (2010). The Manufacturing Fallacy, *Project Syndicate.* August 27, 2010.

Chang, H.-J. (1994). *The Political Economy of Industrial Policy.* Macmillan.

Chen, E. (1979). *Hyper-Growth in Asian Economies.* Holmes & Meier.

Chu, Y.-w. (2009). Eclipse or Reconfigured? South Korea's Developmental State and Challenges of the Global Knowledge Economy. *Economy and Society, 38*(2), 278–303.

Cole, D., & Lyman, P. (1971). *Korean Development: The Interplay of Politics and Economics.* Harvard University Press.

Evans, P. (1995). *Embedded Autonomy: States and Industrial Transformation.* Princeton University Press.

Fine, B. (2013). Beyond the Developmental State. In B. Fine, J. Sarawati, & D. Tavasci (Eds.), *Beyond the Developmental State* (pp. 1–32). Pluto Press.

Friedman, T. L. (2007). *The World Is Flat: A Brief History of the Twenty-First Century.* Farrar, Straus and Giroux.

Haggard, S. (1990). *Pathways from the Periphery: The Politics of Growth in the Newly Industrializing Countries.* Cornell University Press.

Haggard, S. (2015). The Development State is Dead: Long Live the Developmental State! In J. Mahoney & K. Thelen (Eds.), *Advances in Comparative-Historical Analysis.* Cambridge University Press.

Haggard, S. (2018). *Developmental States.* Cambridge University Press.

Johnson, C. (1982). *MITI and the Japanese Miracle: The Growth of Industrial Policy, 1925–1975.* Stanford University Press.

Kang, D. C. (2002). *Crony capitalism: Corruption and development in South Korea and The Philippines*. Cambridge University Press.
Kim, Y. T. (2005). DJnomics and the Transformation of a Developmental State. *Journal of Contemporary Asia, 35*(4), 471–484.
Kim, S.-Y. (2012). Transition from Fast-Follower to Innovator: The Institutional Foundations of the Korean Telecommunications Sector. *Review of International Political Economy, 19*(1), 140–168.
Kim, E. M. (2014). The South Korean Developmental Alliance between Business, Labor and Government. In I. Yi & T. Mkandawire (Eds.), *Learning from the South Korean Developmental Success: Effective Developmental Cooperation and Synergistic Institutions and Policies*. Palgrave.
Kim, S.-Y. (2019). Hybridized Industrial Ecosystems and the Makings of a New Developmental Infrastructure in East Asia's Green Energy Sector. *Review of International Political Economy*. Published Online https://doi.org/10.1080/09692290.2018.1554540.
Kim, K. M. (2020). *The Korean Developmental State*. Palgrave Macmillan.
Kim, K. M., & Kwon, H.-k. (2017). The State's Role in Globalization: Korea's Experience from a Comparative Perspective. *Politics and Society, 45*(4), 505–531.
Kirk, D. M. (2000). *Korean Crisis: Unraveling of the Miracle in the IMF Era*. Macmillan.
Kong, T. Y. (2000). *The Politics of Economic Reform in South Korea: A Fragile Miracle*. Routledge.
Kwon, O. Y. (2010). *The Korean Economy in Transition: An Institutional Perspective*. Edward Elgar.
Kwon, H.-k. (2021). *Changes by Competition: The Evolution of the South Korean Developmental State*. Oxford University Press.
Kwon, H.-k. (2024). *Openness and Coordination: National Economies of the U.S., Japan, and Germany in a Globalized World*. Palgrave Macmillan.
Larson, J. F., & Park, J. (2014). From Developmental to Network State: Government Restructuring and ICT-led Innovation in Korea. *Telecommunications Policy, 38*(4), 344–359.
Lim, H. (2010). The Transformation of the Developmental State and Economic Reform in Korea. *Journal of Contemporary Asia, 40*(2), 188–210.
Lim, H.-c., & Jang, J.-h. (2006). Between Neo-liberalism and Democracy: The Transformation of the Developmental State in South Korea. *Development and Society, 35*(1), 1–28.
McKinsey & Company. (2003). *Offshoring: Is It a Win-Win Game?* McKinsey Global Institute.
Pack, H., & Saggi, K. (2006). Is There a Case for Industrial Policy? A Critical Survey. *World Bank Research Observer, 21*(2), 267–297.
Routley, L. (2012). *Developmental States: A Review of the Literature*. Effective States and Inclusive Development Working Paper, no. 3. Manchester: ESID.

Sirkin, H. L., Zinser, M., & Hohner, D. (2011). *Made in America, Again: Why Manufacturing will Return to the U.S.* Boston Consulting Group, August 2011 from http://www.bcg.com/documents/file84471.pdf.
Stubbs, R. (2009). What Ever Happened to the East Asian Developmental State? The Unfolding Debate. *The Pacific Review, 22*(1), 1–22.
Thurbon, E. (2016). *Developmental Mindset: The Revival of Financial Activism in South Korea*. Cornell University Press.
Wade, R. (1990). *Governing the Market*. Princeton University Press.
Woo-Cumings, M. (Ed.). (1999). *The Developmental State*. Cornell University Press.
World Bank. (1993). *The East Asian Miracle: Economic Growth and Public Policy*. Policy Research Report. Washington, DC: World Bank.
Yeung, H. W.-c. (2016). *Strategic Coupling: East Asian Industrial Transformation in the New Global Economy*. Cornell University Press.

CHAPTER 2

Korea and the Securitization of International Political Economy

Stephan Haggard

Korea has long occupied a particular position in the field of international political economy. Beginning in the 1980s, tremendous attention was focused on the political and institutional foundations of the country's rapid growth, particularly in the debate about the developmental state.[1] To a surprising extent, this focus continued through the Asian financial crisis up to this day. On the one hand, new work by both economists has revisited the high growth period itself and added new insights on the sources of both policy and growth. Empirical studies using micro data have now demonstrated the effects of industrial policy on output,

[1] Stephan Haggard, *Developmental States* (Cambridge University Press, 2018)

S. Haggard (✉)
School of Global Policy and Strategy and Institute on Global Conflict and Cooperation,University of California San Diego, San Diego, CA, USA
e-mail: shaggard@ucsd.edu

H.-k. Kwon (ed.), *Korean Political Economy from a Comparative-Historical Perspective*, Palgrave Series in Contemporary Korean Studies, https://doi.org/10.1007/978-981-95-9785-7_2

productivity and growth calling into question earlier skepticism about the state's role.[2]

On the other hand, new research by political scientists and others highlighted how industrial policy persisted albeit with changing policy instruments.[3] Industrial policy was deployed to assist upgrading in global value chains and was visible in altogether new activities such as the green energy transition.[4] To be sure, other issues received attention in the IPE literature on Korea, including bilateral trade tensions with the US in the 1980s and 1990s and Korea's unusual level of activity in signing FTA's. Yet even these topics were frequently framed in terms of the persistence of developmentalism.

In this chapter, I argue that a new international political economy of security is emerging, centered in large part on strategic competition between the US and China, and that this securitization of international political economy is highly salient for Korea. For much of the postwar period, the politics of trade and investment centered largely on writing new trade rules—multilaterally, regionally and in bilateral free trade agreements—and negotiating how barriers to closer integration would be reduced. The agenda of such negotiations naturally shifted over time, moving from a focus on trade in goods to a variety of new issues: trade in services, intellectual property, digital trade, and the complex of issues surrounding foreign direct investment. These negotiations were not without conflict; American protectionism and unilateral trade measures tested relations with alliance partners in Asia. And a distinctive literature on economic statecraft, including the use of sanctions and export controls, formed an important subculture within IPE.

But how security calculations played into trade policy was largely implicit. An open world economy, buttressed by multilateral institutions, was seen as advancing US grand strategy in Europe, East Asia and with the

[2] See for example Nathan Lane, "The New Empirics of Industrial Policy," Journal of Industry, Competition and Trade 20: 209–234.

[3] Heyong-Ki Kwon, *Changes by Competition: The Evolution of the South Korean Developmental State*. (Oxford University Press 2021).

[4] E. Thurbon, S.Y. Kim, H. Tan and J. A. Mathews, J.A., *Developmental Environmentalism: State Ambition and Creative Destruction in East Asia's Green Energy Transition*. (Oxford University Press 2023).

developing world more generally. There were an adequate number of followers—including middle powers such as Korea—to provide ballast to an open world economy and to support continued deepening of globalization. This was, visible not only in ongoing policy agreements but in the dramatic increase in trade and capital flows as a share of global output.

The fundamental premises of the so-called liberal international order are increasingly in doubt. One domestic reason is simply backlash, which has generated a significant political economy of its own.[5] Protectionist responses to greater economic openness in the advanced industrial states have been a perennial feature of the trade policy agenda, but have clearly veered into more principled objections to economic openness. Not only has political tolerance for greater exposure to trade declined in the United States, a significant ideological shift is also afoot. The heyday of the Washington Consensus and the market triumphalism of the post-Cold War world has been displaced by set of rival economic ideas, and on both the left and right, that are open to a larger state role in managing foreign economic policy. These shifts can be seen in the US not only in the protectionism of the Trump administration but in the maintenance of those tariffs by the Biden administration and the aggressive pursuit of industrial policy through major pieces of legislation such as the Inflation Reduction and CHIPS Acts.

But the trade policy agenda cannot be fully understood through a standard trade policy lens, as it increasingly intersects with security issues and is driven by them. Various restraints on trade and investment and government interventions in economic activity are motivated and justified by security concerns. No one factor can explain this change; many are at work. The weakening of multilateralism is clearly one. Momentum toward liberalization has long shifted from the WTO to regional and bilateral agreements where geostrategic calculations are likely to play a more significant role.

But There can be little question that the animating factor in the new political economy of national security is not only China's rise, but the fact that its economy has not evolved in the market-oriented direction that had been hoped. China is not only an emerging power with increasingly expansive security ambitions, but one with a statist economic system increasingly at variance with the norms on which the postwar trading

[5] Stefanie Walter, "The Backlash Against Globalization," *Annual Review of Political Science* 24 (2021): 421–442.

regime was built. As the US and Western Europe formulate strategies for dealing with China, Korea will be faced with difficult policy choices about how to balance its strategic interests with respect to the advanced industrial states, China and the developing world.

Before we can address the particular political challenges Korea will face, we need a clearer sense of the policy agenda: how, precisely, trade and investment intersect with national security concerns. I argue that there are five distinct ways in which they do so, each raising somewhat different policy and political concerns. Some of these are longstanding issues in the field of international political economy, but others are not receiving the academic attention they deserve, with important research coming out of think tanks as much as academic research.

A first question is the extent to which the United States is politically capable of sustaining economic commitments that support its grand strategy, both broadly conce the Indo-Pacific more specifically. A second cluster of issues arises around the growing use of economic leverage to achieve political objectives—the weaponization of interdependence—and simultaneous efforts to limit such leverage. These countermoves include increasing the resilience of supply chains and calls for diversification and greater self-sufficiency. A third somewhat distinct objective springs from the logic of denial that motivated the Cold War strategic embargo, although in notably shallower form. How do the United States and its allies limit exports and investments that increase the capabilities of rivals and competitors? A fourth issue is the appropriateness of industrial policy: the extent to which a wider state role is seen as necessary to maintain economic competitiveness in emerging technologies or to anchor national capabilities more broadly.

Finally, we need to consider international institutional questions: the frameworks that provide rules underneath strategic competition. Should the United States, its allies—and China for that matter—seek to revive existing multilateral frameworks? Or are altogether new understandings required to manage the challenges that China poses?

The purpose of this chapter is to provide a brief overview of this securitization of international political economy and the implications of it for Korean studies. Before turning to these issues, it is important to start with a brief exposition of the economic challenges posed by China's rise. An important question—virtually impossible to resolve—is the extent to which China's new statist turn was driven by the hawkish posture of the United States toward the country or by domestic political developments, and particularly the rise of Xi Jinping and his preoccupation with national security. Whatever its sources, however, China's distinctive political economy is increasingly seen as incompatible with basic premises of the international trade and investment regime and fundamental adjustments in those presumptions are required.

Interpreting China

The broad outlines of China's turn to economic reform following Mao's death, the initiation of "reform and opening" under Deng, and the negotiations leading to WTO succession in 2000 are well known and need not be rehearsed here in detail. But it is worth underlining that from the beginning, the leadership saw security and political risks from its new interdependence. Beijing was initially preoccupied with buffering potential shocks associated with closer economic integration, for example with respect to energy dependence and the integration of financial markets, about which the leadership remains extraordinarily cautious. Chinese discussions of economic security during the reform era were also always linked to national security in a broader sense. Chinese writings—drawing on long traditions of "self-strengthening"—emphasized that national power, including military capabilities, rested on an economic foundation.

At the same time, Chinese thinking took a nuanced approach which recognized the strategic value of closer economic integration with the world economy. Such integration not only provided economic benefits but allowed China to capitalize on its rising stature, for example by increasing its leverage with trading partners. The core puzzle for China analysts is why the phase of optimism—in which economic reform, rapid growth and rising international status went together—devolved into a much darker and more threatening picture of the international landscape. Rather than industrial policy receding in the face of continued market-oriented reforms, China has embarked on a giant U-turn, moving away from its commitment to reform and opening and toward greater state and party intervention in the economy.[6]

[6] Barry Naughton, Siwen Xiao, and Yaosheng Xu, "The Trajectory of China's Industrial Policies," Institute on Global Conflict and Cooperation, University of California San Diego Working Paper June 2023, https://ucigcc.org/publication/working-paper/the-trajectory-of-chinas-industrial-policies/

The United States is certainly one factor. Starting with Hu Jintao's turn to industrial policy, but accelerating under Xi Jinping, China's notion of economic security has been driven by the perception that the United States is pursuing a strategy of economic containment. This turn toward securitization has required some subtle but important doctrinal changes, away from the "development-first" policies of the Jiang Zemin era. In 2014, Xi Jinping signaled the new direction with his Comprehensive National Security Concept, which would take "security as the purpose, political security as the basis, and economic security as the foundation." The integrated development-security approach was on full display at the Fifth Plenum of the 19th Central Committee in October 2020 and is now linked to wider political objectives captured in catchwords such as "the strategic rejuvenation of the Chinese people with changes unseen in a century." However, in the 2020's the securitization rhetoric has deepened and is increasingly linked to existential risks: a "turbulent international situation" and the need to maintain a "high-level of alert" for black swan events and even outright conflict. Securitization and "civil military fusion" have now become defining characteristics of the country's national security state.[7]

Some components of the new strategy are well-known and others less so, but for purposes of exposition can be divided into changes in the domestic political economy in a more statist direction and the growing use of trade and investment relations for the purpose of exercising leverage. The explicit turn to a new industrial policy, captured in "Made in China 2025" initiatives, marked a fundamental shift in government-business relations that has affected perceptions of China risk. In addition to the ongoing challenges posed by the theft of intellectual property, state interventions are most readily captured by the massive subsidization of strategic sectors—particularly through government-guided funds—and the attendant surplus capacity they have generated on world markets. Despite Chinese criticisms that the US is pursuing a decoupling strategy, the idea of "dual circulation" implies precisely that, with a strong focus on improving supply-chain and industrial resilience so as to reduce China's vulnerability to western trade and technology sanctions. The turn to industrial policy has also been accompanied by attacks on prominent

[7] Tai Ming Cheung, *Innovate to Dominate: The Rise of the Chinese Techno-Security State.* Ithaca: Cornell University Press, 2022.

Chinese firms as well as continued restraints on the freedom of maneuver of foreign investors.

On the external front, the new industrial policy is explicitly motivated by concerns about the ability of the United States to strangle China's further economic advance through the chokehold it exercises over a number of key technologies, most notably semi-conductor design.[8] In the 14th Five Year Plan (2021–2025), the regime identified four broad categories of risk: those associated with industrial supply chains, food and agriculture, energy and resources, and the financial system. Purely commercial motives—staying internationally competitive—are increasingly coupled to wider security objectives through "civil military fusion."

While fundamentally reordering China's domestic political economy, China has also self-consciously engaged in strategies of "deep coupling," ultimately exploited in the policies characterized by the United States and its allies as "economic coercion" The THAAD controversy was but one example. Nor are these measures ad hoc: the government has sought to institutionalize the new national security agenda through a variety of laws. These include, among others, revisions of foreign trade and investment laws, the creation of an Unreliable Entity List, China's own Export Control Law, Rules on Counteracting Unjustified Extra-Territorial Application of Foreign legislation and an Anti-Foreign Sanctions Law.

The IPE of Security I: Grand Strategy and Economic Order

How do we characterize the new political economy of national security? A first question centers on the political tolerance for increasing economic integration as a component of US grand strategy. As Wertheim has recently outlined in some historical detail, America's postwar planners specifically considered whether it could withdraw into a post-war order anchored primarily in its relations with the Western Hemisphere.[9] The answer was "no": American economic as well as security interests required access to markets in both Europe and Asia.

[8] Chris Miller, *Chip War: The Fight for the World's Most Critical Technology* (New York: Scribner 2022).

[9] Stephen Wertheim, *Tomorrow the World: The Birth of U.S. Global Supremacy* (Cambridge: Belknap 2020).

These ideas were broadly in line with notions of containment advanced by Kennan and others: that American grand strategy rested on denying control over centers of industrial power in Japan and Western Europe to any Eurasian challenger. However, the alliance systems that subsequently evolved in both regions were firmly anchored in economic ties. These ties started with US investment in reconstruction: multilaterally through the Marshall Plan and Organization for European Economic Co-operation in Europe, through bilateral aid to Japan and other allies in Asia. These commitments were further buttressed by the creation of the Bretton Woods institutions and a gradual and cautious process of trade liberalization undertaken through the GATT when the more ambitious International Trade Organization failed to materialize. Beginning in the 1960s, trade ties were augmented by foreign direct investment and other capital flows. From the end of World War II well into the 1970s, however, U.S. imports as a share of GDP were less than five percent and trade with Europe took an intra-industry form that did not generate significant political resistance.

Continuing trade liberalization and the entry of Japan, the East Asian newly industrializing countries into global markets and ultimately China pushed this up to nearly 18 percent by the time of the global financial crisis of 2008 after which the degree of economic openness stalled and even fell back slightly. Over this long period of deepening international exposure, current account deficits widened and employment in manufacturing underwent a secular decline, falling from over 25 percent in 1970 to around 10 percent today.

Whether these developments were causally related is one of the great debates of our time, but one thing is increasingly clear. Economic analysis increasingly acknowledges that while the aggregate effects of trade remain positive, its distributional consequences are real.[10] These distributional costs of trade have become a focus of both political parties and the Republican party now appears more inward-looking than its Democratic counterpart.

The political economy of trade hovers over the security debate because domestic politics impinges on the capacity of the United States to exercise international economic leadership. In the Indo-Pacific, this was visible in the inability of either political party to follow through on the Trans-Pacific

[10] An agenda-setting contribution was David H. Autor, David Dorn, and Gordon H. Hanson, "The China Syndrome: Local Labor Market Effects of Import Competition in the United States." *American Economic Review*, 103, 6 (2013): 2121–68.

Partnership in the late Obama administration, through the sectoral tariffs imposed during the first Trump administration, to the difficulties the Biden administration faced in advancing the relatively modest Indo-Pacific Economic Framework.[11] In the strategic community, these failures were seen as ceding political ground to China not only economically (for example in its ability to propose an alternative in RCEP) but through the political signals these policy failures sent to allies in the region.[12]

Under the second Trump administration, the strategic focus of the United States has shifted in a more fundamental way, effectively undermining core norms on which the postwar trading order was based. While a long-standing bipartisan consensus had seen relatively open trade and investment relations as complementary to American national security interests, the new Trump administration is even more adamant that they are antithetical. Rather than starting with a liberal prior that the US gained from expanding economic ties with allies and partners, Trump has focused on free-riding and used optimal tariff arguments to go after allies as well as adversaries.

In the first Trump administration, this took the form of pressure to renegotiate existing agreements, such as the KORUS and NAFTA, but with relatively minor changes particularly in the US-Korea agreement. Such a tactical use of tariff threats might be seen as falling broadly within the liberal strategic consensus.

Yet there is increasing evidence that Trump's ideas shifted more strongly in the second administration into the view that tariffs are not simply a tool for extracting trade concessions but are a more enduring feature of US foreign economic policy. The Trade Expansion Act of 1962 in Section 232 gave the president substantial discretion in imposing tariffs—and taking liberalizing initiatives—on national security grounds. But initially these were interpreted to rest narrowly on requirements for defense and critical infrastructure. Just weeks after 9/11, however, the Department of Commerce reached the conclusion that "national security" can be interpreted more broadly to include the general security and welfare of certain industries … which are critical to the minimum operations of the economy

[11] Gavin Rade, "How Sherrod Brown Rattled Biden's Summit Agenda," *Politico*, November 14, 2023, https://www.politico.com/news/2023/11/14/electoral-angst-biden-trade-deal-00127064

[12] Michael J. Green and Matthew P. Goodman, "After TPP: The Geopolitics of Asia and the Pacific." *The Washington Quarterly*, 38, 4 (2015): 19–34.

and the government."[13] These justifications were invoked with respect to steel and aluminum tariffs in the first Trump administration, reversed as harming national security under the Biden administration by raising costs and then revived again early in the second Trump administration.

But then came Liberation Day on April 2, 2025 when a completely novel approach to trade was rolled out, grounded in authorities the President believed he had under quite different statute: the International Emergency Economic Powers Act of 1977.[14] The basic idea of the April 2 reciprocal tariffs initiative proved to be in fundamental tension with most-favored nation norms and the entire GATT/WTO framework. Rather than uniform tariffs for all WTO members, each country would face different baseline tariffs, later revealed to be set initially on the relative size of the bilateral trade deficit. This opening bid set the stage for a series of bilateral negotiations with important trading partners, including the EU, Japan and Korea among others, in which tariffs would be partially—but not wholly—"bought down" through the negotiation of bilateral trade deals. These agreements not only included tariff and non-tariff barriers but departed from past norms in requiring that countries make investment commitments in the US. As this chapter goes to press in May 2026, there is still substantial uncertainty about what commitments such as Korea's $350 billion investment pledge even means: whether it is additional to existing planned investment; how it will be monitored; and even who controls the funding. Moreover, it is possible that this initial negotiation is just the beginning of an effort on the part of the Trump administration to link trade policy to other concessions, for example with respect to defense spending or alliance burden-sharing.

It is too early to say that such a fundamental re-orientation of US grand strategy will be enduring or not. The Supreme Court struck down one authority for the reciprocal tariffs, and it could well reverse under subsequent administrations. But from the perspective of US allies, it is not clear that the latter scenario is any more comforting than the former. Korea's

[13] Jonathan Hilman. "Trump's National Security Tariffs," The Council on Foreign Relations, February 12, 2025 at https://www.cfr.org/article/trumps-national-security-tariffs

[14] "Fact Sheet: President Donald J. Trump Declares National Emergency to Increase our Competitive Edge, Protect our Sovereignty, and Strengthen our National and Economic Security," April 2, 2025 at https://www.whitehouse.gov/fact-sheets/2025/04/fact-sheet-president-donald-j-trump-declares-national-emergency-to-increase-our-competitive-edge-protect-our-sovereignty-and-strengthen-our-national-and-economic-security/

alliance relations with the United States have always been subject to a certain degree of volatility. But if we are seeing such a fundamental shift in US foreign economic policy, Korean responses will increasingly be driven by a perception of "America risk" that will motivate ongoing diversification and a deepening of its own Indo-Pacific and Europe strategies.

The IPE of Security II: The Weaponization of Interdependence

The second strand of thinking about the securitization of IPE centers on what Farrell and Newman have called the weaponization of interdependence.[15] This agenda is wide-ranging, and in the United States has taken a variety of forms: from the long-standing attachment to sanctions as a foreign policy tool to the use of trade policy instruments to generate leverage, most notably in the first Trump administration's trade war, in the early flurry of trade policy actions against Canada and Mexico in his second administration, in the reciprocal tariff initiative of April 2025, and in a host of sectoral tariffs that were under investigation from the middle of 2025.[16]

At the core of the weaponization of interdependence is an effort to use the leverage generated through trade and investment ties to secure a policy quid pro quo: restraints are placed on trade and investment but with the openly stated commitment to lift them—at least in part—if the target complies with the demand. The use of these tools has been accompanied by a well-known debate about whether such sanctions "work" and what it means for them to work. Yet we are also seeing growing concern that such instruments may be subject to declining marginal returns with respect to adversaries. Target countries respond to such policies by diversifying,

[15] Henry Farrell and Abraham Newman, "Weaponized Interdependence: How Global Economic Networks Shape State Coercion," *International Security* 44, 1 (Summer 2019) 42–79; Farrell and Newman, *Underground Empire: How the United States Weaponized the World Economy* (New York: Henry Holt 2023).

[16] Bob Davis and Lingling Wei, *Superpower Showdown: How the Battle Between Trump and Xi Threatens a New Cold War* (New York: Harper Business, 2020); Juan Carols Zarate, *Treasury's War: The Unleashing of a New Era of Financial Warfare* (New York: Public Affairs 2013).

pursuing self-reliance and exploiting the massive international underground economy that has emerged in part to skirt sanctions efforts.[17]

With respect to China's behavior, the debate has focused around "economic coercion," and has now swept up a variety of U.S. allies and partners: Korea around the deployment of THAAD, the Philippines around South China Sea claims, Australia for its temerity in challenging China's COVID narratives, and European countries around their human rights preoccupations.[18] As with critics of the U.S. use of these tools, China analysts are arguing whether aggressive economic diplomacy has had the effect of attracting support—as some Chinese scholars appeared to think—or whether it fuels blowback and new anti-coercion instruments.[19]

However, it is important to underscore that the weaponization of interdependence has two sides. On the one hand are efforts on the part of both the United States and China to manipulate their very extensive trade ties for leverage. The United States exploits its unique networks and capabilities, for example with respect to financial clearing; China relies on the substantial dependence it has quite purposefully built among its trading partners.

But on the other hand, are the attempts to *reduce* those vulnerabilities. A significant component of the current debate about economics and security centers on the means for accomplishing this objective, including through so-called supply chain resilience. Multinational enterprises have always had to manage risk in the design of their international production networks, for example through diversification and make-buy decisions. What is new is the focus on political as well as economic risks. Among the strategies in play are encouraging geographical diversification on the part of national firms. These include the pursuit of "China+1" strategies on the part of American investors concerned about the risks of concentrating production in China, "friendshoring" through cooperation with allies to

[17] Daniel Drezner, "The United States of Sanctions: The Use and Abuse of Economic Coercion," *Foreign Affairs* 100, 5 (September/October 2021): 142–154.

[18] Aya Adachi, Alexander Brown and Max Zenglein, *Fasten Your Seatbelts: How to Manage China's Economic Coercion*, MERICS Report August 25, 2022, https://merics.org/en/report/fasten-your-seatbelts-how-manage-chinas-economic-coercion

[19] Yan Xuetong. *Leadership and the Rise of Great Powers* (Princeton: Princeton University Press, 2019); Susan Shirk, *Overreach: How China Derailed its Peaceful Rise* (Oxford University Press, 2022).

outright onshoring back to the United States, which is in effect a strategy of import-substitution.[20]

Nor is China standing still with respect to reducing its external risk. The theory of "dual circulation" has been read as a badly-needed effort to rebalance the Chinese growth model towards increasing domestic consumption. Over time, as argued above, it has devolved into an effort to sustain export growth while simultaneously limiting imports and relying to a greater extent on domestic production. Yet the broader strategy has a foreign economic policy component. As with the U.S. Indo-Pacific strategy and the efforts to "friendshore," China has pursued its own "neighborhood diplomacy," an early initiative of the Xi Jinping administration that is now ten years on.[21] More broadly, the entire Belt and Road Initiative (BRI) could be seen as a grand strategic counterpart to the U.S. focus on "allies and partners."

The policy issues with respect to such "de-risking" center on how to define which risks are tolerable so that desirable economic relationships are sustained, and underlying rules do not erode. For example, the Biden administration sought to focus its efforts on supply-chain resilience on a handful of particular sectors and related objectives: public health and biological preparedness; information and communications technology, including semiconductors; energy, encompassing green transition objectives; and critical minerals and materials.[22] Nonetheless, the International Trade Administration identified no fewer than 2400 "critical" goods and materials under this nominally focused strategy. In the Trump administration, as outlined in the previous section, the effort to de-risk is by no means as discriminating. As I will show, it may have less to do with strate-

[20] Remarks by Secretary of the Treasury Janet L. Yellen on Way Forward for the World Economy," Atlantic Council, April 13, 2022, https://home.treasury.gov/news/press-releases/jy0714

[21] For an introduction to neighborhood diplomacy, see Jacob Stokes, *China's Periphery Diplomacy: Implications for Peace and Security in Asia*, United States Institute of Peace Special Report No. 467, May 2020 https://www.usip.org/sites/default/files/2020-05/20200520-sr_467-chinas_periphery_diplomacy_implications_for_peace_and_security_in_asia-sr.pdf. For evidence of the continuing emphasis given to the concept, see Embassy of the People's Republic of China in the United States, "Outlook on China's Foreign Policy on Its Neighborhood In the New Era," October 24, 2023, which celebrates the tenth anniversary of Xi Jinping's introduction of the concept.

[22] "Executive Order on America's Supply Chains," February 24, 2021, https://www.whitehouse.gov/briefing-room/presidential-actions/2021/02/24/executive-order-on-americas-supply-chains/

gic derisking then with other policy objectives such as outright protection for manufacturing and the generation of revenue.

The IPE of Security III: Export and Investment Controls and the New Politics of Denial

A third strand of the economics/security tangle centers on export and investment controls, the objective of which is not leverage but denial: to prevent strategic competitors from acquiring capabilities and particularly those that will show up in weapons systems or other tools for coercion, including in the cyber domain. The evolution of such controls in the United States had their conceptual origins in the wide-ranging strategic embargos of the high Cold War, which required collaboration with allies through consultative bodies (COCOM and CHICOM) to assure that the embargo would not leak. Subsequently, multilateral export control regimes narrowed the product menu to so-called dual-use goods, services and technologies and tied controls to military end-uses. For example, the product specifications hammered out in the Nuclear Suppliers Group identified inputs that could lead to the generation of fissile material or the production of nuclear weapons and committed members of the group to initiate appropriate licensing over those products.

More recently, the evolution of United States export controls ran through UN Security Council Resolution 1540, which mandated controls to limit proliferation risk in the wake of 9/11. Groundbreaking statutory changes were undertaken by the first Trump administration in 2018 that reformed the export control process and delineated emerging technologies that warranted scrutiny and oversight. Of particular importance were the passage of the Export Control Reform Act (ECRA) and the Foreign Investment Risk Review Modernization Act (FIRRMA), which updated the rules governing the Committee on Foreign Investment in the United States (CFIUS); marginal changes to these initiatives surfaced in the second Trump administration as well. ECRA still focused on core technologies that can pose national security threats to the United States, but also introduced language underlining the importance of maintaining and even developing capabilities in strategic or foundational goods. These new laws broke the link to specific military end-uses since the ultimate value of such technologies for military purposes is, in many cases, difficult to ascertain. Clearly, security considerations were paramount, however, most notably in the targeted semiconductor export controls rolled out by the Biden administration in October 2022 and October 2023.[23]

In describing the policy process, it is worthwhile to note the distinction between export controls and the investment screening process, both with respect to incoming and outgoing investment. In the end, however, the motives of these controls are the same: to assure that technologies are not either exported or acquired by foreign firms in ways that could redound to the military capabilities of adversaries. These motives will increasingly extend to negotiations—and protective actions—with respect to intellectual property as well. Complaints about the theft of intellectual property are by no means limited to purely commercial concerns but increasingly focus on theft of dual-use and military technologies, including through cyberspace.[24]

The main challenge for achieving these denial objectives is akin to the sanctions enforcement problem: how to control leakage given the incentives controls create for diversion. Let me cite an example that attracted scrutiny in the economic press in the United States.[25] We can write a rule that denies a Chinese entity such as iFlytek, a partly state-owned firm, access to Nvidia A100 chips. But will such control incentivize Nvidia to supply chips just shy of technical thresholds or iFlytek to purchase such chips on gray markets? iFlytek can also lease cloud computing services that run on Nvidia chips. Do we regulate or even restrict cloud services?

The answer is not sanctions nihilism: controls are always porous to some extent and raising costs to illicit purchasers might itself be a partial policy win. But sanctions and export controls do incentivize a growing

[23] For an announcement outlining the new restrictions and providing links to the full text of the rules, see: "The Bureau of Industry and Security, U.S. Department of Commerce," October 17, 2023, www.bis.doc.gov/index.php/documents/about-bis/newsroom/press-releases/3355-2023-10-17-bis-press-release-acs-and-sme-rules-final-js/file

[24] On the commercial issues, see for example Jon Bateman, U.S. China Technological "Decoupling": A Strategy and Policy Framework, Carnegie Endowment for International Peace, April 25, 2022, https://carnegieendowment.org/2022/04/25/countering-unfair-chinese-economic-practices-and-intellectual-property-theft-pub-86925. On the pervasiveness of espionage and intellectual property theft related to the military, see Center for Strategic and International Studies. *Survey of Chinese Espionage in the United States Since 2000*, https://www.csis.org/programs/strategic-technologies-program/survey-chinese-espionage-united-states-2000

[25] Eleanor Olcott, Qianer Liu and Demetri Savastopulo, "Chinese AI groups use cloud services to evade US chip export controls," The Financial Times, March 8, 2023, https://www.ft.com/content/9706c917-6440-4fa9-b588-b18fbc1503b9

parallel universe of trade, investment and finance. Particularly given the changed geostrategic environment, China, Russia, North Korea, and Iran tacitly cooperate by turning a blind eye to export controls or even purposefully assisting firms in circumventing them. At a minimum, effective controls require coordination among allies. Yet they may also rest on extraterritorial tools such as the Foreign Direct Product Rule—which effectively grants the United States the power to control exports that embody certain American technologies—or the imposition of secondary sanctions on uncooperative rivals.

As of this writing, US policy with respect to these issues remains in flux, with the administration sometimes tacking in one direction (for example, in an effort to limit high-end chips sales to China) and then tacking back in another direction (by relaxing those controls, but requiring Nvidia to share revenues on licensed sales). A crucial question for Korea is how to manage the cross-pressures such controls generate. On the one hand, Korea may share some US concerns about Chinese military capabilities. On the other hand, both the US and Korea need to appreciate that the capacity of Korean firms to innovate is partly a function of the profitability of its trade and investment relations with China. Such tradeoffs will of necessity be managed by negotiations that seek compromise on what goods it is reasonable to seek controls.

The IPE of Security IV: The Return of Industrial Policy

A fourth basket of issues centers on a significant intellectual shift: a reconsideration of the merits of industrial policy. East Asia was a pioneer in open-economy industrial policy, an approach that combined selective support for manufacturing with broadly export-oriented growth strategies.[26] This developmental state approach fell out of favor as economies became more open—in part because of foreign pressure—and the costs of industrial policy were seen to outweigh the benefits. More recently, however, industrial policy has witnessed a renaissance among the advanced industrial states.[27] The Biden administration's Inflation Reduction (IRA) and

[26] Stephan Haggard, *Developmental States*. Cambridge: Cambridge University Press, 2018.

[27] For example, Mariana Mazucatto, *The Entrepreneurial State: Debunking Public and Private Sector Myths* (Public Affairs, 2015) and *Mission Economy: A Moonshot Guide to Changing Capitalism* (Harper Business, 2021).

Chips and Science Acts (CHIPS Act) increased public investment in green energy, semiconductor research and even production. Moreover, as we noted the experience of industrial policy in Korea has been subjected to extensive economic research and shown to have generated significant benefits both in the short- and long-run.

U.S. trading partners, including Korea, have followed suit by unveiling their own industrial policy initiatives, and not simply by emulation but out of competitive concerns. The Biden administration's pursuit of industrial policy in the IRA and CHIPS Act generated conflict with Korea by making subsidies conditional on domestic production in the United States. The policy thus Korean investment away from the home market or other regional partners. Korea responded not only through corporate decisions about investment but through three pieces of legislation: the KChips Act, which focused on tax breaks to the industry, the Act on Protection of Industrial Technology (ITA), intended in part to prevent leakage of intellectual property, and a more recent and expansive Advanced Industries Act which targeted innovation in sectors ranging from displays, to batteries, biopharmaceuticals, nuclear power and robotics. While the Advanced Industries Act was targeted more narrowly on the stability of supply chains the ITA covered technologies that may have a more foundational impact on growth and national security. These examples show that U.S. policy can generate conflicts with allies, but also how they may respond with industrial policies of their own. The question looming over this example is whether the advantages of greater resilience and capacity outweigh the potential for inter-allied competition and protection, and how those gains might be realized collectively through initiatives such as the Chip-4 alliance among the United States, Japan, Korea and Taiwan.

The return of industrial policy raises perennial political economy questions that mirror debates about the developmental state. Can public investments be efficient or are they necessarily tainted by rent-seeking or government error? How can industrial policies be designed to incentivize firms to greater innovation and productivity?

As of this writing, it is not clear whether the Trump administration is committed to an industrial policy agenda or whether he sees it operating through different policy tools. The administration has expressed hostility to Biden-era policies, particularly with respect to the green energy transition. However, it has also defined the purpose of its new tariff policy in terms of the revival of American manufacturing and has expressed an interest in something resembling industrial policy in several sectors, including shipbuilding (in which Korea would play a pivotal role). Moreover, the administration offered a rare apology following the notorious ICE raid on a Hyundai facility in Georgia that swept up over 200 Korean engineers and skilled workers, suggesting that it is aware of the need for a more nuanced approach.

However, two policy points are worth underlining about the industrial policy agenda. The first is that these efforts are increasingly cloaked in a national security rationale. The second question raised by the resurgence of industrial policy is how to manage the conflicts such policies can generate. Although many policies are relevant here, the proliferation of subsidies, the tendency for them to generate mimicry and the badly fraying WTO subsidies regime deserve mention.[28] Although these issues are most clearly in evidence with respect to the U.S.-China trade war and Europe's growing attention to the challenge, they have also arisen *among* the advanced industrial states as well as Korea has seen repeatedly.

The IPE of Security V: New Governance Structures

The possibility that strategic competition will generate economic races-to-the-bottom segues naturally to the final cluster of issues where economics and security intersect: the role played by international and regional organizations and the effort to craft rules of the road. China's emergence on the world economic stage was capped by its entry into the WTO, which was seen as placing important restraints on Chinese economic policy. Since that time, the WTO has suffered a long slow decline, first through the inability to negotiate a conclusion to the long-running Doha Round and more recently because of debilitating conflicts over the dispute settlement process and the initiation of Trump's reciprocal tariff regime. In principle, WTO commitments remain intact (outside of the US), and an effort has emerged to circumvent US and other objections through the creation of the Multi-Party Interim Appeal Arbitration Arrangement (MPIA). But the inability of the WTO to manage emergent trade policy conflicts with China was increasingly clear well before the onset of the second Trump administration and trade policy action has long shifted to regional, plurilateral and bilateral agreements. The rise of national security

[28] Simon Evenett and Johannes Fritz, *Subsidies and Market Access: Toward an Inventory of Corporate Subsidies by China, the European Union and the United States: 28th Global Trade Alert Report*. London: Centre for Economic Policy Research, 2021.

considerations not only makes it more likely that such groupings will play a central role in world trade but also imbues them with a competitive quality.

An unanticipated outcome of the weaponization of interdependence, export and investment controls and industrial policy is that they can necessitate cooperation. For example, the United States has been forced to think in terms of multilateral frameworks to accomplish export control objectives because of the challenges of leakage, and not only from hostile actors but from allies as well. Among those initiatives are the U.S.-EU Trade and Technology Council (TTC), whose stated objective includes "strengthening our technological and industrial leadership, boosting innovation, and protecting and promoting critical and emerging technologies and infrastructure."[29] In the Asia-Pacific, these efforts have centered more on supply-chain resilience through the Biden-era Indo-Pacific Economic Framework and an aggressive U.S. diplomacy to align allies with its export control agenda, in part through the shadow of U.S. extraterritorial reach provided by the Foreign Direct Product rules.[30]

Will Asian-only trade agreements such as the Regional Comprehensive Economic Partnership (RCEP) shape trade relations in the Indo-Pacific, or will initiatives spearheaded by the advanced industrial states carve out meaningful roles: the Trans-Pacific Partnership (TPP) and its successor the Comprehensive and Progressive Agreement for Trans-Pacific Partnership (CPTPP), the Quad, or the Indo-Pacific Economic Framework (IPEF)? Do Chinese-led initiatives such as BRI provide global public goods or do they embody competing economic norms and security ties that are inimical to Western interests? Of particular interest is whether and how U.S. allies in the region might cooperate on the expansive security agenda just outlined: to anchor alliance relations in expanded economic ties; to exercise leverage collectively; to coordinate around export controls; and to foster innovation.[31] While rule-based initiatives are unlikely to come out of the second Trump administration, such arrangements might

[29] Office of the United States Trade Representative, "U.S.-EU Trade and Technology Council," https://ustr.gov/useuttc

[30] On the definitions of these rules, see "Bureau of Industry and Security, Foreign-Direct Product (FDP) Rules," https://www.bis.doc.gov/index.php/2011-09-13-13-22-03/22-licensing/reexports-and-offshore-transactions/645-direct-product-guidelines

[31] See for example Daniel Liman, Ben FitzGerald, Kristine Lee and Joshua Fitt, *Forging an Alliance Innovation Base*. Center for a New American Security March 29, 2020, https://www.cnas.org/publications/reports/forging-an-alliance-innovation-base

emerge around particular technologies: again, shipbuilding and semiconductors are obvious candidates.

Concluding Thoughts

The central argument of this chapter is that a new international political economy is emerging, focused on the relationship between economics and security. Although there are a handful of new academic contributions in this vein, much of the research is coming out of think tanks and follows closely on the heels of policy initiatives that have political as well as security motivations.

At the most encompassing level, the US long held to the view that an open world economy, supported by multilateral institutions, was broadly in line with US grand strategy interests. The strategic as well as economic gains that the United States, its allies and China reap from closer economic integration are increasing put at risk by the restraints on trade and investment that are motivated by security concerns, concerns that are being defined by second Trump administration in increasingly expansive terms. Efforts to exercise leverage, impose sanctions for political ends and tighten export and investment controls all throw sand in the wheels of global commerce. An important question for future research is whether the new security agenda implies a world economy that is significantly less open.

But the costs of these measures are not simply one-off; they can set in train dynamic processes with unintended consequences. To cite but three examples, U.S. efforts to impose multilateral and bilateral sanctions against adversaries such as North Korea and Russia have contributed to a thriving global underground economy of illicit activities and sanctions evasion, facilitated in part by innovations such as cryptocurrency. Even among allies, sanctions can have perverse effects. Japan's effort to signal displeasure in an ongoing history war with Korea had the unintended effect of pushing South Korea to substitute for Japanese imports in the semiconductor supply chain.[32] And U.S. policies to constrain Chinese trade practices, even if warranted, appear to have pushed Xi Jinping to double-down on his industrial policy bets.

[32] Stephan Haggard and Jeongsoo Kim, "Disrupting Supply Chains: Evidence on the Japan-Korea Conflict," Korea Economic Institute, The Peninsula Blog, April 13, 2020, https://keia.org/the-peninsula/disrupting-supply-chains-evidence-on-the-japan-korea-conflict/

The trade/security agenda is here to stay and the issues in play are by no means limited to the major economic powers; rather they have externalities for countries such as Korea. The study of Korea has played an important role in the field of international political economy because of its rapid growth, its distinctive institutional arrangements, and apparently successful industrial policies. However, the new international milieu poses a range of novel questions as well, and the hope of this chapter is to underscore what some of those might be.

CHAPTER 3

From Compressed Development to Compressed Convergence: Changing Variety of Capitalism in Contemporary Korea

Keun Lee and Djun Kil Kim

Introduction

Beginning with Japan and then followed by the so-called "Four Asian Tigers," the capitalist economies of East Asia achieved a remarkable performance characterized by high growth and low inequality, leading some

This chapter is an updated version of an authors' article published in *Review of Evolutionary Political Economy* (Lee and Kim 2024: Compressed Development, Decompression, and Diverging Convergence in South Korea).

K. Lee (✉)
Chung-Ang University and Seoul National University (emeritus), Seoul, Korea

College of Business and Economics, University of Johannesburg, Johannesburg, South Africa
e-mail: kenneth@snu.ac.kr

D. K. Kim
Center for Economic Catch-up, Seoul, Korea

H.-k. Kwon (ed.), *Korean Political Economy from a Comparative-Historical Perspective*, Palgrave Series in Contemporary Korean Studies, https://doi.org/10.1007/978-981-95-9785-7_3

to refer to this meteoric rise as the "East Asian miracle" (World Bank, 1993). This miraculous performance has often been associated with the role of developmental states (Johnson, 1982; Haggard, 2018; Weiss & Thurbon, 2021). Although South Korea (hereafter Korea), as one of the "Asian Tigers", was once considered an exemplary country of the "East Asian miracle", it now suffers from slow growth and rising inequality. In fact, Korea has exemplified a tumultuous journey, including the economic miracle that began in the 1960s under the authoritarian developmental states, democratization from 1987, the financial crisis of 1997 and subsequent reform and opening, and slowing economic growth and rising inequality in the 2010s and 2020s. In this sense, we are now facing the end of the capitalist model that accompanied the East Asian miracle in Korea.

Despite the turbulent nature of Korea's contemporary political economy, the dominant concept characterizing Korea has been compressed modernity or "compressed development," which focuses on the fact that the country achieved rapid socioeconomic development within a few decades-a feat that took other developed countries over a century (Whittaker et al., 2020). In the literature, compressed modernity has been conventionally defined as "economic, political, and social change that occurred in an extremely condensed manner in both time and space" (Chang, 2022: 19). While such concepts are still useful, there is also a need for a new framework to reflect the contemporary situation of radical opening, slow growth, and increasing equality. In other words, it is now time to ask whether the period of compressed development is over with the waves of democratization, liberalization, and slowing growth. In sum, the literature does not sufficiently elucidate the nature of the socioeconomic changes that have taken place in Korean society since the 2000s. The characterization of recent decades of Korean history as a period of post-catch-up or post-compressed modernity is limited in its explanatory value, as it merely suggests the end of a paradigm without explaining what might follow.

Thus, this chapter adopts a narrow definition of compressed development as a form of late industrialization that lacks political democracy and open markets, and then defines decompression as the process of political democratization and economic liberalization. It then asks whether decompression is leading to Korea's convergence with Western or Anglo-America capitalism or how, why, and to what extent Korea's developmental trajectory has continued to diverge from that of advanced or mature economies in the West. This study will argue that while Korea is undergoing a multifaceted convergence toward different varieties of capitalism, Korea is realizing "divergent convergence" as it remains distinct from any particular form of Western capitalism. For instance, as will be discussed later, Korea joins Japan, Italy and Spain in the "safe capitalism" group in terms of life expectancy and crime rates, while Korea is closer to the Anglo-American model in terms of unemployment and long-term employment rates but is closer to Europe in terms of legal protection against layoffs.

While it is not clear which specific variety of capitalism it is converging, the East Asian miracle seems to be over now, as evidenced by the end of high growth and rising equality. Also, Korea has established itself as one variant of high-income, mature capitalism that displays characteristics resembling a variety of different developed capitalist economies. In sum, synthesizing existing studies and compiling new information and materials, this chapter applies the framework of "compressed development, decompression, and divergent convergence" to analyze and interpret the dynamics of Korea's political economy since the 1980s after the death of the modernizer-dictator, President Park Chung-hee. Our goal is to explain the evolutionary outcome of Korea's distinctive political-economic development trajectory since the end of WWII, and its recent arrival upon a development stage best described as "diverging convergence." Specifically, this chapter aims to fill the following lacunas in the literature.

First, there is a need for a more explicit and focused analysis of the transition from compressed development to decompression, in particular, the linkage between economic achievement under compression and democratization (political decompression). This linkage is highly relevant to debates in the literature about whether political democracy—or "inclusive institutions," following Acemoglu and Robinson (2012)—is a necessary pre-requisite of economic prosperity or whether economic growth can be achieved even under authoritarianism and serve as a catalyst for democratization (Lipset, 1959). This chapter explores the hypothesis that compressed economic development enabled the formation of a critical mass of middle-class Koreans who demanded a level of political freedom commensurate with their economic prosperity (Eichengreen et al., 2015, p. 27).

Second, this chapter attempts to account for the recent changes involving the linkage between decompression and convergence. Gone are the days when Korea could boast of its fast growth rates. Rather, the country is now facing slowing growth and rising inequality, which has led some to speculate about whether Korea has left the model of East Asian capitalism and is now converging with the Anglo-American system (Lee & Shin, 2021). In fact, Korea has dramatically transformed from a society known for high fertility, a high marriage rate, and a low divorce rate into one with the world's lowest fertility rate, widespread singlehood, and a rising divorce rate—all trends that resemble other typical high-income societies (Chang, 2022, p. 18). Therefore, an interdisciplinary approach is needed to analyze the interactions between socio-political and economic factors from the perspective of not only compressed development but also "compressed convergence."

In what follows, Section "Evolution of Capitalism in Korea and the New Departures" reviews the past performance of Korea and the literature to sort out the research gaps and discuss the need for a new framework to deal with new issues. Then, the following three sections discuss each of the three new issues. Section "Linking Compressed Development with Political Decompression" focuses on the linkages from compressed growth to the unfolding of peaceful and radical democratization process. Section "Economic Decompression, Crisis, and the Seeds of Convergence" focuses on the long-term consequences of the post-crisis reforms that ended the East Asian miracle but planted the seeds of convergence. Section "Defining the Variety of Capitalism in Korea after Decompression: A Diverging Convergence" discusses the nature of evolving and contemporary capitalism in Korea, playing with the notion of diverging convergence. Section "Summary and Concluding Remarks" concludes the chapter with a summary and outlook.

Evolution of Capitalism in Korea and the New Departures

Evolution of Capitalism in Korea

Korea underwent a process of compressed development that saw the country achieving rapid development within just a few decades—an accomplishment that took other developed countries over a century. In terms of GDP per capita based on purchasing power parity (PPP), which is a basic measure of living standards, Korea represents a paradigmatic example of quick economic catch-up. For comparison, Korean GDP per capita based on PPP was around 10% in the 1960s. Since then, it rapidly increased to nearly 20% of US levels around 1980. Despite the political turbulence following Park's death in 1979 and the rise of the democratization movement in the mid to late 1980s, the economy continued to catch up, reaching 40% of US levels by the mid-1990s.

In fact, in the late 1980s, chaebols took advantage of the favorable external conditions known as the "three lows" (low oil prices, low interest rates, and the low price of Korean currency) to continue their expansion by increasing R&D and moving into high value-added sectors. Thus, Korea's per capita GDP in PPP terms, which was about 25% of the US level in the late 1980s, continued to climb, reaching 40% of the US level (regarded as the threshold for high-income status) in the mid-1990s and enabling the country to join the OECD. In sum, it was the relatively peaceful process of democratization based on political compromise that did not disrupt economic growth, enabling Korea to join the ranks of the high-income countries.

The initial momentum for this political decompression originated in the ten years that began with the 1987 democratization movement, which restored direct election for the presidency. This period also included the first wave of economic liberalization. The second and more decisive period of economic decompression began with the 1997 financial crisis that paved the way for a transition of political power from the liberal rightist to the liberal leftist government and the radical liberalization of the economy pursuant to IMF-reforms which imposed some of the institutions of Anglo-American capitalism and thus set the country on a trajectory of convergence with Anglo-American capitalism. Further, in the 2000s Korea has initiated and concluded a series of the negotiations for the Free Trade Agreements with the US (2006–2012), India (2006–2010), EU (2007–2015), and China (2012–2015). Thus, Korea has ended up being one of the most open economies in the world, whereas it used to be one of the most protected markets.

Although the 1997 Asian financial crisis dropped Korea's growth rate to −5% rate in 1998, the country quickly recovered, and by 1998, it had returned to a catch-up trajectory. Korea's GDP per capita reached nearly 60% of the US level by the early 2010s following the global financial crisis of 2008 and 2009. This swift catch-up during these periods of crisis is comparable to the catch-up Korea achieved over the 15-year period from the early 1980s to the mid-1990s, during which time Korean GDP per capita grew from 20% to 40% of the US level. Korea's GDP per capita eventually reached 70.2% of the US level in 2020, putting Korea on par with Japan, the United Kingdom, and France and demonstrating that

Korea had achieved convergence with the income levels of other "rich countries."[1]

However, Korean capitalism has still not yet fully converged to with Anglo-American capitalism. This is due to enduring historical legacies and path-dependences associated with institutional inertia and vested interests. On the one hand, the driving forces for convergence appear to be ongoing financialization and the rise of shareholder capitalism, which are perceived as the causes of low investment and high inequality (Lee et al., 2020). On the other hand, the majority of the largest firms in Korea continue to be family-controlled chaebols, and family and kinship linkages remain an important factor in contemporary in Korea (Ha, 2023). Although one might assume that state dominance over the financial system would have ended with the rise of liberalization and globalization, the influence of the government endures, albeit in a new form including industrial policy (Thurbon, 2016; Thurbon & Weiss, 2021; Kwon, 2021; Kastelli et al., 2023).

Nowadays, maturing Korea faces social problems similar to those in Western societies, including youth drug addiction (Chang, 2022). Then, we are facing a paradox of nominal convergence in Korea—that is, the existence of slowing growth, rising unemployment, and higher socio-economic inequality, alongside the persistence of underlying institutional frameworks, such as chaebol dominance, bank–government relations, labor market systems, and the role of the government in the economy. In terms of labor market outcomes, Korea is an extreme outlier with longest working hours and largest gender gap in wages. However, in terms of social wellbeing indicators, such as life expectancy and crime rates, Korea is doing very well and similar to Italy, Spain, and Japan (see Section "Economic Decompression, Crisis, and the Seeds of Convergence" later).

So, there is a need to go beyond the simple dichotomy of convergence versus divergence. The diversity and heterogeneity shown in various aspect of Korea imply that it is an oversimplification to state that Korean capitalism is converging with, or is consistently similar to, any particular type of capitalism or countries. In this sense, we can refer to this phenomenon as "diverging convergence," which is to imply that while Korea is converging with some advanced capitalisms according to certain indicators, it also continues to remain distinct from other forms of advanced capitalism. In

[1] See Figure 1 of Lee and Kim (2024).

other words, Korea is undergoing a multi-faceted convergence toward different types of mature capitalism.

The Literature and This Study

The literature on contemporary Korea have tended to deal individually with distinct phases within the history of Korean capitalism, such as the decades of "miraculous" economic growth, periods of crisis, and the recent era of growth slow-down and rising inequality. Research by the first generation of Korean studies focused on socio-economic changes during the "miracle" economy of the pre-1997 period (Amsden, 1989; Jones & Sakong, 1980; Song, 1990; Woo, 1991; Chang, 1994). The second generation studies have focused on the financial crisis of 1997 and post-crisis transformation (Chang, 2003), while Eichengreen et al. (2015) and Shin (2014) examined the Korean economy during and after the global financial crisis of 2008 and 2009. The second generation also includes studies debating the perceived continuity or discontinuity of the Korean developmental state (Thurbon, 2016; Kwon, 2021) or the nature of the welfare state (Yang, 2017).

This chapter attempts to herald a third generation of Korean studies by focusing on the recent issue of the possible convergence (or divergence) of Korean capitalism with Anglo-American capitalism or other variety of mature Western capitalism (Lee & Shin, 2021). This approach departs from that of the second generation, as it forgoes focusing on the causes of the crisis, instead choosing to explore the sources of convergence beginning with the neoliberal reforms imposed by the IMF. It also departs from the first generation by extending the discussion of compressed development to include the linkages between the economic achievements of this period and democratization which we consider political decompression. Whereas scholars of the second generation are critical of the economic performance before and during the crisis period, they do not address the questions of post-crisis transition and the possible convergence with Anglo-American capitalism.

So, this chapter will re-interpret long term evolution of capitalism in Korea using the framework of compressed development, decompression and diverging convergence, and focus on the following linkages in the evolution. First, compressed economic growth since the 1960s laid the groundwork for political decompression (democratization). Second, an ill-managed first wave of economic decompression (liberalization) resulted in a financial crisis. Finally, post-crisis reforms (a second, more radical decompression) planted the seeds for convergence.

Exploring these linkages is important because the progression from decompression to convergence with Anglo-American capitalism is not an inevitable relationship. In the Korean context, economic decompression since the 1997 crisis was not a gradual internal process driven by political consensus among Koreans. Rather, Anglo-American economic institutions and financialization were implanted in Korea by an external force, the IMF, as part of post-crisis reforms. Contribution of the chapter lies in unraveling the linkages that connect compression to decompression and then decompression to convergence and thereby specify the nature and varieties of capitalism (Soskice & Hall, 2001) in contemporary Korea.

Linking Compressed Development with Political Decompression

This chapter began by defining compressed development as economic growth without democracy, economic liberalization, or worker's rights. The watershed moment in Korea's transition toward democracy was June 1987, when mass demonstrations, referred to as the June Democratic Struggle, brought about the return of free and direct elections for the presidency, marking the restoration of procedural democracy in the post-Park era. However, the nature of the linkages between economic growth and political democracy are not well understood within the literature. In this context, one of the important contributions of this chapter is to argue that the Korean middle class emerged as a result of rapid growth and served as a key intermediary in the relationship between economic growth and political democratization.

Indeed, compressed economic growth resulted in a large middle class employed in decent jobs (Koo, 2022; Shin, 2003). This phenomenon is reflected in both the perceptions of everyday Koreans and in objective data. First, poll data reveals that middle-class consciousness increased among the population, with 70% or more of Koreans regarding themselves as middle class in the late 1980s (Koo, 2022: Ch. 1). Although there is some variation between survey findings, Koo (2022) has reported a continuous increase in the share of people who considered themselves to be middle class. Koo found that this ratio increased from 40% in the 1960s to about 60% in the 1970s, 60% to 70% in the 1980s, and finally 70% to

80% in the late 1980s and 1990s. According to Shin (2003), among the three components of the middle class, the share of the new middle class—meaning those employed as skilled or educated white-collar workers in urban areas—has driven this increase, with their share increasing from a mere 6.6% in 1960 to 14.2% in 1970 and 26.1% in 1990, followed by a slight decrease to 25.5% in 1995.

However, the question that follows from this is about the relationship between this new urban middle class and democratization, which is less explored in the literature, including in the work of Koo (2022). A survey show that the new middle class maintained strongly negative impression of the military regimes (Teichman, 2016, p. 148). Then, Shin (2003) shows that the Korean middle class's critical attitude toward the authoritarian regime and embrace of democratic values was due to their university education and student movement experiences on campuses. Indeed, during the time that the authoritarian regime was violently suppressing anti-government organizing, the university emerged as an important space where political speech and actions critical of the government were somewhat tolerated. As the new middle class became increasingly confident of its economic power and motivated by democratic values, they came out to challenge the military regime.

Actually, it was the middle class—not radical organized labor—that was the primary group of the pro-democracy demonstrations in the June 1987 Mass Resistance. In the Korean media, these middle-class protestors have been referred to as the so-called "necktie brigade" (Chang, 2017; Ahn, 2010), as they were primarily white-color office workers. The middle-class composition of the pro-democracy demonstrations is also reflected in the leadership of the movement; Several progressive groups were united to form the National Headquarters (for the demonstration), and the eleven selected leaders are Christian pastors, Buddhist monk, journalists, intellectuals including college professors, poets, lawyers and congressmen. There was no labor leader among the leadership.

This middle-class nature of the demonstrations also explains its peaceful nature, as the movement announced a clear and simple objective that focused on procedural democracy without incorporating leftist demands. Furthermore, as South Koreans became increasingly confident in the country's economic wellbeing and security relative to North Korea, it became possible to challenge the military regime without provoking fear that bringing down the current government, as well as the resulting turmoil, might induce North Korea to contemplate a military attack. This argument for the linkage between economic growth and democracy is consistent with Lipset's (1959) assertion that economic growth reduces the political costs of overthrowing authoritarian regimes (Chen & Feng, 1996).

Alarmed by the increasing scale of the demonstration, President Chun Doo-whan and his crony presidential candidate Roh Tae-woo accepted popular demands for constitutional reform. On June 29, Roh Tae-woo, the presidential candidate for the ruling party, declared the government's intention to amend the constitution to ensure direct presidential elections. However, the victory of ex-military general Roh Tae-woo in the 1987 presidential election allowed the clique of ex-military politicians to maintain its rule of the country. It took Korea another five years to elect civilian pro-democracy activist Kim Young-sam as president, which was made possible by an unlikely coalition between democracy fighter Kim Young-sam's and ex-military Roh Tae-woo's respective parties.

Although the first stage of political decompression was gradual and based on compromise (or the strange merge of the two parties), its later stages were rather radical. During his term, Kim Young-sam oversaw a decisive purge of the military elite who had run the country for nearly three decades. Subsequently, former pro-democracy activists emerged as new political elites, completely replacing ex-military politicians within the National Assembly and in important positions across Korean society.

A focused look at the composition of the National Assembly since the 1980s reveals that democratization in 1987 and the subsequent general election in 1988 was a turning point in Korean politics, as the composition of the political elite shifted from a small cadre of military officials to pro-democracy leaders and student activists. During this period, National Assembly seats included about 250 members. The composition of the National Assembly for each general election to illustrate the proportion of ex-military members and democracy activists regardless of party affiliation. The ex-military group includes those who graduated from any of the three military academies in Korea, which are the Korea Military Academy, the Korea Naval Academy, and the Korea Air Force Academy. Democracy activists include former student activists, civil rights activists and people active in NGOs, and those active in pro-democracy organizations, notably the Council for the Promotion of Democracy, which was a major pro-democracy organization formed in 1984 by the two opposition leaders Kim Young-sam and Kim Dae-jung.

As is shown by Lee and Kim (2024, Table 1), the share of pro-democracy activists in the National Assembly doubled from 16 seats (5.6%) following the general election in 1981 to 32 seats (11.2%) in 1985. In the 1988 general election, the number of pro-democracy activists jumped to 51 members (16.7%), reflecting the dramatic shift in the composition of the Korean legislature following the first wave of democratization. This number further increased with 68 members (20%) in the 1992 general elections, meaning that the number of democracy activists was now double that of the 34 seats (10%) held by ex-military members. Ten years later, in the 2000 general election, the share of ex-military decreased to just nine seats (2.7%), whereas the share of democracy activists increased to a remarkable 79 seats (26.3%), many of whom belonged to Kim Young-sam's New Korea Party and other opposition parties.

Another important consequence of political decompression in Korea was the emergence of radical labor unionism and the Korea Democratic Labor Party following the pro-democracy protests of 1987. Indeed, following the ruling military-led party's declaration that it would reform the constitution to guarantee the right to political association, a wave of illegal strikes, often referred to as the "Great Labor Struggle," rocked the country from July to September of 1987, which was followed by formation of an increasing number of labor unions. Eventually, by the end of 1988, the total number of new labor unions had risen to 6164, a sharp increase from the 2675 that existed at the end of 1986. These new labor unions were united to form a national-level umbrella organization, called Confederation of Trade Union (KCTU), which finally, in January 2000, established its own party, the Democratic Labor Party (DLP), with the former KCTU chairman Kwon Young-Ghil as the first leader of the party. In the 2004 general election, two DLP candidates, including party head Kwon Young-ghil, were successfully elected to two constituency seats and eight proportional representation seats, with the party receiving 13% of the national vote. Thus, in 2004, the DLP won a total of 10 seats.

In sum, although the first stage of political decompression was a rather gradual process of compromise, its later stage had a very radical ending. First, Kim Young-sam's decisive purge of ex-military elites ended the three-decade rule by the military. Second, former democratic activists assumed new positions as political elites and replaced ex-military politicians in the National Assembly and other sectors of Korean society. Finally, the rise of radical labor unionism since the late 1998 and the creation of their political party in 2000 marked the completion of this radical process of political decompression.

Economic Decompression, Crisis, and the Seeds of Convergence

The 1997 Financial Crisis and the IMF-Imposed Reform

As the first civilian president of the post-Park era, pro-democracy activist Kim Young-sam contributed to consolidating Korea's democratic institutions by eradicating the power base of the military. Perhaps feeling confident from this political victory, President Kim aimed to make Korea a member of the OECD. However, entry into the OECD required that a country have a substantially open and free market economy. In the early to mid-1990s, however, conditions were not ideal for initiating financial liberalization, as the Korean economy was suffering from trade deficits associated with the country's overvalued currency and weak exports. Despite this, the Kim government initiated a series of financial liberalization to deregulate the flow of capital in and out of Korea, creating conditions that would lead to the 1997 financial crisis. The post-crisis reforms imposed by IMF brought Korea into a second, more radical wave of liberalization, or economic decompression.

Given that the origins of these crises have been sufficiently addressed in the literature, this chapter focuses on the medium and long-term consequences of IMF-imposed reform in Korea. In particular, we ask to what extent this reform transformed the Korean economy, pushing it to become more similar to the Anglo-American economic system, while also addressing the costs and benefits of such changes.

The radical unfolding of economic liberalization (decompression) in Korea differs somewhat from that of democratization (political decompression). While the latter was driven primarily by domestic factors and players, the former was driven by the IMF, or the so-called "Wall Street–Treasury–IMF complex" (Wade & Veneroso, 1998; Bhagwati, 1998). Therefore, this post-crisis reform package was inevitably subject to external interests. Scholars continue to debate whether this bailout package was in Korea's best interests and, if not, then whose.

The IMF bailout plan possessed the power to impose specific loan conditions, the details of which were subject to negotiation between stakeholders. The conditions for the Korean IMF bailout were particularly comprehensive and included capital market liberalization, corporate governance reform, and labor market deregulation intended to increase flexibility. Capital market liberalization was based on four key elements: a shift from a managed to a free-floating exchange rates system, liberalization of capital mobility, removal of restrictions on the foreign ownership of stocks, and deregulation of bond markets to allow more foreign participation.

As a consequence of the reform package, the Korean economy began transitioning from an East Asian to an Anglo-American model of capitalism. The former is characterized by a bank-based financial system, relatively high savings, a high debt ratio, high investment, managed exchange rate system, limited capital account openness, and restricted foreign ownership, whereas the latter is characterized by a capital market-based financial system, low savings, low debt ratio, low investment ratio, a floating exchange rate system, full capital account openness, and unrestricted foreign ownership. Given that slower growth and high inequality are common characteristics of the Anglo-American system, it would not be surprising to see such symptoms in Korea following the imposition of the Anglo-American model. Indeed, Korea did experience a growth slowdown beginning in the 2000s. There are two mechanisms that can be identified as the causes for this slowdown of growth.

First, shifting from a high-debt, high-investment economy to a low-debt, low-investment economy tends to have a direct impact on growth potential. During the pre-crisis era of the 1990s, Korean firms displayed extremely high debt-to-equity ratios as well as a tendency to engage in excessive investment, which have been criticized as the underlying factors of the 1997 crisis. Post-crisis reforms, meanwhile, required that Korean firms reduce their debt-to-equity ratios to below 200%—a demand that firms soon realized through restructuring. However, this also meant less investment and, consequently, less growth (Wade & Veneroso, 1998).

Second, IMF reforms stipulated that the Korean corporate sector, in particular chaebols, be made to follow the rules and norms of shareholder capitalism, a core component of the Anglo-American system. These changes in business practices accompanied the rise of foreign ownership in corporate Korea. As noted above, the share of foreign ownership in the stocks of listed Korean firms rose to over 40% by 2003.[2] Interestingly, this

[2] Information from the site of the Korea Stock Exchange (http://krx.co.kr/)

rise in foreign ownership appeared to be negatively associated with the ratio of gross domestic investment to GDP. An econometric analysis by Kim and Cho (2008) using firm-level data proved this assumption to be true, verifying that listed firms with high ratios of foreign-owned equity tended to display low investment. The authors suggested that these firms were subject to demands by shareholders to increase dividends.

Although Korea was previously seen as a country where corporations paid low dividends, this perception has changed, with more firms adopting higher dividend policies, including large chaebols such as Samsung. This trend can be comparable to global trends by referencing data from the OECD National Account, which shows the increasing trends of the ratio of net dividend payment to net value-added in non-financial sectors in Korea (Shin & Lee, 2019). Indeed, this ratio has increased rapidly in Korea, from approximately 6% in 2000 to 11% in 2015, getting close to the ratios in the United States.

This tendency of paying more dividends can also be interpreted as a consequence of financialization. That is, the Korean stock market is increasingly coming to resemble those of the United States and the United Kingdom, as it is functioning less as a source of additional funding for listed companies and more as a channel of value extraction in the form of stock repurchases and dividends (Lazonick & Shin, 2019). This tendency of value extraction can be confirmed by looking at the data on the funds flowing in and out of the listed firms. Up until 2002, listed firms in Korea enjoyed a net positive *inflow* of money with more funds flowing in from issuing new stocks than the amount they paid as dividends or stock repurchase. However, since 2003, there has been a net *outflow* to markets as firms pay higher dividends and use their own profits to purchase their own (treasury) stocks to increase prices and, thereby, further enrich shareholders. In fact, Korea at one time had imposed some restrictions on the purchase and burning of treasury stocks; however, such regulation was relaxed in October 2000.[3]

One consequence of the rise of shareholder capitalism—which values distributing profits as dividends to shareholders over funding reinvestment—appears to be sluggish investment, which, in turn, results in

[3] The maximum amount of the treasury stock repurchases has been expanded to 100% of profits, and decision about retiring treasury stocks can now be made exclusively by the board of directors rather than by shareholders at general assemblies. Accessed in July 2023 at https://n.news.naver.com/article/008/0000022827

slowing economic growth rates.[4] The gross domestic investment to GDP ratio was above 35% during the pre-crisis period in the 1990s but declined to 30% in the 2000s. It continued declining in the 2010s. The above-mentioned symptoms associated with financialization are some of the many causes of increasing income inequality. A study (Shin & Lee, 2019) demonstrated that in OECD countries (including Korea), the increased shares claimed by the stockholders in profits or in financial resources of non-financial sectors led to led to rising inequality in terms of the share of wealth held by the top 10%.

In the meantime, the IMF also demanded Korea to strengthen the capacity of its newly reformed employment insurance system to help stabilize recently terminated workers while they pushed for further initiatives to improve labor market flexibility. The urgent need to restructure industry led the government to legalize redundancy layoffs and the hiring of temporary, at-will workers. In less than 12 months, the number of the unemployed increased by nearly 1.3 million, and the number of employed workers dropped by roughly 2 million (Lee et al., 2008). Notably, the majority of the pain that resulted from labor market reforms and increased flexibility was borne not by workers at large firms but rather by those in less protected segments of the markets, including those at SMEs and young workers, with joblessness rising sharply among unskilled workers, in particular (Lee et al., 2008). Moreover, the "employed" pool contained a significant proportion of part-time workers and day laborers. Consequently, on the macro level, labor flexibility measures were not applied equally across the entire labor market. This strengthened the two-tiered structure of the labor market, polarizing the workforce between a core of unionized workers with relatively robust job protections and precarious workers in at-will employment (Lee et al., 2008; Lee & Lee, 2008).

Thus, the major consequence of restructuring and labor force polarization was rising income inequality, as reflected in Korea's increasing Gini coefficient. Korea's Gini coefficient had been declining in the 1980s and early to mid-1990s before beginning to increase in 1997, a trend that lasted until the late 2000s. Specifically, it rose from 0.283 to 0.320 between 1997 and 1999, slowly decreased to 0.312 in 2002, and then

[4] Of course, growth slowdown at later period or since the 2010s was also caused by Korea's rapidly aging population and the sinking birth rate.

rebounded to 0.306 and 0.310 in 2003 and 2004, respectively.[5] Other indicators of economic equality, such as the share of total wealth held by the top ten richest individuals and the labor share of GDP, all show a similar pattern of improving income equality from the mid-1980s to the late 1990s and then a reversal of this trend that lasts until the end of the 2000s.

In sum, the radical reforms after 1997 had several long-term costs, such as enabling increased ownership in and influence over Korean firms by foreign investors, which resulted in the rise of shareholder capitalism. The Korean economy had become subject to lower investment and slower growth, and rising inequality associated with increasing labor market segmentation and asymmetric sharing of the burden of labor market flexibilization measures.

End of the East Asian Miracle and a Seed for the Anglo-American Capitalism

The literature on Varieties of Capitalism (VoC) pioneered by Soskice and Hall (2001) classifies economies around the world in terms of several key institutions (such as labor–management relations, vocational training and education, corporate governance and finance, inter-firm relations, and relationship with employees). VoC identifies several representative types of capitalism, such as liberal market economies (LMEs), coordinated market economies (CMEs), and mixed market economies (MMEs). LMEs tend to be found in the UK or former UK colonies such as the US, whereas CMEs are found in Continental European and East Asian countries. France, Italy, and Spain tend to be classified as MMEs.

East Asian economies have boasted a remarkable performance of high growth and low inequality, as captured by the phrase "East Asian miracle" (World Bank, 1993). Thus, they have been designated as the "East Asian capitalism group" within the typology of the varieties of capitalism (VoC) literature (Storz et al., 2013). However, the post-crisis reforms imposed by the Wall Street–Treasury–IMF complex introduced various Anglo-American institutions into Korean society, leading to a "new normal" of slow growth and rising inequality. The new situations characterized by

[5] The source of Gini coefficient is http://kosis.nso.go.kr. An updated trend of the labor income shares is from Lee and Kim (2024), and the top 10 shares are from Shin and Lee (2019).

slow growth and rising inequality lead to questions on whether Korea faces the end of East Asian capitalism (characterized by high growth and low inequality) and converges toward the Anglo–American systems (characterized by low growth and high inequality). Lee and Shin (2021) verified that this is true at least in terms of several indicators.

Whereas VoC literature tends to use the variables representing the underlying institutional characteristics of economies, Lee and Shin (2021) used outcome variables to compare economic performance, such as growth rate of GDP per capita, employment rate, and top 10% income share. A statistical analysis, specifically the cluster analysis, is conducted to statistically classify economies into several types over a long period of time. Table 3.1 shows the differences among the four types of capitalism, including East Asian capitalism, in terms of three outcome variables. Their average values are the average of those economies belonging to each cluster. The LME group is associated with slow growth, high inequality, and sound level of employment, whereas CME has a modest growth, low inequality, and sound level of employment rates. Between these two are MMEs with lowest rates of employment that probably reflect labor market rigidity. The East Asian group exhibits the highest growth and lowest inequality.

Table 3.1 Four types of capitalism and their economic outcomes

Period	*CME (Coordinated Market Economy): modest growth; high employment; low inequality)*	*LME (Liberal Market Economy): low growth; high employment; high inequality)*	*MME (Mixed Market Economy): low growth; low employment; low inequality)*	*East Asian Capitalism: very high growth; high employment; very low inequality)*
GDP growth (%)	2.10	1.41	1.64	6.83
Employment (%)	60.32	59.23	47.15	59.54
Top 10% income share (%)	30.15	39.66	31.91	28.47

Source: Table 1 of Lee and Kim (2024)), which is a simplified and integrated version of Tables from Lee and Shin (2021), Lee et al. (2020)

The analysis by Lee and Shin (2021) found that the East Asia cluster became empty in the 2000s with no member economies, which indicates the demise of East Asian capitalism. South Korea and Japan used to be a pioneering economy in the East Asian cluster but joined the LMEs group with the US and UK. This result suggests that the type of capitalism in several East Asian and European countries have become similar to that of the US, which is consistent with the convergence hypothesis toward "bad capitalism" that feature low growth and high inequality. Slow growth and rising inequality have actually been recent trends in both Japan and Korea. The top 10% share of the national income has increased globally, particularly in the US and East Asia, since the 1980s. The US exhibits the highest ratio of over 45%, followed closely by South Korea reaching 45% in 2010 and Japan with 40%.

The discussion above provides an intriguing perspective on capitalism in Korea that goes beyond the simple dichotomy of convergence versus divergence. First, in terms of macro variables such as growth, inequality, and employment rates, Korea now belongs to the Anglo-American capitalism cluster characterized by slow growth and high inequality. This macro-level convergence is matched by firm-level convergence, meaning that chaebols now tend to borrow and invest less and grow slowly while tending to have higher profitability and dividend payments (Im & Lee, 2021). This constitutes a sizeable departure from their operations up until the 1990s, when they used to borrow and invest heavily but paid fewer dividends in order to achieve fast growth.

Defining the Variety of Capitalism in Korea after Decompression: A Diverging Convergence

The preceding section suggests a possible convergence of Korea toward the Anglo-American capitalism as Korea is now experiencing slow growth and rising inequality. This shocking argument raises an important puzzle of how Korea can be considered as converging to the US or UK, despite the possible existing differences in its underlying institutions, such as labor market institutions, corporate governance, and political institution, as well as the state-finance relationship and the techno-industrial governance sphere (Thurbon, 2016; Thurbon & Weiss, 2021). Given this, it is our view that varieties of capitalism should be assessed in broad indictors comprising outcomes, institutions and even policy preferences by the state. Therefore, this section examines more diverse variables regarding labor market institutions, social welfare spending, social wellbeing, labor market policies and democracy.

Social Wellbeing Indicators: Korea as "Safe Capitalism"

This chapter now considers several social welfare indicators, including life expectancy, crime rates, birth rates, gender inequality, and divorce rates. A total of 15 OECD countries will be compared in terms of these five indicators (see Table 3.2). To identify similarities and differences between these

Table 3.2 Birth rate, divorce rate, crime rate, gender inequality index, life expectancy, 2005, 2016

	Birth rate	Divorce rate	Life Expectancy	Crime rate	Gender inequality
	2016	2016	2016	2016	2016
Canada	10.60	1.7	82	1.7	0.10
Germany	11.80	2.0	81	1.2	0.08
Finland	9.60	2.5	81.5	1.3	0.06
Netherlands	10.10	2.0	81.7	0.6	0.05
Denmark	10.80	3.0	80.9	1.0	0.04
Group Average	10.14	2.24	81.42	1.16	0.06
Australia	12.90	1.9	82.4	0.9	0.11
France	11.80	1.9	82.7	1.4	0.08
Sweden	11.80	2.4	82.4	1.1	0.04
Norway	11.30	1.9	82.5	0.5	0.05
UK	11.80	1.8	81.2	1.2	0.14
Group Average	11.92	1.98	82.24	1.02	0.08
Italy	7.80	1.6	83.4	0.7	0.08
Japan	7.80	1.7	84.1	0.3	0.11
Spain	8.80	2.1	83.5	0.6	0.08
Korea	7.90	2.1	82.4	0.7	0.07
Group Average	8.07	1.87	83.35	0.57	0.08
USA	12.2	3	78.7	5.4	0.23

Source: Adaptation of Table 3 of Lee and Kim (2024)

countries, a cluster analysis was conducted, dividing countries into several groups. Cluster analyses identified four major clusters. The first group includes four northern European countries (Denmark, Finland, the Netherlands, and Germany) and Canada. The second group is somewhat mixed and includes two northern European countries (Sweden and Norway), one continental European country (France), and two Commonwealth countries (UK and Australia). The third group includes two East Asian countries (Japan and Korea) and two southern European countries (Spain and Italy). The last group has only one member country—the United States. In other words, the United States is an outlier, representing an exceptionally dangerous form of capitalism with the highest crime rates, shortest life expectancy, highest divorce rates, and highest gender inequality.

While the third group may sound odd, these four countries share important commonalities that can be described as features of "safe capitalism"—that is, these countries have the lowest crime, divorce, and birth rates, a medium level of gender inequality, and the longest life expectancy. Although these southern European countries have been perceived as somewhat poorly performing economies, they demonstrate good performance in terms of social wellbeing indicators. It could be postulated that their slow economic growth has been the price of maintaining a certain level of safety regarding their welfare systems. In contrast, the Nordic countries, which are considered to have pioneered welfare capitalism, seem to have somewhat gone astray, as they now have very high crime rates and divorce rates and slightly lower life expectancy (slightly below 82 years) compared to southern Europe (about 83.5 years).

It is interesting to note that the Korea's social wellbeing indicators are similar to those of Japan and southern Europe but differ significantly from those of the United States. Thus, it can be said that in terms of social welfare variables, Korean capitalism does not converge with the Anglo-American model. Instead, Korea has converged with a different set of countries that demonstrate better social welfare performance—that is, southern European countries and Japan. In particular, life expectance has continually improved in Korea, increasing from 78.2 years in 2006 to 82.4 years in 2016, meaning that the country has achieved one of the longest life expectancies in the world (Table 3.2).

Korea's decent performance in terms of welfare indicators is surprising given the country's characterization as a "small welfare state" (Yang, 2017), where social welfare expenditures are substantially lower than the

OECD average. Korea spent 9.7% of its GDP in 2014 on social welfare, compared to the OECD average of 21.1% (Yang, 2017, p. 1–2). Although Korea's welfare expenditures are relatively low by comparison, the positive indicators outlined above seem to be a result of the country's increasing welfare expenditures since the 1990s, which have contributed to stopping the rise of the Gini coefficient in the country since the 2010s (Wong & Lee, 2018). The share of public expenditures on social protection as a percentage of GDP reached 2% in the early 2000s and then tripled to 6% in 2014. This remarkable jump far outpaces the growth rate of the R&D to GDP ratio, which was 2% in the early 2000s, 3% in the late 2000s, and then 4% in the mid-2010s (Wong & Lee, 2018).

Yang (2017) observed that Korea's comparatively weak welfare state is intimately related to the legacy of compressed development, which suppressed labor organizations and their struggle for political power, as well as decompression, which divided the working class between well-compensated workers in stable employment at large corporations and precarious workers in poorly paid, non-unionized employment at SMEs. Although workers in the former group held some political power, it did not demand social welfare reform, as they were benefitting from the employee benefits (health care, retirement, paid time off, etc) supplied by chaebol firms. Workers in the latter group, by contrast, were not organized and had no political power with which to demand social welfare reforms (Yang, 2017, pp. 60, 46–52). This polarization in the labor market has led to a corresponding divergence in access to insurance coverage. For instance, at large firms, about 75% of both full-time, tenured workers and precarious, at-will workers are covered by employment insurance. In the SME sector, however, the ratio is 64% for tenured workers and 37% for precarious workers (Table 1.1 from Yang, 2017, p. 20).

Following the implementation of nation-wide universal health insurance by Park Chung-hee in 1971, the enactment of the NBLSA by the Kim Dae-jung government constitutes the second major milestone in enhancing Korea's social welfare system (Kim, 2020, p. 87). The NBLSA is a public assistance program that provides cash and in-kind benefits to people living in households with incomes below a certain national standard. In this way, it guarantees a minimum standard of living regardless of age or employment status. The post-crisis liberal-left governments of Kim Dae-jung and Roh Moo-hyun, in fact, introduced various welfare programs (Kim, 2020, pp. 78–79). In particular, the Kim government improved the social welfare system by reconsolidating the health insurance system and restructuring social insurance schemes. Subsequently, the Roh Moo-hyun government oversaw a remarkable expansion in social services, such as child and elderly care. This trend even continued under the two consecutive presidencies of Lee Myung-bak and Park Geun-hye, with both administrations expanding the scale of social welfare coverage (Kim, 2020, p. 78).

Labor Market Outcomes and Institutions

Now let us examine several indicators of labor market institutions. In this context, key variables include working hours, as well as the age and gender wage gaps.[6] The cluster analysis generated four groupings. The first cluster includes the United States, Japan, Canada, Australia, Spain, and Italy. The second cluster includes the United Kingdom, France, and Finland. The third cluster includes the five northern European countries of Sweden, Denmark, Netherlands, Norway, and Germany. Finally, Korea is the outlier that forms its own group. This implies that Korea still conforms to the model of East Asian capitalism, which is characterized by long working hours and large age and gender wage gaps.

This outlier status is due to Korea having extremely high gender and age wage gaps, as well as excessively long working hours. In 2018, among the countries in the table, Korea had the longest average annual working hours at nearly 2000; the United States had the second longest hours at 1780. The salaries of Korean men are almost 34% more than those of women. That said, men and women tend to work in different industries, and therefore, this gap does not necessarily apply to men and women working the same job. As of 2018, Korean seniors (55–64 years old) were paid 19% more than younger workers (25–54 years old) on average. However, a positive sign is that all three of these indicators improved between 2006 and 2018.

The above results are comparable to the results from a similar cluster analysis done by E. Jung (2020), which included many indicators. If the variables are limited to those reflecting labor market outcomes, such as unemployment rates, long-term employment rates, wage inequality, working hours, and wage gaps, then Korea and the United states both fall into the same cluster, which puts them in the company of other Anglo-American economies. Such an outcome is consistent with the results of

[6] The data below are from Table 4 of Lee and Kim (2024).

our cluster analyses using labor market institutions, such as the level of collective bargaining and unionization rates. For instance, the collective bargaining coverage and unionization rates in Korea are 14.8% and 11.6%, respectively. This situation is comparable with the United States, where the numbers are 11.7% and 10.1%, respectively. These figures are extremely low compared to the average of the four continental European countries, where they were 80.0% and 20.7% as of 2018. In northern European countries, the average rates of unionization are much higher at over 50%, except for in the Netherlands.

However, legal protections against layoffs are somewhat higher in Korea than in typical Anglo-American economies. For instance, as of 2018, the average index value for the strictness of employment protections was 0.93 for tenured workers and 0.44 for temporary workers in Anglo-American-style economies. The comparable figures for Korea are 2.42 and 2.13, respectively. On this basis, Korea's labor market can be characterized as a (neo)liberal regime with considerable regulation (Jung 2020).

However, further qualification is needed because, in terms of the degree of active (or passive) LMPs (labor market policies), Korea is closer to European economies than Anglo-American economies.[7] In 2018, the share of expenditures on both active and passive LMP measures to GDP in Korea were both 0.36%. These figures are much higher than the rates of 0.15% and 0.10%, respectively, in the United States. However, the numbers for Korea are still very low compared to European countries. For instance, in 2018, the averages for the four continental European countries were 0.64% and 1.32%, respectively, whereas those for the northern European countries were 0.99 and 0.89%, respectively. Passive LMP measures primarily address distributional concerns and mitigate the adverse effects of unemployment and poverty, and therefore, they function more like a social safety net. Active LMP measures, in contrast, aim to directly reduce unemployment, match labor supply and demand, and enhance individuals' employability and job opportunities and the specific tools include support for worker training, employment incentives, direct job creation, and startup incentives.

Korea still has considerable room for improvement; this applies not only to Korea's shortcomings in LMP expenditures but also to the actual

[7] The share of the expenditure on labor market policy, such as safety nets, worker training, etc., in GDP has increased rapidly from 0.11% (active measures), and 0.17% (passive measures) in 2004 to 0.35%, and 0.32% in 2015 (June 2020).

types of measures. According to the same OECD data, compared to Europe, active LMP measures in Korea are skewed more toward direct job creation by public spending and less toward training and employment incentives.[8] In fact, whereas Korea spends only 0.06% of GDP on worker training, the four continental and five Nordic European countries spend 0.17% and 0.20%, respectively. In contrast, Korea spends as much as 0.15% of GDP on direct job creation, which is approximately 2.5 times more than Korea spends on training. By comparison, the four continental and five northern European countries spend approximately 0.08% and 0.11%, respectively, on job creation.

Political Institutions and Democracy

Finally, this section now addresses factors related to political institutions, such as democracy, freedom, and corruption. Table 3.3 shows indicators of these aspects and rankings of diverse countries, most of which belong to the OECD.

First, in terms of the level of democracy, Korea scores 8.03 out of 10 points and, therefore, ranks 24th out of over 100 countries. This level is comparable to continental European countries, such as France (8.07, 22th), Italy (7.69, 34th), and Spain (8.07, 22th), as well as Japan (8.33; 16th). That said, Korea is much lower than typical northern European countries. However, Korea's level of democracy is higher than that of the United States (7.85, 30th) and much higher than Singapore (6.22, 70th).

Second, if we compare Korea to other countries in terms of the political freedom index, which is a measure of political rights and civil liberties, a similar result emerges. That is, Korea's point is 83 out of 100, which is comparable to several continental European countries but is lower than northern European countries (97 to 100). However, Korea and comparable European countries are all classified as politically "free" countries with points above 80: Korea (83), France (89), and Spain (90). Again, the United States does not rank that well, with a score of just 83. Singapore is worse off at 47 and, therefore, is classified as only "partly free."

Third, according to the corruption index, Korea is again comparable to continental European countries with a score of 63, placing it 31st among all countries. For comparison, France scored 72 (22nd), Spain scored 60

[8] The sources for the data are the same as other tables, which is the OECD (https://stats.oecd.org/)

Table 3.3 Democracy Index, global freedom status, and Corruption Perception Index of countries

Country	*Democracy Index (country ranking)*	*Global freedom status*	*Corruption Perception Index (ranking)*
South Korea	8.03/10 (24)	83/100 (Free)	63/100 (31)
Singapore	6.22/10 (70)	47/100 (Partly Free)	83/100 (5)
Japan	8.33/10 (16)	96/100 (Free)	73/100 (18)
U.S.	7.85/10 (30)	83/100 (Free)	69/100 (24)
U.K.	8.28/10 (18)	93/100 (Free)	73/100 (18)
Canada	8.88/10 (12)	98/100 (Free)	74/100 (14)
Australia	8.71/10 (15)	95/100 (Free)	75/100 (13)
France	8.07/10 (22)	89/100 (Free)	72/100 (21)
Germany	8.80/10 (14)	94/100 (Free)	79/100 (9)
Italy	7.69/10 (34)	90/100 (Free)	56/100 (41)
Spain	8.07/10 (22)	90/100 (Free)	60/100 (35)
Sweden	9.39/10 (4)	100/100 (Free)	83/100 (5)
Netherland	9.00/10 (9)	97/100 (Free)	80/100 (8)
Denmark	9.28/10 (6)	97/100 (Free)	90/100 (1)
Finland	9.29/10 (5)	100/100 (Free)	87/100 (2)
Norway	9.81/10 (1)	100/100 (Free)	84/100 (4)

Source: Table 6 of Lee and Kim (2024) which is based on the data from Democracy Index 2022 (Economist Intelligence Unit.); Global Freedom Status (Freedom House); 2022 Corruption Perception Index (Transparency International)

Notes: The Democracy Index represents the achievement of democracy in the range of 1 to 10. Transparency International's Corruption Perception Index scores (2022) range from 0 (Highly Corruptive) to 100 (Very Clean) for 180 countries

(35th), and Italy scored 56 (41th). Here, as well, Korea scores much worse than northern European countries yet is similar to the United States (69, 24th). It is interesting to note that according to the corruption index, Singapore is ranked as very clean with a score of 83 (5th), which is comparable to northern Europe.

The above results imply that Korea belongs to the group of "free but not-so-clean" democracies together with several continental European countries and the United States. It is not all that surprising that the level of democracy in Korea is comparable to that of the United States and several European countries. For example, Korea has elected a female head of state, former president Park Geun-hye—something that the United States has yet to do. Korean later impeached President Park Geun-hye on March 10, 2017, through a formal and orderly process as outlined in the Constitution. It can be argued that political systems in Korean are healthier than those in the United States in terms of the degree of plutocracy. Indeed, Korea has sent many former presidents to jail—including Chun Doo-hwan, Roh Tae-woo, Park Geun-hye, and Lee Myung-bak—as well as many CEOs of large corporations, such as Samsung, SK, and Hyundai.

Although it was not until the late 1980s that the democratization movement was able to secure procedural democracy and the direct election of the president (see section 3), Korea's democracy has since quickly progressed, achieving a more balanced distribution of power among the executive, legislative, and judicial branches. That is, this democratic maturing was achieved by granting the legislative and jurisdictive branches increased power to compensate for the rather dominant position of the executive in the past. In current times, it is the legislature that has the final say on many issues despite the executive branch being responsible for implementing policies and proposing bills and acts.

Martial Law and Impeachment in 2025 and Risk of Capitalism in Korea

In 2025, an impeachment of the president was again executed in an orderly fashion. This time, the case involved Korea's 20th president, Yoon Suk-yeol, who took office in 2022. In the presidential election, Yoon secured a narrow victory with a 0.7% margin over his opponent, Lee Jae-myung. While he represented conservative voices in Korean politics, his party was a minority in the National Assembly (see the chronology at the end of this volume). Many of the policy initiatives proposed by him and his party were rejected by the National Assembly, which was led by the opposition party. This led to a state of profound exasperation for the president, who even labeled the situation a "legislative dictatorship" by the majority opposition party. He stated that the primary motivation behind the declaration of martial law on December 3, 2024, was the perceived necessity of safeguarding public safety and maintaining order through the deployment of military forces.

While there were heated debates, the court's decision was not unexpected in hindsight, given that the grounds for declaring martial law were perceived as unsubstantiated and contentious. The 21st presidential election in Korea took place on June 3, 2025, offering voters the chance to express their views on President Yoon's use of military force to address political challenges within the legislature. The majority of Korean voters expressed support for the principles of liberal democracy by electing Lee Jae-myung, despite the fact that he was subject to five litigation cases.[9] Following his assumption of the presidency, these legal proceedings were postponed indefinitely or ceased altogether. These decisions by the court were also controversial, and critics argued that the judiciary had become politicized and had lost its independence.

The swift progression of events from the declaration of martial law to the impeachment and election of a new president within a four-month period may indicate the stability and resilience of Korea's political system and democracy. After martial law was declared at 10 PM on December 3, 2024, the ROK Army entered the National Assembly by 12 AM but failed to arrest parliamentary members and halt the passage of the motion to lift martial law, which occurred at 1 AM on December 4. There were instances of soldiers not adhering strictly to the directives issued by high-ranking generals, who, along with President Yoon, were instrumental in the imposition of martial law. The Korean people and society, including soldiers, had successfully prevented a potential regression into a military-led government.

The political turmoil that followed the imposition of martial law may suggest the immaturity of Korea's political and legal systems. It's arguable that the system failed to effectively resolve political tensions between the incumbent and opposition parties within parliament. It's also worth considering that some Korean politicians and military elites may, at times, have believed in the efficacy of martial law for resolving political deadlocks. The potential politicization of the judiciary could be indicative of underlying risks within Korean society. This situation has revealed the "diverging convergence" nature of Korea's political system. From another perspective, it seems that "Korea is not simply a risk society similar to Western societies, but a complex risk society experiencing accidents and hazards common to advanced industrial and underdeveloped societies, plus those unique to South Korea" (Chang, 2025, p. 19). We concur with Chang's view that Korea's multifaceted risk structure has not been fully alleviated, despite its development into a high-income capitalism in the twenty-first century.

[9] One of these cases related to the dissemination of what was considered false information in violation of the Public Official Election Act, and he received a guilty verdict at the Supreme Court on May 1, 2025. His case was then transferred to the High Court for sentencing.

Summary and Concluding Remarks

This chapter has analyzed the long-term development of capitalism in Korea using a new framework of compressed development, decompression, and diverging convergence.

First, the middle class emerged in Korea in the 1980s as a result of compressed growth since the 1960s and served as a key intermediary in linking economic growth to democratization. The process of political decompression, or democratization, was peaceful because it was demanded and led not by the working class but by the middle class. Political decompression in Korea, which began gradually and in a compromised manner involving the merge of the pro-democracy party and the ex-military party, culminated in a radical transformation involving the purge of the ex-military elites and their replacement by new democratic elites. It can be considered a "political miracle" rarely seen in the history of the latecomer countries that gained independence after the World War II.

Second, an ill-managed first wave of economic decompression (liberalization) led to a financial crisis, and then post-crisis reforms (a second, more radical decompression) imposed by the IMF planted the institutional seeds for convergence toward Anglo-American capitalism characterized by slow growth and rising inequality. The economic decompression since the 1997 crisis was not a gradual internal process driven by political consensus among Koreans, but was forced by external forces, the IMF, to implant Anglo-American economic institutions and financialization. The new economic system emerged after the IMF program lowered the propensity for investment and growth in the Korean economy, while still failing to save the country from another crisis in 2008 and a near-crisis during the COVID-19 pandemic in 2020.

Third, it is an oversimplification to say that Korean capitalism is converging with or consistently resembling any particular type of capitalism or group of countries. But it can still be argued that we are now facing the end of the capitalist model that accompanied the East Asian miracle in Korea, as evidenced by the end of high growth and increasing equality. Therefore, it is more accurate to say that Korea is undergoing a multifaceted convergence toward different types of mature capitalism, with Korea having established itself as a variant of high-income mature capitalism that has characteristics similar to a variety of different developed capitalist economies. Thus, while we need to move beyond a simple dichotomy of convergence versus divergence, the term "compressed development" is outdated. Therefore, we use the term "diverging convergence" to characterize the nature of contemporary Korean capitalism.

That is, we seek to rationalize the strange coexistence of Korea's convergence with Anglo-American capitalism, characterized by slow growth, worsening inequality, and "free but not so clean" democratic institutions, alongside Korea's other convergence with the "safe capitalism" of continental European countries in terms of social welfare and well-being indicators, as well as some indicators of labor market policies. One source of this diverging convergence may be the planting of Anglo-American institutions through post-crisis reforms and the subsequent responses and demands by workers and civil society activists for a stronger social safety net and welfare protection in the context of rising labor market insecurity and worsening income inequality.

The underlying mechanism driving this trend may also be the increasing financialization in Korea, which is leading to slow growth and higher inequality. The high level of inequality, as measured by the share of income held by the top 10%, appears to be associated with low unionization; this inequality may also be partly responsible for Korea's moderate level of democracy, as inequality tends to be associated with more corruption and weaker protection of civil and political rights. In contrast, Korea's divergence from the United States as a "safe capitalism" with low crime and divorce rates and high life expectancy seems to be associated with the large difference in health insurance coverage as well as ethnic and cultural homogeneity.

In a sense, a fundamental force driving Korea's convergence with advanced capitalism in the West seems to be the general rise in Korean income levels. As Koreans have become richer, their behavior has come to resemble that of members of affluent societies. In addition, the rapid decline in the birth rate, which has now fallen below 0.8 births per woman, seems to be related to the rise in income levels. Declining fertility is a common phenomenon in affluent East Asian societies. First in Japan, then in Korea, Taiwan, and now even in China.

It is also interesting to note that this diverging convergence has occurred in the relatively short period of just a few decades. Therefore, while this chapter began with the initial three-part framework of "compressed development, decompression, and diverging convergence," it could be said that Korea's long-term evolution may be summarized with one term: compressed convergence. Consequently, the term "compressed development" is perhaps not the most accurate way to describe contemporary Korean society. However, it would be remiss if we do not acknowledge the significant challenges that Korean society has faced, particularly in the period stretching from the imposition of martial law in December 2024 up to April 2025. These events have highlighted the ongoing presence of "risks of compressed modernity," to borrow a term from Chang (2025), and they underscore the importance of vigilance in navigating the complexities of social and political transformation.

Finally, it may be advisable for Korea to seize the COVID-19 pandemic and deglobalization since the US-China tension as opportunities to revitalize the economy by adopting policies that can curb the ongoing trend of financialization, restore the original strength of Asian capitalism, and return Korea to a trend of high growth and healthy social equity. The retreat of globalization provides a golden opportunity to restore autonomy in domestic economic policymaking on issues such as interest and exchange rates, while imposing adjustments to excessive capital mobility. However, instead of trying to return to the old model of East Asian capitalism, Korea should pursue a hybrid capitalism that rebalance elements of shareholder and stakeholder capitalism while keeping East Asian capitalism at its core.

These reform agenda discussed above for future capitalism in Korea has been overshadowed by a new wave of challenges, signaled by the global shock of universal and sectoral tariffs imposed by the Trump administration in the United States since 2025. Korea now faces three distinct forces leading to the hollowing out of its economy and industry.

The first force is the hollowing out driven by US tariffs and pressure for increased investment in the United States. In response, major businesses, such as Hyundai Motors, are investing heavily and expanding production in their US factories while reducing domestic output. Consequently, exporting "made in Korea" goods has become more expensive due to tariffs, making production and sales within the United States more economically viable. The second force originates from China, where its economy is weakening due to US measures, including high tariffs and restrictions on access to American technology. Facing sluggish demand, China's oversupplied goods, such as steel and petrochemical products, are aggressively seeking overseas markets, including Korea. This influx of increasingly competitive Chinese goods has severely impacted Korean firms, forcing companies like POSCO and Hyundai Steel to close factories and production lines, respectively. The third and final force is domestic, stemming from population aging and the resulting hollowing out of specific regions, particularly the southern provinces. This demographic shift has led to the closure of more schools due to a lack of students and an increase in unoccupied homes.

While Korea has historically been known for its successful late industrialization and has maintained a relatively high share of manufacturing, it is now heading toward a unique form of de-industrialization. This process, which may be considered another sign of diverging convergence, shares some features with de-industrialization in Western advanced economies but is distinct due to the influence of recent geopolitical changes and the rise of China as a manufacturing powerhouse with immense production capacity. Solving these challenges requires new deals between management and workers, and between the central and provincial governments and their people.

References

Acemoglu, D., & Robinson, J. A. (2012). *Why Nations Fail.* Crown Publishing Group.

Ahn, B.-O. (2010). Hanguk minjuhwa undong e daehan pyongga wa insik eui jeonhwan eul wihayeo [For a Change of Evaluation and Conception of Korea's Democratization Movement], *Yeoksa wa Hyeonsil* [History and Reality] 77, 17–40.

Amsden, A. (1989). *Asia's Next Giant.* Oxford University Press.

Bhagwati, J. (1998). The Capital Myth: The Difference between Trades in Widgets and Dollars. *Foreign Affairs, 77*(May/June), 7–12.

Chang, H.-J. (1994). *The Political Economy of Industrial Policy.* Macmillan.

Chang, S.-J. (2003). *Financial Crisis & Transformation of Korean Business Groups.* Cambridge University Press.

Chang, J. H. (2017). 1987 nyeon minjuhwa undong eui seonggyeok kwa yeonghyang: [The Character and Influence of the 1987 Democratization Movement], *Hwonvophag yeongu* [The Constitution Study] 23(3), 115–144.

Chang, K.-S. (2022). *The Logic of Compressed Modernity.* Polity Press.

Chang, K.-S. (2025). *The Risk of Compressed Modernity.* Polity Press.

Chen, B., & Feng, Y. (1996). Economic Development, Political Cost and Democratic Transition. *Journal of Economic Development, 21*, 2.

Eichengreen, B., et al. (2015). *The Korean Economy.* Harvard University Asia Center.

Ha, Y.-C. (2023). *Late Industrialization, Tradition, and Social Change in South Korea.* University of Washington Press.

Haggard, S. (2018). *Developmental States.* Cambridge University Press.

Im, B., & Lee, K. (2021). From Catching Up to Convergence of the Latecomer Firms. *Journal of Open Innovation, 7*(3), 1–23.

Johnson, C. (1982). *MITI and the Japanese Miracle*. Stanford University Press.

Jones, L. P., & Sakong, I. (1980). *Government, Business and Entrepreneurship in Economic Development: The Korean Case*. Harvard University Asia Center.

Jung, E-H, (2020), Typology of Korea's Labor Market Regimes Revisited, *Nodong Yeongu (labor studies)*, 41: 5-39.

Kastelli, I., Mamica, L., & Lee, K. (2023). New Perspectives and Issues in Industrial Policy for Sustainable Development. *Rev Evol Polit Eco, 4*, 1–25. https://doi.org/10.1007/s43253-023-00100-2

Kim, A., & Cho, M. H. (2008). Types of Foreign Investors, Dividends and Investment Policy: An Empirical Study of Korean Firms. *Journal of Strategic Management (in Korean), 11*(1), 25–42.

Kim, Y.-S. (2020). Civic Movements and the Detour to Welfare State Building in South Korea. In J. Yang (Ed.), *The Small Welfare State*. E. Elgar.

Koo, H. (2022). *Privilege and Anxiety: The Korean Middle Class in The Global Era*. Cornell University Press.

Kwon, H.-K. (2021). *Changes by Competition: Evolution of South Korean Developmental State*. Oxford University Press.

Lazonick, W., & Shin, J.-S. (2019). *Predatory Value Extraction: How the Looting of the Business Corporation Became the US Norm and How Sustainable Prosperity Can Be Restored*. Oxford Press.

Lee, K., & Lee, C. H. (2008). The Miracle to Crisis and the Mirage of the Postcrisis reform in Korea. *Journal of Asian Economics, 19*(5–6), 425–437.

Lee, K., & Kim, D. K. (2024). Compressed Development, Decompression, and Diverging Convergence in South Korea: Which Varieties of Capitalism in Contemporary Korea? *Review of Evolutionary Political Economy's (REPE's), 5*, 173–200.

Lee, K., & Shin, H. (2021). Varieties of Capitalism and East Asia. *Structural Change and Economic Dynamics, 56*, 431–437.

Lee, K., Kim, B. K., Lee, C. H., Yee, J., et al. (2008). Visible Success and Invisible Failure in Post-Crisis Reform in the Republic of Korea. *Journal of Asian Sociology, 37*(1), 23–53.

Lee, K., Ho-Chul, S., & Jongho, L. (2020). From Catch-up to Convergence?: Recasting the Trajectory of Capitalism in South Korea. *Korean Studies, 44*, 54–79.

Lipset, S. M. (1959). Some Social Requisites of Democracy: Economic Development and Political Development. *American Political Science Review, 53*, 69–105.

Shin, A. (2003). The Growth of the Korean Middle Class and its Social Consciousness. *The Developing Economies, XLI*(2), 204.

Shin, J. S. (2014). *The Global Financial Crisis and the Korean Economy*. Routledge.

Shin, H., & Lee, K. (2019). Impact of Financialization and Financial Development on Inequality. *Asian Economic Papers, 18*(1), 69–90.
Song, B.-N. (1990). *The Rise of the Korean Economy*. Oxford University Press.
Soskice, D., & Hall, P. A. (2001). *Varieties of Capitalism: The Institutional Foundations of Comparative Advantage*. Oxford University Press.
Storz, C., Amable, B., Casper, S., & Lechevalier, S. (2013). Bringing Asia into The Comparative Capitalism Perspective. *Socio-Economic Review., 11*(2), 217–232.
Teichman, J. (2016). *The Politics of Inclusive Development*. Palgrave Macmillan.
Thurbon, E. (2016). *Developmental Mindset: The Revival of Financial Activism in South Korea*. Cornell University Press.
Thurbon, E., & Weiss, L. (2021). Economic Statecraft at the Frontier: Korea's Drive for Intelligent Robotics. *Review of International Political Economy, 28*(1), 103–127. https://doi.org/10.1080/09692290.2019.1655084
Wade, R., & Veneroso, F. (1998). The Asian Crisis: The High Debt Model Versus the Wall Street—Treasury—IMF Complex. *New Left Review, 288*(March/April), 3–23.
Weiss, L., & Thurbon, E. (2021). Developmental State or Economic Statecraft? *New Political Economy, 26*(3), 472–489. https://doi.org/10.1080/13563467.2020.1766431
Whittaker, D. H., Sturgeon, T. J., Okida, T., & Zhu, T. (2020). *Compressed Development*. Oxford University Press.
Wong, C. Y., & Lee, K. (2018). Projecting The Arena of Inclusion: The Case of South Korea in Pursuing a Phased Inclusive Growth Process. *The Review of Policy Research, 35*(4), 590–616.
Woo, J.-e. (1991). *Race to the Swift: State and Finance in Korean Industrialization*. Columbia University Press.
World Bank. (1993). *The East Asian Miracle*. Oxford University Press.
Yang, J.-j. (2017). *The Political Economy of the Small Welfare State in South Korea*. Cambridge University Press.

CHAPTER 4

Divergent Evolution of Statist Coordination Models: A Comparison of Japan and Korea

Kyung Mi Kim and Hyeong-ki Kwon

Since the 2008 global financial crisis, distrust in the neoliberal order has deepened, while state-led industrial policies and economic coordination have regained renewed attention. The growing frequency of global economic crises and pandemics, the instability of the world economy driven by U.S.–China rivalry, and the intensifying technological competition among nations spurred by the digital revolution have collectively called for a restructuring of existing global supply chains. In turn, this call for restructuring has prompted both developing and advanced economies to competitively adopt proactive industrial policies (Kwon, 2024). Even international organizations such as the World Bank have shifted from a previous neoliberal stance toward supporting industrial policy (Noman & Stiglitz, 2017).

K. M. Kim (✉)
Sapienza Università di Roma, Rome, Italy
e-mail: kyungmi.kim@uniroma1.it

H.-k. Kwon
Seoul National University, Seoul, Korea
e-mail: kwonhk@snu.ac.kr

H.-k. Kwon (ed.), *Korean Political Economy from a Comparative-Historical Perspective*, Palgrave Series in Contemporary Korean Studies, https://doi.org/10.1007/978-981-95-9785-7_4

In this context, East Asian developmental states, which have successfully achieved economic development through industrial policies, are once again receiving attention. In particular, Japan and South Korea, regarded as archetypes of the East Asian developmental state, have continued to adopt state-interventionist industrial policies, as evidenced by their high-tech policies since the 2000s (Schaede, 2020; Watanabe, 2020; Kalinowski, 2015; Kim, 2020; Kwon, 2021). For example, Japan's biomedical industry and South Korea's robotics industry have been fostered through active industrial policies (Ibata-Arens, 2019; Thurbon & Weiss, 2021).

How can statist coordination, perceived as effective only during the catch-up phase of late-developing economies, remain relevant in advanced capitalist economies in an era of intensified globalization and digitalization? Many scholars argue that despite globalization, the escalation of national rivalry due to new external threats has made formation of a new competitive state or new state-business alliances increasingly important to sustain and enhance national competitiveness. They emphasize that external competitive threats, such as the rise of China, drive states to pursue new interventionist industrial policies to strengthen national competitiveness (Kalinowski, 2019, p. 217; Kang & Jo, 2021, pp. 717–718; Doner et al., 2005; Waldner, 1999, pp. 125–152).

However, Japan and South Korea, despite their similar statist coordination institutions, have followed markedly different development trajectories and patterns over the past 30 years. Japan has suffered from prolonged economic stagnation—often referred to as the "lost decades," spanning from the early 1990s to the late 2010s. In contrast, South Korea has maintained relatively steady economic growth, even in the face of the late 1990s financial crisis.

The two countries' diverging trajectories since the 1990s indicate that national rivalry and external factors alone cannot fully account for the renewed effectiveness of the statist coordination model. Despite their similar institutional arrangements of statist coordination, why has Japan been slow to adapt to globalization and rapid technological changes such as the digital revolution, while Korea has adapted quickly? As Atul Kohli (1999) and others argue, Korea's developmental state is rooted in Japan's. How, then, have these two countries evolved such distinct developmental trajectories and patterns?

Japan and South Korea pose a significant challenge to prevailing theories on an efficient market economy. Neoliberal theorists argue that in globalization and digital transformation the free-market model is the only viable option, and that state-led interventionism is no longer effective. However, they struggle to account for the continued effectiveness of state intervention in Korea and post-Abenomics recovery of the Japanese economy.[1] Furthermore, the hollowing out of U.S. domestic production due to "uncoordinated" globalization highlights the limitations of the neoliberal perspective (Kwon, 2024).

Institutional approaches, which offer alternatives to neoliberal theories to explain the diversity of capitalism, emphasize that East Asian economies have not fully converged with the neoliberal model but continue to maintain unique institutional arrangements and practices (Thurbon, 2016; Klingler-Vidra & Pardo, 2020; Nagel, 2024, p. 252). They underscore the enduring institutional legacy of meritocratic bureaucracy and state--driven industrial policy in both Japan and Korea (Kang et al., 2023; Kikuchi, 2023; Thurbon & Weiss, 2021). However, they still fail to account for the diverging patterns of the two statist coordination economies in the economic performances and reform politics since the 1990s.

This chapter focuses on the differences in how these two similar statist coordination models operate. It highlights that, despite their similar institutions and practices, Japan and Korea have developed distinct policy regimes, leading to different political coordination capabilities across periods in each country. Japan's policy regime has historically evolved into a horizontal consensus model integrating political, bureaucratic, and business elites. In contrast, Korea has developed a hierarchical, presidentially driven policy regime. Although both regimes possess distinct advantages and limitations, their contrasting policy regimes led to divergent reform performances during the 1990s and 2000s.

To understand the diverging patterns in Japan and Korea, we first offer a brief overview of dominant theories on national economic development in the era of globalization and digital transformation. We then examine similarities between Japan and Korea's statist coordination models, and their divergent development trajectories and outcomes of reform politics over the past 30 years. Finally, to explain the reasons behind these differences, we focus on differences in their policy regimes.

[1] Abenomics refers to the economic policies led by Shinzo Abe, who had been appointed as Prime Minister of Japan in his second term from 2012 to 2020.

Literature Review and an Alternative

Neoliberals have argued that, due to globalization, East Asian developmental states are no longer viable, and they cannot avoid embracing liberal norms. They claim that most countries cannot escape pressures such as expansion of global value chains and financial liberalization (Katz, 2003, p. 22; Johnson, 2016; Yeung, 2014; Alami et al., 2023; Nölke & Vliegenthart, 2009). Within this international economic context, they assert that Japan and South Korea will inevitably abandon their traditional developmental models and converge toward a neoliberal free-market model (Katz, 2003; Jayasuriya, 2005; Rosenbluth & Thies, 2010; Nagel, 2024, p. 251).

Neoliberals and global value chain (GVC) theorists argue that the free flow of goods, labor, and capital in an open market maximizes national competitiveness and efficiency (World Bank, 2020; Friedman, 2005; Farrell et al., 2003; Sirkin et al., 2011; Ramaswamy & Rowthorn, 2000; Bhagwati, 2010). Neoliberals claim that creative allocation of resources should occur solely through free market mechanisms, and that state intervention, nonmarket constraints, and social regulations hinder the optimal allocation of resources (Pack & Saggi, 2006, p. 276). The GVC literature emphasizes the superior efficiency of global value chains and adopts the neoliberal perspective on comparative advantage and skepticism toward state intervention (Singh, 2023, pp. 4–5; Werner, 2016, pp. 458–460). Based on this premise, it advocates for policies such as trade and investment liberalization and integration into global networks (World Bank, 2020; Yeung, 2022; Bair, 2009; Gibbon et al., 2008).

However, contrary to the optimism of neoliberal and GVC research, not all national economies benefit positively from corporate globalization. While globalization of national corporations follows similar trends, some national economies, such as Germany, have successfully strengthened their industrial competitiveness through globalization, whereas others, like the U.S., have not (Kwon, 2024).

Contrary to neoliberals' claim of universal validity of free markets, upgrading from a low-value-added economy to a high-value-added economy does not occur automatically through free markets and uncoordinated integration into global value chains. For example, in the process of free-market-driven and uncoordinated globalization, the U.S. lost its domestic industrial and innovation commons (Pisano & Shih, 2012). Since the 1990s, the U.S. trade balance in advanced industries has deteriorated significantly, shifting from a 1990 $3.5 billion surplus to a 2020 $178.1 billion deficit. The U.S. goods trade deficit surged from $198 billion in 1996 to $1.09 trillion in 2021 (U.S. Census Bureau, n.d.).

Economist Gregory Tassey points out that this growing trade deficit is linked to American companies' increased R&D spending overseas and the decline in domestic R&D investment (Tassey, 2010, pp. 283–333). Empirical studies from MIT and Harvard indicate that the decline in U.S. R&D is associated with loss of industrial commons, including the reduction of domestic component suppliers and highly skilled labor, as U.S. companies shifted operations abroad (Berger, 2013, pp. 20, 204–205; Porter & Rivkin, 2012, pp. 54–62). Against this backdrop, the recent introduction of new U.S. industrial policies and stronger protectionist trade measures, amid intensifying hegemonic competition with China, reflect a reassessment of these issues (Kwon, 2024).

In contrast to the U.S. free-market system, South Korea's statist coordination and Germany's social coordination systems have more effectively addressed collective action problems among individual firms that arise in globalization. These systems have successfully enhanced industrial commons, which are more likely to be formed through cooperation of key stakeholders, as they emerge from broader social coordination. Furthermore, Japan has recently restored its economic vitality through evolutionary adaptation of its statist coordination model, not through convergence toward the free market model (Kim & Kwon, 2017; Kwon, 2024).

Contrasted with neoliberal convergence theory, studies emphasizing the persistence of diverse patterns of economic development in globalization focus on distinct domestic institutions and practices. They highlight the institutional continuity of merit-based bureaucracy and state-led industrial policies in Japan and Korea (Kang et al., 2023; Kikuchi, 2023; Woo, 2018; Beeson, 2002; Thurbon & Weiss, 2021).

According to these studies, such institutional characteristics in East Asia persist due to cultural traditions and norms formed in their historical experiences. Some cultural approaches attribute the differences between East Asian developmental states and Western economies to Confucianism. They emphasize that the ethical values rooted in the Confucian cultural tradition have formed the foundation of East Asian economies (Moon & Hwang, 2019; Sue, 2022). Other scholars contend that both elites and the public internalized a developmental mindset and strong trust in state-led growth during the industrialization era, and that this shared orientation has sustained the continuity of developmental state institutions and practices in South Korea (Thurbon, 2016; Yoon, 2016; Cho, 2003).

However, while such institutional and cultural approaches are effective in explaining the institutional similarities and continuity in Japan and Korea, they fall short in accounting for the divergent political and economic outcomes after the 1990s. As will be discussed in the following section, the economic performances of Japan and South Korea have diverged since the 2000s. This reflects Japan's failure and South Korea's success in implementing reforms during the crises of the 1990s. Moreover, the two approaches fail to explain why both of Japan and Korea have exhibited different outcomes in different periods with the same institutions and cultural foundations. Since the 2010s, Japan has shown economic recovery through administrative reforms to strengthen the leadership of the Prime Minister's Office, whereas South Korea has experienced an economic slowdown due to the weakening of presidential leadership amid a crisis of political polarization.

Despite the similar statist coordination models, why have Japan and Korea faced different patterns of adaptation to globalization and digitalization? Why did Japan, despite the prolonged crisis since the late 1980s, experience a delay in implementing substantial reforms, while South Korea, in contrast, succeeded in carrying out comprehensive economic system reforms—including in the corporate, financial, and labor sectors—following the severe economic crisis of the late 1990s?

Although Japan and Korea share similar institutional traditions and practices, their statist coordination systems function in markedly different ways. To explore this divergence, we compare the two countries' distinct policy regimes, focusing on who is involved in these policy regimes and how they interact with one another. For this, we will analyze Japan's policy-making process, highlighting how Japan's reform stagnation during the prolonged crisis was driven by its consensus regime centered on the Liberal Democratic Party (LDP), bureaucrats, and business elites. In contrast, we will examine how South Korea's relatively successful reform politics have been driven by strong initiatives of the president and the presidential office.

Similarity and Divergence

Before examining the policy regimes of Japan and Korea, we will explore their similarities in institutions and practices and their divergent development patterns and reform results after the crises in the 1990s.

Similarities in Institutions and Practices

In the political economy literature, Japan and South Korea have been classified as typical developmental states, distinct from Anglo-Saxon liberal market economies and European social coordination models (Woo, 2018, p. 170; Beeson, 2002, p. 4). Japan and South Korea share several key characteristics, including government's economic interventions, elite bureaucracy, close cooperation between state and business, and political exclusion of labor by the state (Johnson, 1982; Amsden, 1989; Wade, 1990). South Korea's system is said to be transplanted from Japan, with South Korea replicating significant aspects of Japan's industrial policies and governance on business (Kohli, 1999, p. 95; 2004).

During their industrialization, Japan and South Korea pursued an export-led growth model through strategic industries and large corporations selectively nurtured and actively promoted by a strong state. Based on a state-controlled and bank-centered financial system, both governments were able to actively coordinate corporations (Wade, 1990; World Bank, 1993). Corporations prioritized access to government financial support and trade quotas by aligning their strategies with government policies rather than focusing solely on market profitability (Moon et al., 2021, p. 654; Schaede, 2012, p. 168; Kim, 2002, p. 253).

Despite the retreat of bureaucratic industrial policy in globalization and liberalization, Japan and South Korea have maintained their statist coordination practices in modified form, distinguishing them from Anglo-American free-market economies (Lechevalier et al., 2019; Watanabe, 2020; Fukuda, 2020; Kim, 2020; Kwon, 2021). Although matured economies can no longer pursue traditional industrial policies, due to their integration into global value chains, Japan and South Korea have developed new statist coordination policies and economic statecraft to enhance industrial competitiveness of national economies amid intensified international competition in cutting-edge technologies.

Watanabe (2020) and Kalinowski (2015) argue that while Japan may no longer fit the classic bureaucratic-led developmental state observed by Johnson (1982), it has developed a new statist coordination model, or neodevelopmental state, that grants a greater role to interest groups. As seen in the Abe administration's Japan Revitalization Strategy, the Japanese government has pursued a state-led growth strategy by promoting industry-academy cooperation and supporting startups in high tech industries since the 2010s (Kwon, 2024, pp. 154–171). For example, Japan has actively promoted bio-related startups to strengthen the country's innovation capacity in biomedical and other high-tech industries (Ibata-Arens, 2019).

Similarly, despite democratization and globalization, South Korea has developed a reconfigured statist coordination system (Kim, 2020; Kwon, 2021; Chu, 2009; Thurbon, 2016). Due to democratization, the South Korean government no longer exercises such direct authoritarian control or discretionary power as it did earlier. Additionally, financial liberalization and globalization have disallowed direct financial control over chaebols (Korean conglomerates) as before.

However, despite changed political and economic conditions, the Korean government has initiated the national growth strategy shift, from input-oriented to innovation-driven, to enhance industrial competitiveness. The government now focuses on building an innovation ecosystem based on broader and more inclusive corporate networks in strategic industries, instead of concentrating support on a few selected conglomerates as before (Kim & Kwon, 2017). Thurbon and Weiss (2021) show that the South Korean government has been developing robotics as a cutting-edge industry to strengthen international competitiveness. Sung-Young Kim (2019) demonstrates that South Korea's green energy policy was not market-neutral but rather a developmentalist strategy to strategically foster smart microgrids.

These statist coordination systems in Japan and Korea depend on a similar merit-based bureaucracy. Meritocracy has been credited with providing the bureaucracy in both countries with plan rationality and a degree of relative autonomy, preventing it from being co-opted by social and interest groups.

In Japan, a national exam-based and selective system for merit-based bureaucracy was established under the Imperial Constitution. Then-Prime Minister Hirobumi Ito introduced the system to avoid criticism of clan politics and to ensure the administration's absoluteness and superiority over parliament (Kikuchi, 2023, p. 102). As a result, Japan's administrative system has very few politically appointed positions compared to the executive branches of other countries (Pempel, 1974; Peters & Pierre, 2004; Kikuchi, 2023, p. 106).

In South Korea, the Higher Civil Service Examination (HCSE) was introduced in 1949, and since then the government has maintained a high level of quality control over its merit-based system. According to an analysis of 1022 ministerial positions from the Rhee government to the Moon government (1948–2019), ministerial appointments in South Korea were predominantly based on competence, not loyalty (Kang et al., 2023, pp. 361–363).

Diverging Patterns

Despite similar legacies and continuity of their developmental states, Japan and Korea have exhibited significantly different development trajectories and patterns over the past 30 years in response to globalization and digitalization. Japan has experienced a prolonged economic recession since the 1990s, while South Korea has maintained continuous economic growth, despite recent signs of slowing down. Since the 1990s, Japan and South Korea's economic growth indicators have diverged dramatically. Japan's real growth rate has averaged less than 1 percent per year since the 1990s (Calder, 2017, pp. 5–6). As a result, Japan's share of the global economy declined from 15 percent in 1990 to just 8 percent in 2012 (Kazuhiko, 2015, p. 56). Japan's nominal GDP per capita decreased from approximately $37,780 in 2000 to $33,834 in 2023. In contrast, South Korea's nominal GDP per capita grew from around $11,347 in 2000 to $33,121 in 2023. In terms of real GDP per capita, as of 2023, South Korea reached $44,600, surpassing Japan's $41,900. In terms of purchasing power parity (PPP), South Korea's per capita GDP in 2023 was $54,033, also surpassing Japan's $51,128.

More importantly, the trade balance of high-tech industries in Japan and South Korea followed different trajectories between 2000 and 2022. Japan's high-tech industries experienced a continuous trade balance decline, shifting from a surplus of $54.98 billion in 2000 to a deficit of $32.29 billion in 2022. In contrast, South Korea's high-tech industries saw significant growth in trade surplus, increasing from $14.12 billion in 2000 to $52.99 billion in 2022. With their economic downturn, Japanese corporations, which dominated global markets until the 1980s, experienced significant stagnation and competitive loss in the 2000s and 2010s. For example, the number of Japanese companies listed on Fortune's Global 500 List declined from 141 in 1995 to just 71 in 2010.

Why, then, have Japan and South Korea, despite sharing a similar statist coordination model, followed increasingly divergent development trajectories over the past few decades? While Japan has remained mired in prolonged stagnation for more than thirty years after the bubble burst in the early 1990s, how was South Korea able to overcome the severe crisis of the late 1990s and achieve sustained growth and technological upgrading? Since the 1990s, Japan and South Korea's differing economic performances have reflected their approaches to reform politics. Japan faced new challenges brought by globalization and digitalization, but failed to adapt quickly due to delayed reforms. South Korea successfully responded with flexible adaptation through swift reforms. Before examining, in the following sections, the differences in policy decision-making regimes that influenced the reform politics of Japan and South Korea, we will first explore how the speed and outcomes of political and economic reforms have differed between the two countries since the 1990s.

Empirical studies highlight that South Korea's reforms after the 1997–1998 crisis led to fundamental changes, while Japan missed opportunities for substantial transformation due to delayed reform. For example, Tiberghien (2007), in a comparative analysis of corporate governance reforms in the 2000s across Japan, South Korea, and France—countries with a state-led coordinated capitalism model—describes the outcomes of these reforms as follows:

> Japan, South Korea, and France all actively pursued reforms related to transparency, accounting, the promotion of foreign direct investment, and the protection of minority shareholders. However, there are significant differences regarding reforms that directly impact the balance of power within corporations, such as labor, privatization, and mergers and acquisitions. Japan did not implement these measures, whereas South Korea attempted fundamental changes by utilizing all available means. France falls somewhere in between. (Tiberghien, 2007, p. 8)

In reality, the corporate governance and economic system reforms that took place in Japan after the late 1990s were limited to partial and technical adjustments, such as formal introduction of outside director systems, without bringing about fundamental changes to its bank-centered corporate governance. According to Calder (2017), Japan's bank-centered circles of compensation resisted adapting to global standards even after globalization, and continued to maintain an economically outdated but politically influential financial nexus. Based on stable relationships among existing insiders, they reinforced rigidity and conservatism, hindering adaptation to change (p. 165). As a result, Japan failed to establish a new system to replace the previous capital evaluation framework, while traditional long-term credit banks disappeared (p. 43).

South Korea, meanwhile, undertook radical corporate restructuring. According to Gourevitch and Shinn (2005), South Korea rapidly adopted shareholder reforms shortly following the Asian financial crisis (pp. 124–131). Although South Korea attempted reform measures to change the closed patterns of corporate governance in the Kim Young-sam administration (1992–1997), corporate governance reforms, so-called "chaebol reforms," were carried out in a rapid and bold manner during the Kim Dae-jung administration, particularly in response to the crisis (Gourevitch & Shinn, 2005, p. 127).

Labor market reforms also show contrast between Japan and South Korea. In Japan, despite long-term economic crises, the practice of long-term employment remained largely intact. After the collapse of the economic bubble in the early 1990s, a series of labor market reforms were needed to revive the sluggish economy, but fundamental reforms including employment flexibility were delayed. To safeguard employment for insiders, Japan adopted a strategy to increase the number of nonregular "outsider" workers. The Liberal Democratic Party (LDP) pursued labor market liberalization primarily for nonpermanent workers, but rarely challenged the protection of regular workers (Schaede, 2020; Song, 2012, pp. 161–162).

South Korea, even under the center-left governments of Kim Dae-jung (1997–2002) and Roh Moo-hyun (2002–2007), took a different approach from Japan under the conservative Liberal Democratic Party (LDP) government. Instead of increasing nonregular workers, South Korea implemented fundamental reforms by easing regulations on the dismissal of regular workers. Rather than prioritizing the protection of insiders, South Korea focused on increasing labor market flexibility and restructuring employment relations. Additionally, performance-based wage systems became more widespread (Woo, 2018; Song, 2012, p. 162).

Moreover, the active government-initiated globalization policies in South Korea in the 1990s bears a significant impact on national competitiveness through the global movement of ideas, capital, and products. In South Korea, following the globalization policies of the Kim Young-sam administration in the mid-1990s, there was a surge in foreign language learning, a sharp rise in the number of students studying abroad, and a greater influx of international students compared to Japan. According to a 2008 UNESCO report, Japan had 60,225 students studying abroad, including those in short-term programs. In contrast, South Korea—with less than half of Japan's population—had 101,913 students studying abroad. A similar disparity is observed in the 2014–2015 period, when 63,710 South Korean students were enrolled in U.S. schools compared to just 19,064 from Japan (Dujarric & Takenaka, 2019, p. 276). In the 2015 DHL World Survey on Global Connectedness Rankings, Japan ranked 38th, significantly lower than South Korea at 18th, and Germany at 7th (Calder, 2017, p. 156).

In sum, Japan and South Korea have exhibited divergent patterns of growth over the past several decades, reflecting distinct reform politics in the political economy, including corporate governance and labor market systems. This suggests that, although both countries share a similar statist coordination model, the way it actually works differs in practice.

Different Policy Regimes

Even when cultural and institutional conditions appear similar, the patterns and mechanisms through which cultures and institutions function can differ significantly. These differences can be observed not only across countries but also within the same country over different periods. The divergent reform outcomes in Japan and Korea were the result of political conflicts among groups with differing interpretations and perspectives on reform pressures. The way these conflicts are resolved is closely related to the policy-making regime.

Japan and Korea share similarities in the relative autonomy of their state bureaucracies and in their interventionist traditions; however, they differ significantly in how the state formulates and implements plan-rational policies to address market failures. The Japanese policy regime seeks a consensus among bureaucrats, politicians, and business leaders. In contrast, Korea's policymaking centers around the presidential office, where the state agenda is established and implemented in a hierarchical manner. The differences in their policy regimes contributed to the variations in reform in the two countries since the 1990s, by influencing state's coordination capability.

Japan's Policy Regime

Why did Japan, with prolonged economic stagnation and a widespread sense of crisis, fail to implement timely reforms and open new pathways for transformation? The reasons cannot be attributed simply to cultural factors such as Confucianism or conservative traditions, nor to institutional path dependency. Over the past 30 years, Japanese society has been deeply divided between reformists and antireform forces, struggling with intense conflicts rather than being dominated by a single cultural influence like conservatism or Confucian values. The issue is not conflict itself but the capability of conflict resolution. Political conflicts among key actors can delay reforms, but can also serve as catalysts for new alternatives when they are successfully coordinated. Japan's reform failures and prolonged stagnation suggest that its policy regime was unable to effectively mediate internal conflicts.

Japan's policy regime is characterized by a consensus model based on a decentralized and fragmented structure of policymaking. Japan's long-dominant Liberal Democratic Party (LDP) is a power-sharing organization composed of multiple factions, and its Prime Minister is chosen through interfactional negotiations rather than through individual dominance. The LDP's oligopolistic faction leaders act as a check on the Prime Minister's unilateral exercise of power, functioning as shadow shoguns who effectively control the party's operations (Schlesinger, 1997). As a result, the LDP's central leadership cannot enforce party discipline in the Diet or in electoral campaigns (Krauss & Pekkanen, 2010).

Additionally, the prime minister's authority to appoint and dismiss cabinet ministers was significantly constrained by the need for approval from factions. Especially, after the LDP regained power in 1994 through a three-party coalition, it continued to govern in coalition, diluting its effectiveness of political influence as before. Due to the principle of jurisdictional authority, each ministry's head was restricted from interfering in the affairs of other ministries, which meant that the prime minister's direct involvement in ministry-specific matters was also limited (Han et al., 2019, p. 83).

The Japanese prime minister and cabinet also had limited authority over the bureaucracy. Cabinet decisions were based on consensus, but in reality, bureaucrats coordinated key agendas in advance. As a result, the cabinet's role was largely formal, merely approving decisions already made. The Vice Ministers' Meeting, held before the official cabinet meeting, served as the actual decision-making venue, and any issue that had not been coordinated in this meeting was unlikely to be presented in the cabinet meeting at all (Han et al., 2019, pp. 83–84).

Japan's consensus-based model, grounded in a horizontal and decentralized structure, contributed to reconciling conflicting interests and promoting national economic development during the period of high growth up to the 1970s.

Since the 1980s, however, Japan's policymaking process has gradually begun to change. The initiative in policy decision-making began to shift from bureaucrats to the LDP (Curtis, 1988, pp. 123–131). One major background for this shift was that, following the 1973 oil shock, Japan transitioned from a high growth economy to a low growth economy, where bureaucrats no longer had sufficient economic resources to accommodate the demands of conservative politicians or interest groups. During this period of low growth, LDP lawmakers became the central actors in policy formation, turning policymaking into a process dominated by intraparty bargaining (Nakamura & Takeshita, 1995, pp. 19, 49).

As political intervention in resource allocation increased, political compromises within the LDP became crucial. In particular, political influence shifted toward the LDP's Policy Affairs Research Committees (PARCs), which emerged as the primary arena for coordinating diverse political interests. Every LDP lawmaker was required to belong to at least one subcommittee. Due to the principle of seniority, many of them remained in the same subcommittee for an extended period, acquiring deep expertise and becoming recognized authorities in specific policy areas (Nakamura & Takeshita, 1995, p. 54).

The LDP's PARCs were not merely internal party organs; they evolved into key institutions that actively shaped national policy. Now, bureaucrats in central ministries drew advantage in obtaining LDP approval before seeking Diet deliberations, making parliamentary approval easier. The PARCs served as the LDP's key working-level body for reviewing policies, making it critical for bureaucrats to pass their proposals through PARC deliberations before reaching the Diet. From the 1980s onward, bureaucrats increasingly turned to the PARCs to resolve difficult policy issues, especially those involving interministerial conflicts (Nakamura & Takeshita, 1995, p. 52).

Along with this, factional politics, so-called zoku politics, developed. Zoku politics is a form of pressure politics, as part of the party's internal interest coordination process, in which LDP lawmakers represent specific interest groups in different policy areas (Nakamura & Takeshita, 1995, p. 55). For example, the LDP's Commerce and Industry Subcommittee became dominated by lawmakers representing large corporations and the Ministry of International Trade and Industry (MITI), forming the so-called "Commerce Tribe" (shoko-zoku). Similarly, the Construction Subcommittee represented the construction industry and the Ministry of Construction, evolving into the "Construction Tribe" (kensetsu-zoku) (Nakamura & Takeshita, 1995, pp. 57–58, 66–67).

These policy tribes solidified their influence through alliances with business associations and the relevant central ministries, forming a strong power bloc, the so-called "Iron Triangle" of politicians, bureaucrats, and business leaders. When vested interests were threatened, these three groups—led by the zoku lawmakers—closed ranks in coordinated defense. Their primary role was to block any attempt to undermine their existing advantages and ensure the continued protection of vested interests. The problem was that such zoku lawmakers were spread across a wide range of industrial sectors, leading to a highly fragmented political landscape (Nakamura & Takeshita, 1995, pp. 20–21, 47).

The zoku politics of this iron triangle effectively prevented Japan from implementing fundamental reforms during the prolonged crisis. The strong ties between the LDP's PARCs and their affiliated policy tribes became even more entrenched during the low-growth era, when vested interests faced greater risks of being challenged. The government was forced to continue existing policies, even at the cost of issuing deficit bonds (Nakamura & Takeshita, 1995, p. 21).

However, with growing criticism over the lack of political leadership and delayed reforms, Japan's policymaking process began to shift toward a cabinet-centered governance system in the late 1990s. The 1994 electoral reform, which introduced single-member districts for the House of Representatives, weakened the factional structure of the LDP, which had previously been built on the multimember district system. Furthermore, through the administrative reforms after the 2000s, Japan has gradually concentrated power in the Prime Minister's Office (Kantei) as part of a broader remedy to the country's stalled reform efforts (Ito, 2006; Park, 2008, p. 116).

The 2001 administrative reforms strengthened the functions of the cabinet and reorganized government ministries by reducing the number of ministries and agencies from 22 to 12. This restructuring aimed to eliminate bureaucratic silos between ministries. Additionally, the Administrative Vice Ministers' Meeting, which had symbolized bureaucratic dominance, was replaced by a new Political Ministers' Meeting led by deputy ministers. Furthermore, the appointment process for senior officials was reformed. Previously, each ministry would recommend a single candidate, and the cabinet would approve the nomination in a formal manner. Following reform, however, ministries were required to recommend multiple candidates, allowing the Prime Minister greater discretion in selecting senior officials (Han et al., 2019, pp. 87–88).

Under the Abe administration, the cabinet's strategic planning and coordination functions were expanded to further strengthen the Prime Minister's role in setting the national policy agenda. This marked a shift from a traditional bottom-up agenda-setting process, dominated by bureaucratic agencies, to a more centralized, top-down approach led by the Prime Minister and the cabinet.

In 2012, the Abe administration further reinforced Kantei[2]-centered governance. The number of political advisors supporting the Prime Minister increased, including five Special Advisors to the Prime Minister and deputy ministers and parliamentary vice ministers. Moreover, the "Six-Person Meeting" (Rokunin Kaigi), which convened daily in the Prime Minister's office, brought together the Chief Cabinet Secretary, three Deputy Chief Cabinet Secretaries, and government secretaries to discuss core policy matters (Han et al., 2019, p. 92).

To further strengthen the Prime Minister's executive capacity, the Cabinet Secretariat and Cabinet Office were significantly expanded. In 2000, the Cabinet Secretariat had 377 regular staff members and 445 dispatched officials (a total of 822 personnel). By 2013, this number had surged to 808 regular staff and 1645 dispatched personnel (a total of 2453 personnel). One of the most significant enhancements to executive leadership was the Cabinet Office (Naikakufu), a powerful agency directly under the Prime Minister's authority. While the Cabinet Office was subordinate to the Cabinet Secretariat (Naikakukan), it functioned above other ministries and agencies. Within the Cabinet Office, several Ministers of State for Special Missions were appointed to support the Prime Minister. When a

[2] "Kantei" (官邸) is the Japanese term for the Prime Minister's Office.

policy decision required interministerial coordination, the Cabinet Office served to resolve conflicts between ministries and handle final adjustments. With this reversal of the traditional power dynamic, ministries began to seek approval from the Cabinet Secretariat and Cabinet Office to designate their major policies as national priorities (Han et al., 2019, p. 93).

In 2014, the government established the Cabinet Bureau of Personnel Affairs, which enabled the Prime Minister to exercise direct authority over high-ranking bureaucratic appointments. This reform expanded the scope of political appointments within ministries and formalized the Prime Minister's direct involvement in hiring and dismissing senior bureaucrats (Han et al., 2019, pp. 95–96).

However, whether Japan's political reforms since the 2000s can bring about a fundamental transformation of its economic system still depends on their ability to reform its structured clientelism. According to Reed (2021), Japanese clientelism is a party-organization patronage system, with the LDP as patron and the interest group as client. This institutionalized clientelism was a key factor in the LDP's long-term dominance until the 1980s.

Japan's long-term economic stagnation significantly reduced public resources, which became inadequate to sustain the traditional system of clientelist politics. As Japanese corporations became more globalized and dependent on international financial markets, the patterned pluralism that had once functioned smoothly through public financial support mechanisms became increasingly difficult to sustain (Muramatsu, 1993). Moreover, the electoral reforms implemented after 1993 accelerated the weakening of Japan's traditional system of political patronage (Reed, 2021).

However, despite these changes, the LDP's traditional clientelist networks did not disappear entirely. The LDP's recent return to power demonstrates a modified restoration of this clientelism. The LDP regained power after 2012 with clientelism emerging in a newly modified form. The LDP's monopoly on access to the public policymaking process enabled the party to sustain its rule. After the 2012 election, the LDP secured landslide victories in three consecutive elections, reestablishing its predominant position, largely due to institutionalized connection between the party and interest group organizations (Reed, 2021, p. 83).

In summary, the Japanese policy regime is characterized by a consensus model, in which power is decentralized and distributed among multiple pluralistic actors, as noted in Muramatsu's (1993) "patterned pluralism" and Aoki's (1998) "bureau-pluralism." In this system, economic bureaucrats engage in discussions with politicians and business. The consensus-based model allowed Japan to achieve stable economic development through close cooperation and information exchange among insiders under the international economic order until the 1970s. However, since the 1980s, the changes of domestic and international environments, such as declining growth, deepening globalization and rapid technological advancements, have slowed the consensus model's adaptability. Due to vested interests among the closed circles of insiders, Japan has struggled to accept new innovations and ideas, leading to delayed reforms and falling into the so-called "Galapagos Syndrome" (Kazuhiko, 2015; Kushida, 2011; Calder, 2017).

Korea's Policy Regime

In contrast to Japan's incomplete and delayed reforms, South Korea swiftly reformed into a more open and innovative economic system after the crisis of the late 1990s (Kwon, 2021; Kim, 2020). Korea's reform politics has relied on a distinct policy regime, even under a statist coordination model similar to Japan's. Even after democratization and globalization, policymaking in Korea continues to be led primarily by the president and the executive branch, with only minimal direct participation from other social groups, the legislature, or political parties. Moon (2016) and Moon and Hwang (2019) conceptualize this as a "president-led policy nexus triad." In this system, the president, bureaucrats, and civil society form a distinctive mode of interaction, while the role of the legislature and political parties remains secondary.

In the Korean policy regime, the president and the Office of the President set the national agenda and oversee its hierarchical implementation with strong initiatives and leadership. This arrangement is supported by the Korean presidential system based on a winner-take-all regime. A change of president implies not only a reorganization of government ministries but also shifts in the goals and priorities of economic policy. The presidency, a powerful institution, exercises extensive discretionary authority through four key administrative agencies: the National Tax Service, the National Intelligence Service, the National Police Agency, and the Prosecutors' Office. Moreover, the president secures control over the bureaucracy and the capacity to coordinate across ministries through the authority to appoint and dismiss senior officials. The presidential office possesses strong policy capacity and exercises dominant administrative power over civil servants (Moon & Hwang, 2019, p. 73). In the process of economic policy coordination, issues that cannot be resolved by the Prime Minister or the Office for Government Policy Coordination are often finally settled by the Senior Secretary for Economic Affairs, leveraging presidential authority (Jeong, 2002, pp. 35, 234).

As a result, even after democratization, all political competition and struggle in Korea remains concentrated around the presidency. Within this structure, political power in Korea is organized through support–patronage (clientelist) networks centered in the president. When a new president comes to power, existing networks are dismantled and reorganized around the new center of authority. In this process, members of the National Assembly function as "clients" of presidential candidates, securing political benefits in exchange for their support (Park, 2008, pp. 115–116, 123–124).

The presidential, centralized, and hierarchical model reflects the continued weakness of parties and the legislature in policymaking. Unlike the counterparts in Japan and the United States, the Korean legislature has not established itself as a central actor in policymaking. Since democratization, the National Assembly has strengthened its political oversight of the executive, but its capacity for policy making and oversight remains limited.

The weakness of the National Assembly's policy leadership can be attributed to legislators' lack of policy expertise and to the structural limitations of the standing committee system. Unlike Japan's LDP Policy Affairs Research Council or the standing committees of the U.S. Congress, both grounded in seniority norms, the standing committees of the Korean National Assembly are characterized by the short terms of the members. In Korea, legislators' turnover rate in committees is over 50 percent, preventing growth in policy expertise. Especially, Korea's Budget and Accounts Committee lacks both expertise and continuity, as members serve only one-year terms, although the budget settlement review is considered the legislature's most powerful tool to check executive policies. The turnover rate of the committee members is 70 to 80 percent, much higher than the 57 to 58 percent observed in the other standing committees. Such frequent replacement of members undermines the continuity of deliberations and thwarts accumulation of expertise, thereby fundamentally impeding substantive review of the budget. In reality, often large numbers of bills are passed in bulk at the end of a session without sufficient deliberation. Rarely does substantive debate take place, even during plenary reviews (Park, 2002).

In addition, while in the U.S. and UK the government auditing agencies belong to the legislature, the Korean Board of Audit and Inspection, which supports government financial audits, belongs to the executive branch. As the Board of Audit and Inspection holds auditing authority but is part of the executive, the National Assembly has no power to require it to conduct regular audits. Consequently, the National Assembly is unable to exercise auditing authority that would substantively guarantee its budget settlement review powers (Park, 2002, pp. 57–58).

The legislature's independent policymaking capacity also is weak in the lawmaking process. The increased proportion of bills initiated by legislators since democratization cannot be interpreted as a strengthening of the Assembly's independent legislative capacity. The increase is due mainly to a rise in cases where bureaucrats introduce bills through ruling party legislators to facilitate their passage (Interview with formal director at the Korean Ministry of Commerce Industry and Energy on June 17, 2015; Interview with former Vice Minister of Knowledge Economy on June 22, 2015). While this new practice indicates that the status of the National Assembly has been enhanced compared to the period before 1987 democratization, it also underscores the Assembly's relatively weak policy capacity compared to the executive's policy expertise.

Finally, the role of civil society and interest groups in Korea's policy regime also remains highly limited. The main civil society actors that influence policymaking can be divided into economic interest groups such as business associations and civic organizations aiming at public interests. Business associations are typically established on the basis of industrial and sectoral interests, such as the Automobile Manufacturers Association, the Small and Medium Business Association, and the Medical Association. By contrast, most civic organizations—such as the Citizens' Coalition for Economic Justice, or the Korean Federation for Environmental Movements—emerged after democratization and aim to improve public interests.

Interest groups in Korea, particularly those centered on business associations, have continued to function as corporatist policy-execution partners even after democratization, remaining highly subordinate in their relationship with the state. Although now formally liberalized, Korean business associations still depend heavily on legal authorization and government approval procedures. According to one study, even after democratization the Korean government continues to pursue industrial policies—such as selection and cultivation of new growth engines—based on a corporatist mindset, with the central government remaining deeply involved in the establishment and operation of business associations to carry out these policies (Kim, 2003). According to data compiled by the Fair Trade Commission, as of 1999 approximately 6300 business associations were in existence, most of them established under the Cooperative Association Act for Small and Medium Enterprises or other special laws related to specific industries, thereby embedding government intervention institutionally (Jeong, 2001).

Korean business associations also have limited financial independence, with most of them carrying out government-delegated projects (Cho, 1994; Kil, 1997; Jeong, 2002, 2011). Their finances rely primarily on membership fees (60%) and service revenues (29.9%). However, the bulk of these service revenues comes from handling government-delegated responsibilities, such as reporting, job training, and licensing. The government selectively delegates authority to specific business associations in line with policy priorities, and supports them in carrying out the corresponding administrative functions (Jeong, 2011, p. 16).

As a result, unlike in Japan or Western parliamentary-centered systems, Korean interest groups overwhelmingly concentrate their lobbying and contact activities on the executive rather than on the legislature or political parties. As we saw, in the practice of Japanese zoku politics, the main counterparts of interest groups are the specialized subcommittees and expert legislators of the ruling LDP (Kikuchi, 2023). By contrast, Korean interest groups have continued to follow an executive-centered pattern of interest representation even after democratization. According to a multiple response survey, the main institutional targets of contact for Korean business associations were the central government (88%), followed by the legislature (44%) and local governments (32%). In terms of perceived influence, the central government ranked highest at 71 percent, compared with 51 percent for the legislature and 30 percent for local governments. Notably, even civic organizations of a social movement character that emerged after democratization were found to contact central and local governments far more frequently than legislatures or parties. In influence evaluations as well, these organizations perceived the executive to exert far greater power than the legislature (Jeong, 2011).

In sum, even after democratization, Korea's policymaking regime has continued to be led by a strong presidential leadership based on the highly centralized and hierarchical structure, while the roles of legislature and civil society remain limited. Despite inherent tensions with democracy, this regime has persisted due to its advantages. With the election of a new president, strong centralized leadership comes into play, allowing policymaking and implementation to advance with remarkable speed and efficiency. This structure enabled the Korean government to successfully pursue state-led reforms, even in the context of democratization and globalization. For example, during the 1998 financial crisis, the Korean government swiftly implemented sweeping reforms—including major chaebol restructuring and corporate governance reforms, bank restructuring, and labor market flexibility. This reform stands in contrast to Japan's decentralized and consensus-based policymaking regime, which since the 1990s has experienced reform paralysis at the hands of closed circles of insiders (Gourevitch & Shinn, 2005, pp. 124–131; Tiberghien, 2007, p. 8).

However, Korea's policymaking system, highly concentrated in the presidency and executive branch, has revealed serious weaknesses under conditions of divided government and extreme ideological polarization, leading to stalemate. Over the past decade, deepening polarization in Korean democracy has severely undermined the president and the government's policy capacity. In the past, bills initiated by the president and executive branch were almost routinely passed in the National Assembly. Even in the early 2000s, nearly all executive-initiated bills were approved, with only about 25 to 30 percent subject to amendments (Park, 2002, p. 25). By contrast, as political polarization in the legislature and civil society intensified, only about 58 of 490 government-initiated bills—roughly 12 percent—were passed during the final two years (2020–2021) of the Moon Jae-in administration. The situation worsened further during the first two years of the Yoon Suk-yeol administration (2022–2023), when just 18 out of 341 government-initiated bills, less than 5 percent, were passed (Park, 2024). Recent Korean politics thus starkly reveal the vulnerabilities of a policy regime that remains extremely centralized.

This system, despite its hierarchical and centralized nature and the tensions it entails with democracy, has long been socially justified on two grounds. First, in Korean democracy, the president—directly elected by the people—has been regarded as a symbol of democracy itself. Koreans believe that through the president they have chosen, they can realize their own will. Second, strong leadership centered on the president and the executive has facilitated the formulation and implementation of policies, enabling Korea to respond swiftly to pressures of change such as globalization and digitalization. However, amid the deepening political polarization in recent Korean politics, this system has come under crisis, and increasingly perceived as neither democratic nor effective.

Conclusion

This chapter aimed to demonstrate that Japan and South Korea's state coordination models operate in fundamentally different ways by comparing their distinct policy regimes. As Atul Kohli (1999, 2004) argues, Korea's developmental state originated from the Japanese model; the two models share similar institutional practices and legacies. Yet they developed distinct paths and approaches to economic transformation during the past decades. While Japan has struggled to adapt to rapid technological changes in globalization and digital revolution, Korea has adapted much faster.

This divergence cannot be explained solely by cultural differences or historical legacies of the developmental state. Korea's divergence was the result of political adaptation processes shaped by conflicts and competition among bureaucrats, politicians, civil society, and interest groups in response to globalization and economic liberalization. The determining factor in political adaptation is the difference in policymaking regimes, how key actors interact, and which groups are best positioned to adapt to new challenges.

Compared to Japan's consensus-based policymaking, Korea's policy formation process is hierarchical and dominated by unilateral presidential initiatives. Despite democratization, the Korean legislature has not developed strong policy leadership, as with Japan's PARCs. Unlike Japan's zoku lawmakers, Korean legislators rotate frequently across committees, limiting their ability to develop policy expertise. And unlike Japan's business associations which actively engage in policymaking, Korean business associations function as extensions of government, primarily handling tasks rather than shaping policy.

While bureaucratic competition between ministries exists in both Japan and Korea, the Korean presidential office plays a far stronger role in resolving disputes and making final decisions. As a result, Korea's policymaking remains highly centralized around the presidency. When a newly elected president has strong public support and a parliamentary majority, rapid and sweeping reforms can be implemented—as seen in the 1998 financial crisis response which included major chaebol reforms, introduction of liberal corporate governance, and liberalization of capital and labor markets.

However, this hierarchical decision-making system comes with major weaknesses. As political and ideological polarization intensifies, and in cases of divided government (where the opposition controls the legislature), the Korean system loses its ability to implement policies effectively. Instead of rapid reform, the country experiences political stalemate. Recent political trends have revealed vulnerabilities, including extreme ideological polarization; a divided legislature; and declining presidential approval ratings. Under these conditions, Korea's centralized policymaking model struggles to function effectively, leading to governance paralysis.

Ultimately, while both Japan and Korea emerged as developmental states with strong government intervention, their responses to globalization and economic crises diverged due to differences in policymaking structures and political adaptation processes. Japan's consensus model enabled stability but slowed reform. Korea's centralized, president-driven model allowed rapid adaptation, but at the cost of political vulnerability in times of polarization.

As Korea faces increasing legislative gridlock and economic stagnation, the limitations of its president-centric policy regime become more apparent. Korea's challenge moving forward will be to maintain its capacity for rapid reform while developing more stable, pluralistic decision-making mechanisms.

Acknowledgments This research was supported by the Ministry of Education of the Republic of Korea and the National Research Foundation of Korea (NRF-2020S1A3A2A01095861).

References

Alami, I., Alves, C., Bonizzi, B., Kaltenbrunner, A., Koddenbrock, K., Kvangraven, I., & Powell, J. (2023). International Financial Subordination: A Critical Research Agenda. *Review of International Political Economy, 30*(4), 1360–1386. https://doi.org/10.1080/09692290.2022.2098359

Aoki, M. (1998). *Unintended fit: Organizational evolution and government design of institutions in Japan.* In M. Aoki, H. Kim, & M. Okuno-Fujiwara (Eds.), The role of government in East Asian economic development: Comparative institutional analysis (pp. 233–253). Clarendon Press.

Amsden, A. H. (1989). *Asia's Next Giant: South Korea and Late Industrialization.* Oxford University Press.

Bair, J. (2009). Global Commodity Chains: Genealogy and Review. In J. Bair (Ed.), *Frontiers of Commodity Chain Research.* Stanford University Press.

Beeson, M. (2002). *Reconfiguring East Asia: Regional Institutions and Organizations after Crisis.* Routledge.

Berger, S. (2013). *Making in America: From Innovation to Market.* The MIT Press.

Bhagwati, J. (2010, September 1). The Computer Chip vs. Potato Chip Debate. *The Moscow Times.*

Calder, K. E. (2017). *Circles of Compensation: Economic Growth and the Globalization of Japan.* Stanford University Press.

Cho, S. J. (1994). *Hanguk haengjeong jojiknon* [Theory of Korean Administrative Organization].

Cho, H. Y. (2003). Jeongchi sahoejeok damron ui gujo byeonhwa wa minjujuui ui donghak: Hanguk hyeondaesa sogeseo ui jibae damron gwa jeohang damron ui sangho jagyong eul jungsim euro [Structural Change of Political-Social Discourses and the Dynamics of Democracy: Focusing on the Interaction between Dominant and Resistant Discourses in Modern Korean History]. In H. Y. Cho (ed.), *Hanguk ui jeongchi sahoejeok jibae damron gwa minjujuui donghak* [The Dominant Political-Social Discourses and the Dynamics of Democracy in Korea]. Hamkke Ilneun Chaek.

Chu, Y.-w. (2009). Eclipse or Reconfigured? South Korea's Developmental State and Challenges of the Global Knowledge Economy. *Economy and Society, 38*(2), 278–303.

Chung, D. K. (2002). *Hanguk-ui gyeongje jeongchaek gyeoljeong gwajeong: Jeong Deok-gu gyosu-ui gangui noteu* [The Process of Economic Policy-Making in Korea: Lecture Notes by Professor Chung Duck-Koo]. Seoul National University.

Curtis, G. (1988). *The Japanese Way of Politics.* Columbia University Press.

Doner, R., Ritchie, B., & Slater, D. (2005). Systemic Vulnerability and the Origins of Developmental States: Northeast and Southeast Asia in Comparative Perspective. *International Organization, 59*(2), 327–361.

Dujarric, R., & Takenaka, A. (2019). Parochialism: Japan's Failure to Internationalize. In J. Kingston (Ed.), *Critical Issues in Contemporary Japan.* Taylor & Francis.

Farrell, D., Baily, M., Agrawal, V., Bansal, V., Beacom, T., Kaka, N., Kejriwal, M., Kumar, A., Palmade, V., Remes, J., & Heinzl, T. (2003). *Offshoring: Is It a Win-Win Game?* McKinsey Global Institute.

Friedman, T. (2005). *The World Is Flat: A Brief History of the Twenty-First Century.* Farrar, Straus and Giroux.

Fukuda, K. (2020). Science, Technology and Innovation Ecosystem Transformation Toward Society 5.0. *International Journal of Production Economics, 220*(C). https://doi.org/10.1016/j.ijpe.2019.07.033

Gibbon, P., Bair, J., & Ponte, S. (2008). Governing Global Value Chains: An Introduction. *Economy and Society, 37*(3), 315–338.

Gourevitch, P., & Shinn, J. (2005). *Political Power and Corporate Control: The New Global Politics of Corporate Governance*. Princeton University Press.
Han, S. J., Choi, H. S., & Lee, C. J. (2019). Haengjeong suban ui gwanryoje hyoyong gwa tongje jeollyak: 2001-nyeon ihu Ilbon ui chongni jidocheje bunseok [The Chief Executive's Strategy of Utilization and Control over the Bureaucracy: Analysis of Leadership System of Japan's Prime Minister Since 2001]. *The Korea Association for Policy Studies, 28*(4), 75–109.
Ibata-Arens, K. (2019). *Beyond Technonationalism: Biomedical Innovation and Entrepreneurship in Asia*. Stanford University Press.
Ito, M. (2006). Kanteishudokata seisaku kettei to jiminto [Prime Minister's Office-Led Policy-making and the LDP]. *Leviathan, 38*, 7–40.
Jayasuriya, K. (2005). Beyond Institutional Fetishism: From the Developmental to the Regulatory State. *New Political Economy, 10*(3), 381–387. https://doi.org/10.1080/13563460500204295
Jeong, S. H. (2001). Saeobjadancheleul Tonghaeseo Bon Hanguggwa Ilbonui Iigjeongchi [Business Associations and Interest Politics in Korea and Japan]. *The Journal of Asiatic Studies, 44*(1), 67–98.
Jeong, S. H. (2002). Hangug Jungsogieob Jibdanui Iigjeongchi: Junggihyeobeul Jungsimeulo [The Interest Politics of the Korean Small and Medium Business Group: Focused on the KFSB]. *Korean Political Science Review, 36*(4), 193–210.
Jeong, S. H. (2011). Hangugui Minjuhwawa Iigjeongchiui Byeonhwawa Yeonsogseonge Daehan Yeongu [Changes and Continuities of the Interest Group Politics in Korean Democratization]. *Korean Party Studies Review, 10*(1), 5–33.
Johnson, C. (1982). *MITI and the Japanese Miracle: The Growth of Industrial Policy, 1925–1975*. Stanford University Press.
Johnson, J. (2016). *Priests of Prosperity: How Central Bankers Transformed the Postcommunist World*. Cornell University Press.
Kalinowski, T. (2015). Crisis Management and The Diversity of Capitalism: Fiscal Stimulus Packages and the East Asian (Neo-)developmental State. *Economy and Society, 44*(2), 244–270.
Kalinowski, T. (2019). *Why International Cooperation Is Failing: How the Clash of Capitalisms Undermines the Regulation of Finance*. Oxford University Press.
Kang, N., & Jo, K. (2021). State-Business Relations in Flux: Capturing the Structural Power of Business in South Korea's Green Industrial Policy. *Journal of Contemporary Asia, 51*(5), 713–736.
Kang, H., Kim, B. S., & Kim, M. H. (2023). Presidential Appointments of Ministers in South Korea: beyond the Dichotomy of Loyalty and Competence. *Asian Journal of Political Science, 31*(3), 351–371.
Katz, R. (2003). *Japanese Phoenix: The Long Road to Economic Revival*. Routledge.

Kazuhiko, T. (2015). The Curse of "Japan, Inc." and Japan's Microeconomic Competitiveness. In Y. Funabashi & B. Kushner (Eds.), *Examining Japan's Lost Decades*. Routledge.
Kikuchi, M. (2023). Patronage Appointment in Japanese Politics: Political Representation in a Large Bureaucracy. In G. Peters, C. Knox, & B. Kim (Eds.), *Political Patronage in Asian Bureaucracies*. Cambridge University Press.
Kil, J. B. (1997). *Jeongbu buche sanha wiwonhoe jedoui unyeonge gwanhan yeongu [A Study on the Operation of Committee Systems under Government Ministries]*. Master's Thesis,. Korea University.
Kim, Y. (2002). Ilbon gwa Hanguk-ui saneop jeongchaek gyeoljeong gwajeong bigyo yeongu: junghwahak gong-eophwa jeongchaekeul jungsim-euro [A Comparative Study on the Industrial Policy-Making Processes of Japan and Korea: Focusing on the Heavy and Chemical Industrialization Policy]. *Jeongchi Bipyeong* 2002 (First Half), 252–283.
Kim, J. K. (2003). Saeobjadanchewa Jeongbuganui Gwangyee Daehan Yeongu: San-Eobjawonbu Sanha Johab Mich Hyeobhoeleul Jungsimeulo [Linking Government and Business Associations: State Corporatism Revisited in Korea]. *Journal of Regulation Studies, 12*(2), 3–32.
Kim, S. (2019). Hybridized Industrial Ecosystems and the Makings of a New Developmental Infrastructure in East Asia's Green Energy Sector. *Review of International Political Economy, 26*(1), 158–182.
Kim, K. M. (2020). *The Korean Developmental State*. Palgrave Macmillan.
Kim, K. M., & Kwon, H. K. (2017). The State's Role in Globaliza-tion: Korea's Experience from a Comparative Perspective. *Politics and Society, 45*(4), 505–531.
Klingler-Vidra, R., & Pardo, R. (2020). Legitimate Social Purpose and South Korea's Support for Entrepreneurial Finance Since the Asian Financial Crisis. *New Political Economy, 25*(3), 337–353. https://doi.org/10.1080/13563467.2018.1563058
Kohli, A. (1999). Where Do High Growth Political Economies Come From?: The Japanese Lineage of Korea's 'Developmental State'. In M. Woo-Cumings (Ed.), *The Developmental State* (pp. 93–136). Cornell University Press.
Kohli, A. (2004). *State-Directed Development: Political Power and Industrialization in the Global Periphery*. Cambridge University Press.
Krauss, E., & Pekkanen, R. (2010). *The Rise and Fall of Japan's LDP*. Cornell University Press.
Kushida, K. (2011). Leading Without Followers: How Politics and Market Dynamics Trapped Innovations in Japan's Domestic 'Galapagos' Telecommunications Sector. *Journal of Industry, Competition, and Trade, 11*, 279–307. https://papers.ssrn.com/abstract=1861208
Kwon, H. K. (2021). *Changes by Competition: The Evolution of the South Korean Developmental State*. Oxford University Press.

Kwon, H. K. (2024). *Openness and Coordination: National Economies of the U.S., Japan, and Germany in a Globalized World*. Palgrave Macmillan.
Lechevalier, S., Debanes, P., & Shin, W. (2019). Financialization and Industrial Policies in Japan and Korea: Evolving Institutional Complementarities and Loss of State Capabilities. *Structural Change and Economic Dynamics, 48*, 69–85.
Moon, M. J. (2016). The Evolution of the Developmental State and Government Capacity in Korea. In K. Park, W. Lee, & S. Lee (Eds.), *Understanding Korean Public Administration*. Routledge.
Moon, M. J., & Hwang, C. H. (2019). The Scholar-Official Policy Nexus and Confuscian Policy Styles in South Korea. In M. Howlett & J. Tosun (Eds.), *Policy Styles and Policy-Making: Exploring the Linkages* (pp. 70–88). Routledge.
Moon, M. J., Suzuki, K., Park, T. I., & Sakuwa, K. (2021). A Comparative Study of COVID-19 Responses in South Korea and Japan: Political Nexus Triad and Policy Responses. *International Review of Administrative Sciences, 87*(3), 651–671.
Muramatsu, M. (1993). Patterned pluralism under challenge: The policies of the 1980s. In G. D. Allinson & Y. Sone (Eds.), *Political dynamics in contemporary Japan* (pp. 50–71). Cornell University Press.
Nagel, M. (2024). Tilting the Playing Field: Government Strategies to Bolster Control Over Policy Paths in Japan and South Korea. *The Pacific Review, 37*(2), 245–276.
Nakamura, A., & Takeshita, Y. (Eds.). (1995). *Ilbon ui jeongchaek gwajeong* [The Policy Process in Japan]. Translated by S. W. Lee and C. D. Kim. Daeyoung Munhwasa.
Nölke, A., & Vliegenthart, A. (2009). Enlarging the Varieties of Capitalism: The Emergence of Dependent Market Economies in East Central Europe. *World Politics, 61*(4), 670–702. https://doi.org/10.1017/S0043887109990098
Noman, A., & Stiglitz, J. (2017). *Efficiency, Finance, and Varieties of Industrial Policy*. Columbia University Press.
Pack, H., & Saggi, K. (2006). Is There a Case for Industrial Policy? A Critical Survey. *World Bank Research Observer, 21*(2), 267–297.
Park, C. P. (2002). *Hangug Uihoejeongchiwa Minjujuui* [National Assembly and Democracy in Korea: In Comparative Perective],, Oruem Publishing House.
Park, C. P. (2008). A Comparative Institutional Analysis of Korean and Japanese Clientelism. *Asian Journal of Political Science, 16*(2), 111–129.
Park, J. K. (2024, May 22). Yoon Suk Yeol jeongbu 2nyeongan Wonandaelo Tonggwahan Jeongbu Beob-an 18gaeppun [In Two Years of the Yoon Administration, Only 18 Government Bills Passed as Originally Proposed]. *Naeil Newspaper*. https://m.naeil.com/news/read/511041
Pempel, T. (1974). The Bureaucratization of Policymaking in Postwar Japan. *American Journal of Political Science, 18*(4), 647–664.

Peters, G., & Pierre, J. (Eds.). (2004). *The Politicization of the Civil Service in Comparative Perspective*. Routledge.

Pisano, G., & Shih, W. (2012). Does America Really Need Manufacturing. *Harvard Business Review, 90*(3), 94–102.

Porter, M., & Rivkin, J. (2012). The Looming Challenge to U.S. Competitiveness. *Harvard Business Review*, 90(3). https://hbr.org/2012/03/the-looming-challenge-to-us-competitiveness.

Ramaswamy, R., & Rowthorn, R. (2000). Does Manufacturing Matter? *Harvard Business Review*, 2000 (November–December).

Reed, S. (2021). Patronage and Predominance: How the LDP Maintains Its Hold on Power. *Social Science Japan Journal, 25*(1), 83–100.

Rosenbluth, F., & Thies, M. (2010). *Japan Transformed: Political Change and Economic Restructuring*. Princeton University Press.

Schaede, U. (2012). From Developmental State to the 'New Japan': The Strategic Reflection Point in Japanese Business. *Asia Pacific Business Review, 18*(2), 167–185.

Schaede, U. (2020). *The Business Reinvention of Japan: How to Make Sense of the New Japan and Why It Matters*. Stanford University Press.

Schlesinger, J. (1997). *Shadow Shoguns: The Rise and Fall of Japan's Post-War Political Machine*. Simon and Shuster.

Singh, S. (2023). Global Value Chains, Neoliberalism and Develop-ment Practice: Reflections on Kenya's Experience. *Journal of International Development*. https://doi.org/10.1002/jid.3786

Sirkin, H., Zinser, M., & Hohner, D. (2011). *Made in America, Again: Why Manufacturing Will Return to the United States*. Boston Consulting Group. http://www.bcg.com/documents/file84471.pdf.

Song, J. (2012). The Diverging Political Pathways of Labor Market Reform in Japan and Korean. *Journal of East Asian Studies, 12*, 161–191.

Sue, W. (2022). An Exploration of the Relationship between Confucianism and Economic Modernization in East Asia. *BCP Social Sciences & Humanities, 19*, 560–568.

Tassey, G. (2010). Rationales and Mechanisms for Revitalizing US Manu-facturing R&D Strategies. *Journal of Technology Transfer, 35*, 283–333.

Thurbon, E. (2016). *Developmental Mindset*. Cornell University Press.

Thurbon, E., & Weiss, L. (2021). Economic Statecraft at the Frontier: Korea's Drive for Intelligent Robotics. *Review of International Political Economy, 28*(1), 103–127.

Tiberghien, Y. (2007). *Entrepreneurial States: Reforming Corporate Governance in France, Japan, and Korea*. Cornell University Press.

U.S. Census Bureau data. (n.d.). https://data.census.gov/

Wade, R. (1990). *Governing the Market*. Princeton.

Waldner, D. (1999). *State Building and Late Development*. Cornell University Press.

Watanabe, H. (2020). *The Japanese Economy*. Agenda Publishing.
Werner, M. (2016). Global Production Networks and Uneven Develop-ment: Exploring Geographies of Devaluation, Disinvestment, and Exclusion. *Geography Compass, 10*(11), 457–469.
Woo, J. (2018). Labor Market Regime in Korea and Japan: Focusing on Policy Response after the Economic Crisis. *East Asian Studies, 37*(2), 169–219.
World Bank. (1993). *The East Asian Miracle*. Oxford University Press.
World Bank. (2020). *World Development Report 2020: Trading for Development in the Age of Global Value Chains*. World Bank.
Yeung, H. (2014). Governing the Market in a Globalizing Era: Developmental States, Global Production Networks and Inter-Firm Dynamics in East Asia. *Review of International Political Economy, 21*(1), 70–101. https://doi.org/10.1080/09692290.2012.756415
Yeung, H. (2022). *Interconnected Worlds: Global Electronics and Production Networks in East Asia*. Stanford Business Books.
Yoon, S. W. (2016). Hanguk seongjangjuui ideollogi ui yeoksajeok byeoncheon gwa jaesaengsan [The Historical Transformation and Reproduction of the Growth-Oriented Ideology in Korea]. *Hanguk Sahoe* [Korean Society], 17(1), 3–38.

CHAPTER 5

The Developmental States of South Korea and Taiwan: Core Features and Divergent Trajectories

Yin-wah Chu

Introduction

South Korea (hereafter Korea) and Taiwan are, after Japan, prime examples upon which the concept of the developmental state (hereafter DS) has been constructed and elaborated. Built initially on the experience of economic development in these Northeast Asian societies since the 1950s and 1960s (Amsden, 1989; Evans, 1995; Gold, 1986; Haggard, 1990; Johnson, 1982; Lim, 1985; Wade, 1990; Woo, 1991), the concept has over the years inspired widespread application within and beyond Northeast Asia, and it has been the subject of extensive theoretical debates

Funding Support
Research Grants Council (Hong Kong), General Research Fund reference number: 12622622.

Y.-w. Chu (✉)
Data Economy Lab, Hong Kong Baptist University, Kowloon Tong, Hong Kong
e-mail: ywchu@associate.hkbu.edu.hk

H.-k. Kwon (ed.), *Korean Political Economy from a Comparative-Historical Perspective*, Palgrave Series in Contemporary Korean Studies, https://doi.org/10.1007/978-981-95-9785-7_5

and re-construction (Block, 2008; Doner et al., 2005; Edigheji, 2010; Jessop, 2016).

This paper will contribute to the ongoing debate by making two main arguments. First, unlike some of the discussion in recent years that focuses on the institutional features of the DS, sometimes even examining it as a model that other emerging economies could emulate (Edigheji, 2010; Kalu & Aniche, 2025; Rahman et al., 2025), this study contends that geopolitical and social structural forces are preconditions that facilitate the emergence of developmental initiatives and factors that shape the policy trajectories at the same time. It will analyze differences in the developmental state policies pursued by Korea and Taiwan up to the 1980s, together with their distributive outcomes, to illustrate this point. Second, this paper contends that the developmental state institutions are not static entities, but they may reconfigure and navigate new policy tools or dissolve in the face of global and national changes. It thus partakes in the debate on whether the Korean and Taiwanese DS have demised in the shadow of the deepening of globalization, opening up of China, emerging US-China rivalry, democratization of the two states, and growth of local enterprises since the mid-1980s. Examining the adaptation of various developmental state institutions in Korea and Taiwan, this paper argues that even as state influence has declined relatively, the institutions remain resilient and have continued to use monetary and non-monetary resources to structure the market and coordinate business actions to desirable ends. Yet again, this paper argues that how a DS adapts depends in part on the geopolitical contexts and social structural conditions. That Taiwan has faced more complex challenges from China's rise and Korea has a more vigorous labor movement have triggered divergent trajectories. This paper will make these arguments by examining the two states' efforts to tackle COVID-19 and the performance of their top R&D enterprises.

The following will start with a brief overview of the evolving debates and recent applications of the notion.[1] After a short statement on data and method, it will examine the core developmental state institutions of Korea and Taiwan and argue how geopolitical and social structural forces have facilitated the emergence of and shaped the policy directions of the two cases' developmental endeavors up to the mid-1980s. The second part of the paper examines the post- mid-1980s' global and national

[1] This study also refers to scholarships that use the term state-directed development, developmental activism, and the like.

political-economic changes as well as their impacts on the developmental state institutions. In addition to analyzing the developmental state institutions' adaptation, it will also highlight the two states' strategies of tackling COVID-19 to illustrate the permeation of the developmental state practices into non-developmental dimensions of state action, hence the practices' deep-seated institutionalization. In turn, the two states' strategies of outward direct investment and the performances of their top R&D firms will be examined to demonstrate the influences exerted by the changes in geopolitical forces and constraints exerted by their preexisting socio-economic structures.

The Developmental State: Debates and Elements of an Empirically Derived Concept

There is a long debate on the state's role in economic development (Jessop, 2016; Polanyi, 1944), though Johnson (1982) is responsible for coining the term developmental state. Early applications of the concept have seen competing attempts among neo-Marxists who analyze the social structural foundations of state autonomy, neo-Weberian who examine the institutional features of the state (Evans, 1995; Gold, 1986; Haggard, 1990; Lim, 1985; Woo, 1991), and others that focus on the geopolitical context (Cumings, 1984). The thriving debate quietened temporarily with the deepening of globalization and eruption of the 1997–1998 Asian financial crises as researchers argue for the DS's demise (Pirie, 2007; Stubbs, 2009).

Nevertheless, the concept has continued to receive widespread academic examination in the last few decades. In addition to debating the continuing relevance of the concept for the East Asian cases (Cho, 2019; Chu, 2009; Kim, 2021; Kim & Kwon, 2017; Thurbon, 2016; Woo-Cumings, 1999), other scholars have critically applied the concept to countries in Africa (Edigheji, 2010; Clapham, 2018; Kalu & Aniche, 2025), Central Asia (Bolesta, 2019), South Asia (Rahman et al., 2025), the Middle East (Mehri, 2015), and even the developed economies (Block, 2008; Maggor, 2021; ÓRiain, 2004; Ornston, 2012). Although there are exceptions, most works have examined the dynamics of the DS, often times in relation to the organization and modus operandi of the state institutions. While appreciative of their nuance and depth, studies that focus exclusively on the capabilities of the civil service, mindset of the bureaucrats, specific policies, and even the alliance between technocrats and business elites might draw attention away from the geopolitical and broader social structural contexts, rendering the DS an abstract model that countries can simply emulate to achieve economic advancement. The resultant understanding could be misleading or, at the very least, incomplete.

There already exists much excellent theoretical exposé and debate on the merits of both social structural and institutional analysis of the DS (Evans, 1995; Skocpol, 1979; Block, 2008). This paper will therefore confine itself to an empirical task. Addressing the cases of Korea and Taiwan, it will show the importance of geopolitical factors in the rise of developmentalism. Relying on the comparative method, it will also contend that, due to differences in their social structural and geopolitical conditions, Korea and Taiwan have pursued divergent policies and, in the face of emerging challenges, adapted in disparate ways despite similarities in their developmental state institutions.

It will draw upon documents that include government policy papers, legislation, and other publications; financial statements and reports released by private corporations; reports by research institutions; league tables prepared by global agencies; news reports; as well as scholarly studies. These will be supplemented by interviews conducted in the last decades with government officials and researchers. Where possible, this study will consult and weigh divergent viewpoints with a view to triangulating the observations.

Elements of a Concept and the Cases of Korea and Taiwan, 1960s–1980s

The literature that contributes to the formation of the concept of DS has mostly identified four elements, namely, the ideational foundation, state institutions, policy tools, and social-structural conditions. This paper will use these elements as heuristic tools to guide comparison between Korea and Taiwan. As the following will suggest, the 1960s–80s Korea and Taiwan were quite similar insofar as the ideational foundation and state institutions were concerned, yet differences in terms of social-structural and geopolitical conditions as well as the deployment of divergent policy tools led to the emergence of rather distinct economic structures and distributive outcomes.

Ideational Foundation

The need for survival and, sometimes, the desire to regain national glory, were considered to have generated the ideational foundation or the "will to develop" that prompted state leaders to give priority to and channel resources to promote economic development. In other words, it was a commitment to facilitating economic development not for the sake of improving the living standard, but for achieving economic security (Castells, 1992; Johnson, 1995; Woo-Cumings, 1999). For some observers, this ideational foundation also persuaded capitalists and workers to comply with state directives (Kim, 1997). Both Korea and Taiwan were devastated by the Second World War. Between the mid-1940s and the unwinding of the Cold War in the 1980s, they were also confronted with political competitions and military threats from their communist counterparts. Economic backwardness and the need to overcome security threats had prompted the emergence of the said ideational foundation, inducing Park Chung-hee and Chiang Kai-shek to give priority to development programs.

State Institutions

Appropriate state institutions are deemed essential for the capacity to make and implement economic policies. In this connection, researchers have emphasized the presence of a small but efficient bureaucracy and, furthermore, the existence of a pilot agency capable of coordinating different offices in the government (significantly, statistics, budgetary, planning, finance, and trade) to attain the supreme goal (Gold, 1986; Johnson, 1982; Lim, 1985; Chibber, 2002). In Korea and Taiwan, the emergence of their modern civil bureaucracies had allegedly benefitted from the societies' high educational levels, their Japanese colonial legacy, as well as the experience of working with various American organizations such as the military in the case of Korea and the Sino-American Joint Commission on Rural Reconstruction in Taiwan. At the same time, Korea's Economic Planning Board (EPB) and Taiwan's Council for Economic Planning and Development (CEPD) have been identified as pilot agencies comparable to Japan's Ministry of International Trade and Industry (MITI).

Some scholars also drew attention to the extensive formal and informal ties that emerged to facilitate coordination among government officials and between the state institutions and business organizations (Evans, 1995). In Korea and Taiwan, apart from alumni, regional, co-ethic and other informal ties (Hamilton & Kao, 2017), the presence of extensive formal ties, such as regular meetings between government officials and business and professional associations (Jones, 1980; Kim, 2011) as well as the introduction of extension services (Hsieh, 2016) have been well documented.

Policies and Policy Tools

Despite adopting the capitalist market economic system, state elites support and guide the private enterprises through the provision of capital, technical know-how, market information, and inducements to move up the value chains.[2] Indeed, both Korea and Taiwan started with the introduction of import substitution industrialization in the 1950s, turned to export promotion in the 1960s, embarked on industrial deepening in the 1970s, and sought to promote technology-based industries since the 1980s. At this general level, the DS of both Korea and Taiwan had pursued similar policy goals.

However, the two cases had adopted divergent policy tools. In Korea, a most notable tool was the provision of bank loans to finance investments in designated economic sectors, though foreign exchange control, accelerated depreciation, tax concession and other tools were used (Amsden, 1989; Jones, 1980; Woo, 1991). The mobilization of bank loans explained in part the high debt-equity ratio that prevailed amongst the Korean *chaebol* until the 1997–1998 financial crises. As for Taiwan, the KMT-state mobilized the state enterprises to pursue some industrial ventures, though the most notable tool to guide the private sector was tax concession made through the Nineteen-point Program of Economic and Financial Reform. In both cases, the list of eligible industries and criteria of eligibility were updated regularly, the purpose of which was to channel limited national (public or private) resources toward industrial sectors that state officials considered to have high value-added and high growth potentials.[3]

[2] Although labor issue is not the focus of the present chapter, it has to be emphasized that state actors in both cases suppressed labor activism and, initially at least, blatantly disregarded labor rights. Whereas Korea relied mostly on the military-police to forbid the formation of autonomous labor unions, Taiwan mobilized KMT party officials and the KMT-linked Chinese Federation of Labor to monitor labor activists (Liu, 2015). By the 1980s, however, some scholars observed that the wages/salaries (of selected employees) increased faster than productivity (Amsden, 1989; Hsu, 2000).

[3] The emphasis on and adherence to the criteria of eligibility are considered by some scholars to explain why corruption and the problem of moral hazard were within control.

Apart from the above, the Park Chung-hee regime in Korea introduced high and increasing export values since the 1970s as the basis for eligibility. This "pick winners" strategy led to the economy's increasing domination by large corporations and, with the "big push" policy for the launch of heavy-and-chemical industries, the *chaebol's* domination was consolidated. In the 1980s and 1990s, the top 10 *chaebol* were known to have contributed some 40 percent of the country's total exports. When the Korean state pushed for the development of the electronics industries in the late 1970s, *chaebol* such as Samsung, LG, and Daewoo spearheaded the investments. Thus said, it remains true that there was no lack of small-and-medium enterprises (SMEs) in the country, which either served the local economy or were incorporated as subcontractors to the larger firms. The production networks thus emerged tended to be hierarchical, characterized by a domineering *chaebol*-SME relationship.

As for Taiwan, even though the government gave priority to state enterprises, tax concessions provided under the Nineteen-point Program did not discriminate against the SMEs. The same was true of other forms of state support (Cheng, 1987). Consequently, although it would be presumptuous to argue that the Taiwan state was pro-SMEs, the objective outcome was a much lower level of big business domination. Indeed, some even argue that, despite the domination of state- and a few private large enterprises in upstream industries (e.g., electricity, telecommunication, steel, plastic), SMEs spearheaded the accession to the thriving overseas markets (Chen, 1994; Feenstra & Hamilton, 2006). Hence, ironically, in the early 1970s when the KMT-state strove to launch the automobile and shipbuilding industries by using its own version of "triple alliance," it found a lack of local business interest and the plans were shelved (Cheng, 1987). Similarly, the KMT-state's bid to introduce technology-intensive industries such as semiconductors had not relied upon or favored private large corporations. Instead, the Ministry of Economic Affairs (MOEA) worked with other stakeholders to form the Industrial Technology Research Institute (ITRI) in 1973 and, a few years later, signed an "IC technology transfer and licensing contract" with the Radio Corporation of America, sending 19 engineers to the US for training by the Corporation. While the ITRI helped these engineers to hone their semiconductor design and manufacturing skills, state officials sought foreign and local investors' support in the establishment of a new semiconductor foundry, namely, the Taiwan Semiconductor Manufacturing Company Ltd.

(TSMC, n.d.).[4] In other words, it still took the form of a "triple alliance." The ITRI has since continued to incubate other technology firms with or without the state's direct funding support (ITRI, 2023).

To a larger extent than Korea, Taiwan was known for the prevalence of production networks. In order to access market intelligence, obtain working capital, enhance flexibility, and acquire new technology, SMEs in Taiwan developed robust business networks that tended to be horizontal in organization, with inter-firm relationships more collaborative rather than domineering in nature. It was suggested that although the lead firm in a production network tended to be strategically placed, the latter could involve technical know-how or market access and might not be the one largest in scale (Chen, 1994). This was different from the oft-mentioned *chaebol*-SME relationship in Korea.

Social-Structural Factors

The differences in specific policies and policy tools adopted by Korea and Taiwan brings the present discussion to the social-structural factors. Unlike Weberian researchers who consider modern bureaucracy sufficient to guarantee autonomous state actions, hence developmentalism (Evans, 1995), neo-Marxist scholars pinpoint social-structural conditions as prerequisites for the emergence of state autonomy, especially state actions that could potentially harm the incumbent class interests (Poulantzas, 1975; cf. Skocpol, 1979). In this connection, they contend that the threat to survival of Korea and Taiwan posed by their communist counterparts prompted the emergence of the "will to develop" amongst their state elites. Likewise, the prospect of US withdrawal from Vietnam in the early 1970s and the Republic of China's loss of its United Nations membership in 1971 impelled them to be proactive and embark on heavy-and-chemical industries in the 1970s and, subsequently, technology-intensive ones. In turn, the absence of social ties between the Park regime and the KMT-state to the incumbent elites in their societies made it possible for the state elites to initiate policies that could harm the established economic

[4] The venture was considered very risky and, as a result, the only foreign firm willing to invest was the Dutch company Philips, which contributed US$58 million or 27.5 percent of the total capital. State officials of Taiwan also mobilized its National Development Fund (48 percent of the total capital) and made phone calls to wealthy Taiwanese, demanding them to invest (ITRI, 2023).

interests, especially the 1950s land reform and subsequent pro-industrialization policies.

But the Korean and Taiwanese cases shed more light on the significance of geopolitical and social-structural factors than the inspiration of developmental activism. Two observations are in order.

In the first place, geopolitical conditions confronting Korea and Taiwan both *facilitated and eased* their developmental activism (Cumings, 1984). The United States (US) provided economic and military aids, hence much needed capital, to both Korea and Taiwan up to the mid-1960s and, until the late 1970s, opened its domestic market to the two economies' manufactured exports, mediated the investment of some US firms (e.g., Singer to Taiwan), and turned a blind eye to what could be considered mercantilist practices of these two economies. This contrasts sharply with accusations of dumping or currency manipulation made in recent decades against Korea, Taiwan, and other newly industrializing economies.

In the second place, social-structural factors that confronted the two states also induced Korea's *chaebol* dominant and Taiwan's SME-led strategies. Despite Park Chung-hee's initial threat to punish the "parasites of the people," only the nation-wide commercial banks were nationalized, whilst most capitalists were pardoned and asked to become partners in the country's development. The relatively cordial state-capital relationships made room for the pursuit of "pick winners" and "big push" strategies in Korea (Amsden, 1989; Lim, 1985). By contrast, the KMT-state was aversive to the grooming of large local business enterprises from the start. Economic chaos including runaway inflation and massive corruption in the last years of the KMT's rule on Mainland China made the party-state wary of large businesses in general. More importantly, the 228 Incident in 1947 generated a tension-ridden relationship between the KMT and local Taiwanese.[5] A strong class of Taiwanese capitalists threatened to challenge the KMT's rule (Cheng, 1987; Hsiao, 1993) and, conversely, the mutual distrust that emerged thereof made it difficult for the KMT to mobilize local business cooperation. Hence, unlike Korea, the KMT-state did not privatize Japanese properties in the 1950s and, as the above discussion has already noted, even though a few large Taiwanese enterprises emerged in the process of the 1950s land reform, the KMT-state's policies allowed for

[5] The 228 incident refers to an island-wide uprising in 1947 erupted amongst the Taiwanese against the KMT government in Taiwan, which at that time was preoccupied with committing the island's resources to fighting with the Chinese Communist Party on the mainland.

the proliferation of SMEs. Furthermore, not only had state enterprises played a major role in Taiwan's import-substitution industrialization, but state institutions also took the place of private large enterprises in spearheading the technology-intensive industries.

To reiterate, the cases of Korea and Taiwan underscored the need to consider the social-political factors in any understanding of the developmental state. Apart from inducing a sense of emergency and generating the "will to develop," geopolitical conditions also shaped the policy directions as in the "heavy-and-chemical industry drive" and, indeed, increased the chances for policy success in these two cases as in the United States' tolerance of mercantilism. Furthermore, class and sub-ethnic relations also shaped the policy directions so that whereas Korea's industrialization was *chaebol* dominant, Taiwan's was SME driven. The significance of geopolitics and social structure is sometimes overlooked by observers too keen on identifying a model of the developmental state or policymakers too eager to spread the model to other late developing economies. Even as the ideational foundation and state institutions were factors that enabled the state actors to actively facilitate economic development, the social-structural forces account partly for the drive and, indeed, shape the contours of the policies and the potential for success. Without an examination of the social-structural forces, the analysis remains partial.

The Developmental State in the Context of Globalization and China's Rise

As if authenticating the above points concerning the significance of geopolitical and social-structural conditions, changes since the 1990s led many observers to question the continuing relevance of the DS in Korea and Taiwan (Stubbs, 2009). This paper contends with other scholars that the developmental state institutions remain resilient (Lee, 2020; Wang, 2016; Kim & Kwon, 2017), even as their influences have declined, and policy directions delimited by the emerging geopolitical and social-structural conditions.

Far-reaching geopolitical and social-structural changes have occurred since the mid-1980s; a few of these changes and their implications for developmental state intervention will be highlighted here. In the first place, if Korea's and Taiwan's pursuit of export-led industrialization was helped by US support in anticipation of the end of economic aids in the mid-1960s, the winding down of the Cold War tension and success of these economies brought a close to this obliging outlook, rendering it more difficult for these East Asian states to device economic support policies. The signing of the Plaza Accord in 1985 and the introduction of trade rules (e.g., against dumping) enforced by the GATT and subsequently the WTO were indicative. Second, the aforementioned changes coincided with China's opening up in the late-1970s. In presenting itself as a massive supplier of inexpensive labor and other resources, the country attracted immense overseas direct investments, including those from Korea and Taiwan. However, as China progressed swiftly along the value chain, Korean and Taiwanese enterprises hastened the extension of their production networks into Southeast Asia. The regionalization and, indeed, globalization of these already sizable business enterprises in Korea and Taiwan progressively "decoupled" them from directives issued by their national states (Yeung, 2016). Third, The situation in Korea was exacerbated by the 1997–1998 Asian financial crises, as the IMF-mandated structural adjustments and corporate management reforms had resulted in the obsolescence of many of the existing policy tools (Pirie, 2007). Fourth, both Korea and Taiwan underwent the transition to democracy in the mid-1980s, leading to intensive electoral competitions and regime transitions that took place regularly. Under favorable circumstances, these would permit the surfacing and settlement of social and economic disagreements. However, if an important source of state capacity in Korea and Taiwan was the elevation of executive power from legislative constraints (Johnson, 1995), democratization threatens to weaken the developmental state's capacity to intervene. In particular, although the transitions in both cases were more appropriately characterized as liberal democracy, the political oppositions have been more inclined to place redistribution on the agenda, thus contesting the developmental state's sole emphasis on economic development. Fifth, whereas China's opening up had initially alleviated geopolitical tensions in the region, the country has subsequently become more assertive. For Taiwan in particular, China as a source of economic-cum-military threat has aggravated overtime in tandem with the electoral successes of the pro-independent Democratic Progressive Party (DPP) and the rise of the Taiwanese (rather than Chinese) identity on the island. The one-China policy not only excludes Taiwan from many global institutions, but it also exerts much constraint on Taiwan's capacity to extend its diplomatic or even economic relationships.

Altogether, these far-reaching political and economic changes have weakened the state capacity of Korea and Taiwan, undermining their ability to initiate state-directed development and, indeed, the feasibility of their prevailing policy tools. However, elements of the DS have not experienced demise but mostly reconstitution and reconfiguration.

The Will to Develop

In the first place, state elites have upheld "the will to develop." Though paying more attention to the provision of welfare, all presidential candidates in both cases have indicated in their platforms the commitment to facilitating if not leading economic development. Regardless of democratization, economic performance has become a basic determinant of the right to rule. In Korea, Kim Dae-jung, Roh Moo-hyun, Lee Myung-bak, and Park Geun-hye are known for their pledge to promote the information technology, cultural, and green energy industries.[6] As for Taiwan, various DPP presidents have used the term "Silicon Island" or its variants to encapsulate their support for the semiconductor and related industries (Wong, 2024).[7] At the same time, state officials in Korea and Taiwan continued to take pride in their responsibility to promote and direct economic development. In research interviews conducted in 2005 in Seoul, officials from the Ministry of Commerce, Industry, and Energy (MOCIE) explained that they "compete to make the best policies" (cf. Cho, 2019; Kwon, 2021) and those from the Ministry of Information and Communication (MIC) suggested that, although the *chaebol* have grown very big and do not need government support, "Korea needs to maintain competitiveness vis-à-vis China and India, … the government still has a role for the economy" (Chu, 2009, 2021). As for Taiwan, visits in the 2010s to the MOEA could not fail to observe how its offices were buzzing with visitors and, in turn, the dynamism of the officials. An official from the Small and Medium Enterprise Administration (SMEA)[8] sug-

[6] Moon Jae-In's case is more controversial. He had initially promoted the "income-driven growth." Though he introduced a 160 trillion won K-New Deal to promote the digital and green industries toward the end of his tenure, it was mostly in response to the economy downturn due to COVID-19 (Kim, 2020).

[7] Examples of the DPP presidents that used the term "Silicon Island" include Chen Shui-bien (2000–2008), Tsai Ing-wen (2016–2024), and Lai Ching-de (2024–).

[8] The SMEA was established in 1981 and its current name is the Small and Medium Enterprise and Startup Administration. The official hinted with pride that the Administration had given support to Hon Hai in the past, hence contributing to its current success.

gested further that technological research is expensive, state support has a role to play even among the large companies (Chu, 2021). In short, despite democratization and the relative growth of private business enterprises, state officials in both economies remain vigilant of the strategic need to maintain economic competitiveness and do not shy away from their leadership roles.

Developmental State Institutions

In the second place, although political changes have led to the restructuring of developmental state institutions in Korea and Taiwan, alternative institutions emerged to take their place and perform comparable functions. Above all, institutions in the sense of established practices of performing a task continue to exert their influence. That is to say, the modes in which actors from different domains interact to achieve shared goals have become one of the "cultural tool kits" (Swidler, 1986).

To begin with, even as Korea's EPB was dismantled in 1994 and regime transition in the country is often associated with the change in prioritized economic sector, economic ministries in the chosen sectors have stepped up to provide "roadmaps" and support.[9] Examples include the MIC (2003–2008), Ministry of Knowledge Economy (2008–2013), and the Ministry of Culture, Sports and Tourism (2013–2017) that facilitated the development of the information technology, green energy, and cultural industries, respectively.[10] To the extent that regime transition has led to drastic change in selected economic sector, such as the shift of emphasis from information technology to green energy, some lower-level organizations such as the National Information Society Agency (NIA) have continued to carry out established policies of the previous regime, thus providing some measures of policy continuity[11] (see also Cho, 2019; Lee, 2020).

[9] As polar opposites to the free market and hated symbols of authoritarian domination, the EPB in Korea and state enterprises in Taiwan dismantled accordingly.

[10] Indeed, one might even argue that Lee Myung-bak Presidential Committee on Green Growth, which devised the Plan and, the Green Technology Council (GTC), which was in charge of the Green Technology agenda, were pilot agencies of sort.

[11] Cho's (2019, pp. 116–129) study of Korea's software industry found that different Ministries interested in steering the development of the information technology sector had established varying degrees of external coordinating capacity (with other public institutions) by the mid-1990s and, at the same time, the career advancement of top state administrators was accompanied by their transfers amongst the Office of the President, Prime Minister's

Taiwan's democratization and regime transition have not been associated with dramatic changes in prioritized sectors or state institutions. Although pharmaceuticals and green energy have been highlighted sometime after the 2000s, information technology has continued to receive special support. Above all, although the CEPD has shifted its attention to more comprehensive social development since the mid-1990s, the MOEA, ITRI, and other institutions have provided continual support for the afore-mentioned economic sectors.

Just as important, institutions in the subtle sense of "cultural tool kits" (Swidler, 1986) or established practices of performing a task have also pervaded in Korea and Taiwan, as seen in their efforts to combat COVID-19. In the face of a calamitous public health hazard, the two states fell back on practices that were reminiscent of their developmental state institutions, namely, formed or mobilized pilot-agency-like organizations to provide leadership, facilitate inter-ministerial coordination, and relied on the "social embeddedness" of the state institutions to work with the private sector (Chu, 2023).

In Korea, the Central Disaster and Safety Countermeasures Headquarters (CDSCH) was assembled with the announcement of level four crisis on 23 February 2020. Headed by the Prime Minister and with the Minister of Health and Welfare and the Minister of the Interior and Safety serving as deputy heads, the CDSCH worked alongside the Korea Centers for Disease Control and Prevention (KCDC) to facilitate disease control and provide administrative assistance, including coordination with local governments. Among other policies launched by these institutions, the KCDC experts met in as early as 2–3 January 2020 to explore methods for the production of diagnostic reagent and, in order to expedite the mass production of diagnostic reagent, the KCDC held a forum on 27 January to share with more than 20 private biotechnology firms information on the virus strains and its own diagnostic test technology, as well as mobilized the Emergency Use Authorization to allow the Korean Food and Drug Administration to expedite the approval of the private firms' test kits. Together, these facilitated the approval of four diagnostic kits in early

Office, the EPB, and other ministerial offices that spanned more than one presidency. Although Cho was arguing for the role of power contention in driving the policies, the information also suggested the prevalence and perseverance of the institutional practices of the DS and explained the possibility of policy continuity.

February and daily shipments of some 100,000 test kits by March (Hur & Kim, 2020).

As for Taiwan, the Central Epidemic Command Center (CECC), formed under the Taiwan Centers for Disease Control (TCDC), was activated on 20 January 2020, three days before the Wuhan lockdown. It came under the commandership of the Minister of Health and received the full backing of senior administrators, including the Premier (TCDC, 2020), which was instrumental for attaining inter-ministerial coordination. The support of the Ministry of Transportation and Communications, the Ministry of National Defense, Coast Guard Administration, and the National Police Agency were crucial in maintaining stringent border control that enabled Taiwan to attain the 253-day record of zero local transmission (EY, 2020). Similarly, the "social embeddedness" of Taiwan's state institutions made possible the production of the much-needed materials for the prevention of disease outbreak. Apart from working with the Taiwan Machine Tool & Accessory Builders' Association to set up 60 face mask production lines within 25 days, the CECC worked with Chunghua Telecom to develop the "cellular tracking method" and relied on the cooperation of five other telecom providers to implement the "electronic fence system" that was instrumental for home quarantine/isolation control (Huang, 2020).

In short, the exemplary performance of Korea's CDSCH and Taiwan's CECC in combatting COVID-19 had relied on the two medical and health institutions' ability in adopting practices reminiscent of the pilot agencies in the heydays of the DS, which were capable of commanding inter-ministerial coordination, on the one hand, and socially embedded so as to work with the private sectors, on the other hand. Even after three decades' democratization, the abolishment or repurpose of the pilot agencies, and the change of personnel in the civil service, the aforementioned established practices (institutions) persevered.

Policy Tools

In the third place, changes in global trade policies, especially WTO regulations, prohibited many policy tools used hitherto by the Korean and Taiwanese states, whereas the emergence of legislative constraints over the executive branch and the growth of local corporations also undermined the power of such tools. In both cases, however, state institutions still possess valuable resources that enable them to prompt and coordinate corporate actions. Three points will be examined here. First, state institutions in Korea and Taiwan continue to make economic plans and, in the case of Korea, roadmaps for the development of selected industries. Tapping on the research competency of the ministries and research institutes, economic plans mostly highlight the prospective growth sectors, and roadmaps[12] seek to outline what some might call "ecosystems" or subsectors in the same industry the development of which would be mutually reinforcing. In line with Hirschman's viewpoint, to the extent that the roadmaps (and accompanying policies) help to reduce the risk of uncertainty associated with the entrance into new (and increasingly unexplored) markets, they facilitate the "coordination" of investments amongst the private enterprises (Chu, 2009, p. 292).

Second, despite the growth of local corporations, the increasing importance of exports, and the availability of investment funds from the global market, which altogether render the economic plans to become indicative rather than directive,[13] the Korean and Taiwanese states still command valuable resources that can induce the private sector to respond. For one, they possess a number of public resources such as land and spectrum,[14] and are responsible for the setting of standards, have the authority to enforce regulations, and are in the position to negotiate external trade and investment relations. All these might be considered the market-making capability of the state (cf. Polanyi, 1944). Indeed, Korean officials interviewed in 2006 explained how spectrum and communication standards could be used to channel investments and, more generally, send messages to market players about the government's priorities as outlined in the roadmaps. In turn, given a government's regulatory function, its participation in joint R&D projects initiated by the private sector could boost confidence in fair play among all participating corporations. According to a Taiwan official interviewed by this author in 2013, R&D investments are costly, and even large corporations have found it expedient to collaborate

[12] The IT839 Strategy prepared by the Roh Moo-hyun government and National Green Technology R&D Master Plan devised during Lee Myung-bak's tenure can be considered examples of such roadmaps (GGGI, 2015, pp. 158–60).

[13] Different from some definitions of indicative planning, economic plans and sectoral roadmaps in Korea and Taiwan do take into consideration technological change and the global economy. At the same time, while quotas are done away with in Korea, individual enterprises still get to perform in order to receive support.

[14] Spectrum refers to the invisible radio frequencies that wireless signals travel over.

with each other. The role of the government is instrumental in facilitating such collaborations (Liu, 2020).[15]

For another, the Korean and Taiwanese states still command public funds and have used them with considerable effects to encourage the development of selected industries. Funding support can take many forms, such as government requisitions and funds for employee training, yet the most salient one in recent years is R&D funds. In both Korea and Taiwan, the amount of general expenditure for research and development (GERD) and its share in GDP increased steadily over the years. In 2020, whereas Korea as a country invested US$111.1 billion or 4.8 percent of its GDP in R&D, that of Taiwan amounted to US$47.9 billion or 3.6 percent of its GDP, respectively (Table 5.1). Korea's rate of R&D investment in 2023 actually topped all OECD countries. To be sure, business enterprises in both cases have grown substantially in recent decades, so that as many as 15 and 5 companies in Korea and Taiwan, respectively, have made it to the list of Global Fortune 500 in 2024. Furthermore, business corporations in both economies have invested heavily in R&D such that the private sector contribution to GERD reached 77% in Korea and 82.5% in Taiwan as of 2020 (Table 5.1). However, despite the relative decline in the public sector's GERD contribution, the absolute amounts of public R&D funds have increased over the years, and the state institutions in both cases have continued to devise R&D programs to facilitate the growth of industrial sectors. One example in Korea is the "Generic Industrial Technology Development Project: Transportation Systems" (GITDP) managed by the Ministry of Trade, Industry and Energy. It made "open calls for research proposals (in 11 pre-selected industrial areas) ... [that aims at] ... greenhouse gas emissions reduction," among others. It provided a "total of 2-3 billion KRW ... to each research project with 3–7-year period" (GGGI, 2015, p. 165). As for Taiwan, the Department of Industrial Technology (DoIT) under MOEA has managed a number of Industrial Development Programs to "subsidize enterprises to conduct R&D into innovative and advanced technologies ... and to connect with R&D systems in multinational corporations," among others. Some of the current programs specify the industrial sector, such as autonomous vehicles; other programs are more generic. Most of the programs pledge to provide 40 or even 50 percent of the R&D expenditure (DoIT, 2024).

[15] The next section will say more about the external trade relations.

Table 5.1 R&D expenditure in Korea and Taiwan (1995–2020)

	Korea			*Taiwan*		
	Expenditure	*% GDP*	*% Private*	*Expenditure*	*% GDP*	*% Private*
1995[1]	13.3 billion USD	2.8	78	5.5 billion USD	1.7	54.1
2000	18.6 billion USD	2.7	72	8.8 billion USD	1.9	65.0
2010	52.1 billion USD	3.5	72	23.8 billion USD	2.9	71.2
2020	111.1 billion USD	4.8	77	47.9 billion USD	3.6	82.5

[1]The 1995 data for Korea is actually those of 1996, source: Bartzokas (2008)

Sources:ROC. National Science and Technology Council. Statistical Dataset, https://wsts.nstc.gov.tw/stsweb/technology/TechnologyStatistics.aspx?language=C&ID=3 & https://wsts.nstc.gov.tw/STSWeb/technology/TechnologyStatistics.aspx?language=C&ID=11 accessed on 9 August 2024. ROC. MOEA. R&D Expenditure Dataset 1997–2022, https://dmz26.moea.gov.tw/GA/visualize/VisDashboard.aspx?d=5, accessed 9 August 2024. Bartzokas, A. (2008). Monitoring and analysis of policies and public financing instruments conducive to higher levels of R&D investments: The "POLICY MIX" Project, https://ec.europa.eu/invest-in-research/pdf/download_en/korea.pdf, accessed 9 August 2024.

The aforementioned growth of local corporations and their access to global investment funds have no doubt increased their leverage and reduced the hold of state funding support. An informant from the Federation of Korean Industries interviewed in the 2010s claimed that the conglomerates had more resources than the government and that they "just wanted to be left alone." In fact, conglomerates in Korea make their own long-term and short-term R&D plans by working with universities and other corporations and one informant from SAIT interviewed in the mid-2000s noted that he was not familiar with some of the government's policy documents, as it had "made so many policies." Hence, it is fair to question whether the economic plans, roadmaps, or even research funding have achieved their purposes.

However, despite the size of the Korean conglomerates, the available public resources are still substantial. In a study of the Green Growth Policy of the Lee Myung-bak era, it was reported that Hyundai Motor's "Core Industrial Technology Development Project" was one the GITDP mentioned above. The *chaebol* led "a consortium of automotive parts manufacturers, universities, and government research institutes … [to conduct a five-year study], the objective of which was to help realize the mass production of fuel cell electric vehicles (FCEVs) by the year 2015, one of the 27 key green technologies selected by the Lee regime (GGGI 2015). Hence, it seems that even for Hyundai Motor, which reportedly spent

2416.2 billion KRW[16] on R&D in 2010 (Hyundai Motor, 2012), it is still worthwhile to bid for a government-subvention project.[17]

As for Taiwan, the above already noted that, given the "smaller" size of most of its corporations, they are not aversive to working with each other and to receiving state funding and regulatory support (Liu, 2020). It was reported that some 769 projects were submitted to its Industrial Technology Foresight Research as of 31 January 2024.[18] Same as Korea, large corporations also make use of government research support.[19] MediaTek, which ranks 54 in EU's 2023 R&D Investment Scoreboard, was reported to have worked with ITRI since 2015 on the development of key 5G technologies (MediaTek, 2017). In turn, Hon Hai Precision, ranks 55 in the EU Scoreboard, was reported to have signed an agreement with Taiwan Biophotonic Corporation and ITRI in February 2022 to develop a long-distance care monitoring platform. Furthermore, close ties amongst the three partners were said to have been made possible by the MOEA-established Taiwan Integrated Biomedical Industrial Center (OCAC, 2022).

This leads to the third point of this discussion. With democratization, there has been an increase in concern with equality and, hence, pressures for the government to provide more support to SMEs. This is especially true in Korea, where government R&D funds *directly* used by large corporations and SMEs in 2018 were 882.1 billion won versus 2122.8 billion won, respectively (KISTEP, 2019, p. 23). That is to say, large corporations got slightly above 29 percent of the funds directly allocated to the

[16] The reported figure was calculated according to the Korean Generally Accepted Accounting Standards (K-GAAP). When using the Korea-International Financial Reporting Standard (K-IFRS), Hyundai Motor's R&D expenditure for 2010 was 1388.8 billion KRW.

[17] It is of interest to note that, whereas Hyundai Motor gave credit to the Polaris project launched in conjunction with the Korean government's G7 Project (1992–2001) for the corporation's ability to independently develop complete fuel cell vehicle systems, it did not mention the Lee regime's National Green Technology R&D Master Plan (Hyundai Motor, 2012).

[18] The DoIT (2024) did not specify length of the period during which the 769 projects were submitted. However, the program in question was launched in 2014, which was a continuation of an earlier program.

[19] It goes without saying that there exists longstanding partnership between ITRI and TSMC. A point of interest is that the shareholdings of the National Development Fund (NDF) of the Executive Yuan ROC has declined persistently from some 48 percent when TSMC was founded to "over 10 percent" in 1999 and about 6.38 percent in 2023 (TSMC, n.d., Various Years).

enterprises (cf. Lee, 2018).[20] Furthermore, large corporations were encouraged to work with SMEs. In the GITDP mentioned above, the MOTIE stipulated that "Matching fund requirements from the private sector recipients vary (25%–50%) according to the number of SMEs participating in the research initiative" (GGGI, 2015, p. 165). That Korea's R&D programs have since the late 1990s prioritized SMEs and encouraged their cooperation with the *chaebol* has been found by other scholars. Cho's (2019, p. 89) study of Korea's software industry since the 1980s found that the issue of polarization was addressed to some extent by the 1995 revision of the Fair Transactions in Subcontracting Act, which included the software industry and, accordingly, rationalized policies on the bidding for state projects and labor cost calculations. The election of President DJ Kim in 1998 was in addition accompanied by the provision of funding support for the creation of small software firms and their R&D projects (Cho, 2019, p. 154). Similarly, Kim and Kwon (2017) reported that, not only has the Korean state prioritized SMEs for R&D support, but the SMEs' involvement in state-initiated R&D programs enabled them to work with the *chaebol*. Altogether, these policies facilitated the retention of manufacturing jobs in the country and enabled Korea to expand its production of component parts.[21]

As for Taiwan, its major R&D subsidy program for SMEs was started in 1999 and provides a maximum of NT$16 million for 36 months for individual applicants that cover three stages from pilot study, R&D, to value-added applications (SMESA, 2024). Unfortunately, the total amount of R&D subsidies provided for SMEs is unknown. However, in view of the greater number of DoIT-operated programs, which do not prioritize the SMEs, and the average of NT$22 million per project subsidy of those programs, it seems that SMEs in Taiwan have not received overwhelming

[20] These figures do not reflect the levels of collaboration with public research institutes and higher education sectors, hence the benefits derived (KISTEP, 2019, p. 23). According to Lee (2018: 3), which apparently includes funding provided to non-profit sectors, "the expenditure for SME-operated government R&D projects recorded 2,897 billion won in 2016, which is equivalent to 15.2 percent of the government's total R&D investment."

[21] Despite the emergence of prominent *chaebol* brand names, studies of four-digit US import statistics in the 1980s found that Korea specialized in the production of final products with few component parts, which were considered to carry genuinely high value-added (Feenstra & Hamilton, 2006).

support, at least in the dimension of R&D.[22] To the extent that the above discussion is accurate, it seems that democratization has exerted greater pressure on successive regimes of Korea than Taiwan to increase its support to SMEs.

Historical Institutionalism and the Enduring Constraints of Social-Structural Factors

The above section has striven to demonstrate the resilience of the DS in both Korea and Taiwan, inclusive of the will to develop, reconfigured state institutions, and commensurate adaptation in policy directions and policy tools. Yet, the *reconfiguration* of the state institutions and *adaptation* of their policies also suggest the constraints exerted by social-structural changes. The following will further this analysis by examining both the characteristics of their top R&D companies and practices of outward direct investment (ODI) as outcomes structured by their respective social-structural circumstances.

Top R&D Companies

The previous section suggests that the Korean state has privileged SMEs in its R&D support policies since the 2000s, whereas the same extent of policy change has not been found in Taiwan. Indeed, compared with Taiwan, Korea has a stronger labor movement (Liu, 2015) and, even though the country's democratization is best described as "liberal" rather than "social," there exists a wide-ranging dissent against the *chaebol* and consequently support to changing the big push policy.

At the same time, despite the policy change, an examination of the characteristics of the top R&D companies in both cases suggests the significance of institutional legacy or enduring constraints exerted by policy differences in the 1960s to 1980s. Since the 1990s, Korea's level of R&D investment has been higher than that of Taiwan, both in absolute terms and as a percentage of their GDP (Table 5.1). This difference repeats itself when examining the aggregate R&D expenditure of the Korean and

[22] This estimation is calculated according to DoIT (2024), which reports that, of the 1627 projects approved, over NT$298 billion investment was induced and, furthermore, NT$8.32 direct and indirect investment was induced per 1 NTD subsidy. To be fair to the Taiwan government, though, it also provides SMEs with investment and financing support.

Taiwanese companies that made their way into the top 1000 list of the 2023 European Union's R&D Scoreboard: whereas Korea's aggregate was 34,014 million Euro, Taiwan recorded just 21,305.5 million Euro (Table 5.2). Despite this, only 17 Korean companies made their way into said list when 23 Taiwanese companies did so. This is due to the high level of concentration of the R&D expenditure in the Korean case. Indeed, the topmost Korean company's R&D expenditure amounted to 54.2% of the aggregate expenditure of the 17 companies on the list, whilst the comparable figure for the Taiwanese company was 23.4%.[23] Having been groomed by two decades' big push policy, the Korean *chaebol* continues to dominate in innovation-based development, and the trend has not been reversed despite policy changes since the 2000s.

Outward Direct Investment

The above also alluded to the intensification of global competition and, around the same time, the "opening up" of China and its rapid progress from a supplier of inexpensive labor to a "global factory" that excels also in skill and technology. In addition to R&D support, the Korean and Taiwanese states have also devised ODI policies, both to improve the competitiveness of their enterprises and to address other impending risks. Without engaging in a comprehensive analysis of their ODI (e.g., timing of increase, sectoral distribution, and objectives), the following will highlight the changing importance of China as an ODI destination.

A notable policy of the Korean state in the 1990s was to encourage the *chaebol* to acquire US and European firms so as to secure technology and gain a foothold in potential markets (Chu, 2021; Kim & Rhe, 2009). With the establishment of diplomatic relationship with China in 1992, business firms also started to invest in the country. Starting from 1% in 1990, the share of Korea's ODI to China peaked in 2007 to reach 31.7% (Fig. 5.1). However, China's restructuring and introduction of the Labor Contract Law in 2008 reduced its attractiveness as a base for production, whereas Vietnam's accession to the WTO in 2007 and the activation of the Korea-ASEAN-FTA in the same year enhanced the prospect for Southeast Asia. Hence, even before the initiation of President Obama's "Pivot to East Asia" or President Trump's "Indo-Pacific strategy," Korean

[23] The comparable figure for 2016/17 was 49.6% in Korea and 17.9% in Taiwan, suggesting an increase in R&D concentration in both cases.

Table 5.2 Top R&D companies in Korea and Taiwan, 2023

Company (Korea)	*2023 EU R&D S*	*2024 Fortune G. 500*	*Sector*[1]	*R&D Exp € milion*	*R&D I.*[2]*%*	*Profit*[3]*%*	*Company (Taiwan)*	*2023 EU R&D S*	*2024 Fortune G. 500*	*Sector*[1]	*R&D Exp € milion*	*R&D I.*[2]*%*	*Profit*[3]*%*
Samsung Electronics	7	31	EEE	18435.43	8.2	14.4	Taiwan Semiconductor Mfg.	42	186	THE	4984.63	7.2	49.6
SK Hynix	59	–	THE	3323.85	10.1	15.3	MEDIATEK	54	–	THE	3568.35	21.3	23.2
LG Electronics	72	209	LG	2745.54	4.4	4.3	Hon Hai Precision	55	32	EEE	3488.46	1.7	2.7
Hyundai Motor	91	73	AP	2468.42	2.3	6.9	Realtek Semiconductor	235	–	THE	918.43	26.9	14.3
LG Chem	177	355	GI	1305.60	3.4	5.8	Delta Electronics (Taiwan)	236	–	EEE	912.14	7.8	11.5
Hyundai Mobis	219	339	AP	1014.17	2.6	3.9	Wistron	285	–	THE	763.53	2.5	2.8
Samsung SDI	271	–	EEE	796.29	5.3	9.0	ASE Technology Holding	291	–	SCS	744.05	3.6	12.3
Korea Electric Power (KEPCO)	374	201	E	561.65	1.1	−45.8	Asustek Computer	335	–	THE	629.70	3.8	2.5
Hanwha	383	372	GI	545.28	1.2	4.0	Compal Electronics	381	–	EEE	547.41	1.7	0.9
SK	395	100	C	516.33	0.5	5.9	Quanta Computer	409	444	THE	499.93	1.3	2.4
Kia	442	162	AP	461.22	0.7	8.4	Pegatron	419	375	EEE	488.93	1.2	2.3
Samsung Electro-Mechanics	480	–	EEE	417.20	6.0	12.6	Winbond Electronics	425	–	THE	482.97	16.7	17.8
POSCO Holdings	498	233	IMM	396.74	0.6	5.7	Novatek Microelectronics	438	–	EEE	465.46	13.9	29.8
NCSOFT	544	–	TL	349.95	18.4	21.7	Innolux	495	–	EEE	398.29	5.8	−12.4
Doosan	599	–	GI	312.30	2.5	6.6	United Microelectronics	499	–	THE	395.49	4.6	36.3
NXC	902	–	SCS	193.05	5.9	22.1	AU Optronics	502	–	EEE	392.87	5.2	−8.4
HL Mando	1000	–	AP	171.88	3.1	3.3	Inventec	521	–	THE	369.29	2.2	1.3

(*continued*)

Table 5.2 (continued)

Company (Korea)	*2023 EU R&D S*	*2024 Fortune G. 500*	*Sector[1]*	*R&D Exp € milion*	*R&D I.[2]%*	*Profit[3]%*	*Company (Taiwan)*	*2023 EU R&D S*	*2024 Fortune G. 500*	*Sector[1]*	*R&D Exp € milion*	*R&D I.[2]%*	*Profit[3]%*
KB Financial Group	–	296	–	–	–	–	Zhen Ding Technology Holding	726	–	EEE	252.79	4.8	13.0
HD Hyundai	–	321	–	–	–	–	Phison Electronics	739	–	EEE	248.24	13.5	11.6
GS Caltex	–	405	–	–	–	–	QISDA	809	–	THE	219.59	3.0	2.6
Korea Gas	–	456	–	–	–	–	Macronix International	959	–	THE	180.53	13.6	21.9
Samsung C&T	–	500	–	–	–	–	Unimicron Technology	972	–	EEE	177.69	4.1	27.6
							Silicon Motion Technology	978	–	THE	176.76	19.9	22.6
							CPC	–	465	–	–	–	–
Total no./ aggregate amt.	17	15	10	34014.9			Total no./ aggregate amt.	23	5	3	21305.53		

Notes:

[1] AP (Automobiles & Parts); C (Chemicals); E (Electricity); EEE (Electronic & Electrical Equipment), GI (General Industrials); IMM (Industrial Metals & Mining); LG (Leisure Goods); SCS (Software & Computer Services); THE (Technology Hardware & Equipment); TL (Travel & Leisure);

[2] R&D Intensity or the company's R&D expenditure divided by its net sales.

[3] Profitability or the company's operational profit divided by its net sales.

Sources:Fortune. (2024). *Fortune Global 500*, https://fortune.com/ranking/global500/search/Nindl, E., Confraria, H., Rentocchini, F., Napolitano, L., Georgakaki, A., Ince, E., Fako, P., Hernández Guevara, H., Gavigan, J., Tübke, A., Pinero-Mira, P., Rueda-Cantuche, J.M., Banacloche-Sánchez, S., de Prato, G., and Calza, E. (2023). *2023 R&D Investment Scoreboard (World 2500)*, https://iri.jrc.ec.europa.eu/scoreboard/2023-eu-industrial-rd-investment-scoreboard

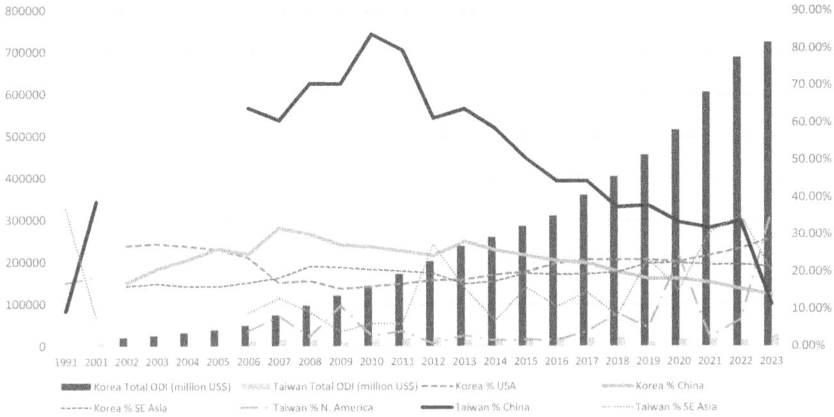

Fig. 5.1 Outward direct investment from Korea and Taiwan (1991–2023)

enterprises had sought to reduce the concentration of their overseas production facilities in China and pursue the "China + 1" strategy. The percentage share of Korea's ODI to China decreased steadily since 2007 to reach 20.1% in 2018, whereas the comparable figure to Southeast Asia fluctuated upward to reach 19.9% in the same year.

Most of Taiwan's pre-1990 ODI were located in Southeast Asia. However, many Taiwan enterprises were soon attracted by China's opening up, even though it was impossible until 1992 to invest directly in the mainland.[24] Indeed, as much as 9.5% of Taiwan's ODI in 1991 went to the mainland and the share continued to surge until it peaked in 2010 at 83.8% (Fig. 5.1). Confronted by China's restructuring and tightening labor law in 2008 as well as increase in US-China tension in the 2010s, Taiwan enterprises did try to lessen their "dependence" on China. However, even though it is possible to see an upward, albeit fluctuating, trend of Taiwan's ODI to Southeast Asia, which averaged at 15.5% between 2017 and 2019, Taiwan's ODI to China in 2018 remained substantial (i.e., 37.3%). This is striking not only in view of the presence of the Chinese overseas communities, but also the "southbound policy" advocated by President Lee Teng-hui and generations of DPP presidents.

[24] In 1992, the Taiwan government presented a "positive list of industries" that Taiwan enterprises were allowed to invest directly (rather than through medium in Hong Kong and elsewhere) in mainland China.

Although there are other contributing factors, the one-China policy, Taiwan's diplomatic isolation, and the resultant exclusion of the island-state from many trade agreements have all undermined the effectiveness of Taiwan's ODI policy. Geopolitical factors remain influential in determining the outcomes of development policies.

Conclusion

This paper contends that, regardless of the depth and nuance achieved by the best recent studies on the developmental state institutions, it remains necessary to address the commensurate geopolitical and social-structural conditions. Without such an effort, any analysis of the East Asian DS would be partial and, at worst, exacerbate the tendency to regard the DS an abstract model that can simply be adopted by countries seeking economic advancement.

Guided by this premise, this paper uses the four elements of the DS as heuristic tools to revisit the 1960s–1980s Korea and Taiwan, arguing that despite similarities in their ideational foundation and state institutions, they adopted very different policies mainly due to divergencies in their social-structural and geopolitical conditions. Referring to the global and local transformations since the mid-1980s, this paper also examines the reconfiguration and adaptation of the ideational foundation, state institutions, development policies, and experience of combating COVID-19 amongst Korea and Taiwan. In so doing, the paper not only demonstrates the prevalence and resilience of the developmental state institutions in the two cases, but also how social-structural factors have contributed to differences in their R&D funding policies. At the same time, highlighting Korea's and Taiwan's levels of ODI to China and R&D performances of their leading enterprises, this paper also tries to illustrate the enduring influence of their geopolitical and social-structural conditions.

References

Amsden, A. H. (1989). *Asia's Next Giant*. Oxford University Press.

Block, F. (2008). Swimming against the Current. *Politics and Society, 36*(2), 169–206.

Bolesta, A. (2019). From Socialism to Capitalism with Communist Characteristics. *Post-Communist Economies, 34*(1), 71–98.

Castells, M. (1992). Four Asian Tigers with a Dragon Head. In R. P. Appelbaum & J. W. Henderson (Eds.), *State and Society in the Pacific Rim* (pp. 33–70). Sage.
Chen, J. S. (1994). *Cooperative Networks and Life Structure (Xieli wangluo yu shenghuo jiegou)*. Linking Books.
Cheng, T.-J. (1987). *The Politics of Industrial Transformation*. PhD Dissertation,. University of California.
Chibber, V. (2002). Bureaucratic Rationality and the Developmental State. *American Journal of Sociology, 107*(4), 951–989.
Cho, S. (2019). *The Transformation of the Developmental State in a Polarizing Global Economy*. PhD Dissertation,. University of Wisconsin.
Chu, Y.-W. (2009). Eclipse or Reconfigured? *Economy and Society, 38*(2), 278–303.
Chu, Y.-W. (2021). Democratization, Globalization, and Institutional Adaptation. *Review of International Political Economy, 28*(1), 59–80.
Chu, Y.-W. (2023). Containing COVID-19 in South Korea and Taiwan. In A. Croissant & O. Hellmann (Eds.), *Democracy, State Capacity and the Governance of COVID-19 in Asia-Oceania* (pp. 92–112). Routledge.
Clapham, C. (2018). The Ethiopian Developmental State. *Third World Quarterly, 39*(6), 1151–1165.
Cumings, B. (1984). The Origins and Development of the Northeast Asian Political Economy. *International Organization, 38*(1), 1–40.
DoIT (ROC MOEA Department of Industrial Technology). (2024). TDP for Industry. https://www.moea.gov.tw/MNS/doit_e/content/Content.aspx?menu_id=5442
Doner, R. F., Ritchie, B. K., & Slater, D. (2005). Systemic Vulnerability and the Origins of Developmental States. *International Organization, 59*(2), 327–361.
Edigheji, O. (Ed.). (2010). *Constructing a Democratic Developmental State in South Africa*. HSRC Press.
Evans, P. B. (1995). *Embedded Autonomy*. Princeton University Press.
EY (ROC Executive Yuan). (2020). Premier Su: Long Holiday Approaching, People Should Take Precaution to Fight the Virus (Su kui: lianjia jiangzhi, guoren ying jieshen kongju zuohao fangyi) (24 December). https://www.ey.gov.tw/Page/9277F759E41CCD91/e33c0935-066c-4a96-bd62-1b014a889e84
Feenstra, R. C., & Hamilton, G. G. (2006). *Emergent Economies, Divergent Paths*. Cambridge University Press.
GGGI (Global Green Growth Institute). (2015). *Korea's Green Growth Experience*. The Institute.
Gold, T. B. (1986). *State and Society in the Taiwan Miracle*. ME Sharpe.
Haggard, S. (1990). *Pathways from the Periphery*. Cornell University Press.
Hamilton, G. G., & Kao, C.-S. (2017). *Making Money*. Stanford University Press.
Hsiao, H. H. M. (1993). The Political Economy of State-Business Relations in Taiwan. *Acta Oeconomica, 45*(1–2), 145–172.

Hsieh, M. F. (2016). Embedding the Economy. In Y.-W. Chu (Ed.), *The Asian Developmental State* (pp. 73–95). Palgrave Macmillan.
Hsu, K. (2000). Beyond Laissez-Faire and Repression [In Chinese]. *Taiwan: A Radical Quarterly in Social Studies* 38: 1–57.
Huang, Y. (2020). Electronic Fence Facilitates Home Quarantine (Dianzi weili xitong youzhu luoshi jujiajianyi) (1 June). https://www.ithome.com.tw/news/137939
Hur, J. Y., & Kim, K. W. (2020). Crisis Learning and Flattening the Curve. *American Review of Public Administration.* https://doi.org/10.1177/0275074020941733
Hyundai Motor. (2012). *Annual Report 2012.* https://www.hyundai.com/content/dam/hyundai/ww/en/images/about-hyundai/ir/financial-statements/annual-report/hw073495.pdf
ITRI (Industrial Technology Research Institute). (2023). *ITRI Innovating a Better Future*, https://50th.itri.org.tw/en/history/
Jessop, B. (2016). The Developmental State in an Era of Finance-Dominated Accumulation. In Y.-W. Chu (Ed.), *The Asian Developmental State* (pp. 27–55). Palgrave Macmillan.
Johnson, C. (1982). *MITI and the Japanese Miracle.* Stanford University Press.
Johnson, C. (1995). *Japan, Who Governs?* WW Norton & Company.
Jones, L. P. (1980). *Government, Business, and Entrepreneurship in Economic Development.* Harvard University Press.
Kalu, K., & Aniche, E. T. (2025). The Political Economy of China's Special Economic Zones and Adaptability of Developmental State Model of Industrialisation in Africa. *Journal of Public Affairs, 25*(1), e70018.
Kim, B. K. (2011). The Labyrinth of Solitude. In B. K. Kim & E. F. Vogel (Eds.), *The Park Chung-hee Era* (pp. 140–167). Harvard University Press.
Kim, J. (2020). South Korea's Moon Stakes Legacy on $138bn K-New Deal. *Nikkie Asia* (14 October), https://asia.nikkei.com/Economy/South-Korea-s-Moon-stakes-legacy-on-138bn-K-New-Deal
Kim, J. M., & Rhe, D.-K. (2009). Trends and Determinants of South Korean Outward Foreign Direct Investment. *The Copenhagen Journal of Asian Studies, 27*(1), 126–154.
Kim, K. M. (2021). Persistence or Change? *Journal of Australian Political Economy, 87*, 121–144.
Kim, K. M., & Kwon, H. K. (2017). The State's Role in Globalization. *Politics and Society, 45*(4), 505–531.
Kim, S. K. (1997). *Class Struggle or Family Struggle?* Cambridge University Press.
KISTEP (Korea Institute of S&T Evaluation and Planning). (2019). *Survey of Research and Development in Korea, 2018*, https://www.kistep.re.kr › reportDownload.
Kwon, H. K. (2021). *Changes by Competition.* Oxford University Press.

Lee, H. K. (2020). Making Creative Industries Policy in the Real World. *International Journal of Cultural Policy, 26*(4), 544–560.
Lee, S. (2018). Government R&D Support for SMEs, *KDI FOCUS*, April 12 (No. 89). https://www.kdi.re.kr/eng/research/focusView?pub_no=15625
Lim, H. C. (1985). *Dependent Development in Korea*. Seoul National University Press.
Liu, C.-K. (2020). Industrial Upgrading and Technology Diffusion in the Taiwan Automotive Parts Sector: From Gunpowder and Gas Cylinders to Airbags. *Taiwanese Sociology, 40*, 47–88.
Liu, H. J. (2015). *Leverage of the Weak*. University of Minnesota Press.
Maggor, E. (2021). The Politics of Innovation Policy. *Politics and Society, 49*(4), 451–487.
MediaTek. (2017). ITRI and MediaTek Join Hands in Announcing in Advance 5G Key Technologies (Gongyanyuan yu Lianfakeji xieshou lingxian fabiao 5G guanjian jishu) (17 December). https://corp.mediatek.tw/news-events/press-releases/itri-and-mediatek-jointly-announce-5g-technology
Mehri, D. B. (2015). Pockets of Efficiency and the Rise of Iran Auto. *Studies in Comparative International Development, 50*, 408–432.
OCAC (ROC Overseas Community Affairs Council). (2022). Hon Hai Eyes Digital Healthcare Device Market in Southeast Asia, *OCAC News* (17 February). https://ocacnews.net/article/302988
ÓRiain, S. (2004). *The Politics of High-Tech Growth*. Cambridge University Press.
Ornston, D. (2012). *When Small States Make Big Leaps*. Cornell University Press.
Pirie, I. (2007). *The Korean Developmental State*. Routledge.
Polanyi, K. (1944). *The Great Transformation*. Farrar & Rinehart.
Poulantzas, N. (1975) *Classes in Contemporary Capitalism*. Verso.
Rahman, M. M., Huque, A. S., & Ahmad, M. M. (2025). Civil Service and Socio-Economic Progress in Bangladesh. *Public Administration and Policy, 28*(2), 191–201.
Skocpol, T. (1979). *States and Social Revolutions*. Cambridge University Press.
SMESA (ROC Small and Medium Enterprise and Startup Administration). (2024). Small Business Innovation Research (SBIR) Program. https://www.sme.gov.tw/article-en-2607-4318
Stubbs, R. (2009). What Ever Happened to the East Asian Developmental State? *The Pacific Review, 22*(1), 1–22.
Swidler, A. (1986). Culture in Action. *American Sociological Review, 51*, 273–286.
TCDC (Taiwan Centers for Disease Control). (2020). In Response to Wuhan Pneumonia Outbreak [...] (23 January). https://www.cdc.gov.tw/En/Bulletin/Detail/iLHMXe2cq6X3V7ayG94C4A?typeid=158
Thurbon, E. (2016). *Developmental Mindset*. Cornell University Press.

TSMC (Taiwan Semiconductor Manufacturing Company Limited). (n.d.) (Various Years). *Annual Report*. https://www.tsmc.com/english/aboutTSMC/dc_annual_report
Wade, R. (1990). *Governing the Market*. Princeton University Press.
Wang, J. H. (2016). Toward a Platform Builder. In Y.-W. Chu (Ed.), *The Asian Developmental State* (pp. 97–115). Palgrave Macmillan.
Wong, R. (2024). The Semiconductor Choke-Point. *The Economist* (13 June). https://www.economist.com/asia/2024/06/13/the-semiconductor-choke-point
Woo, J.-e. (1991). *Race to the Swift*. Columbia University Press.
Woo-Cumings, M. (Ed.). (1999). *The Developmental State*. Cornell University Press.
Yeung, H. W. C. (2016). *Strategic Coupling*. Cornell University Press.

CHAPTER 6

Evolution of Technology Sourcing Strategies of Korean Electronics Companies: The Case of Samsung Electronics

Jaeyong Song

Introduction

According to Romer (1990), the field of endogenous growth theory posits that major technological and industrial fields have long been dominated by firms from a few advanced countries. This domination can be attributed to increasing returns to scale of physical and human resources, the cumulativeness/path dependence of knowledge accumulation, and the localization of knowledge spillover. Consequently, it is challenging for latecomer firms (LCFs) in emerging economies to achieve comparable levels of development. This assertion by Romer has been corroborated by a substantial corpus of empirical studies. Jaffe et al. (1991) employed patent citations as a means to empirically demonstrate the geographical localization of knowledge spillovers, thereby elucidating the sustained advantage of innovation clusters located in advanced countries. As demonstrated by

J. Song (✉)
Graduate School of Business, Seoul National University, Seoul, Korea
e-mail: jsong@snu.ac.kr

H.-k. Kwon (ed.), *Korean Political Economy from a Comparative-Historical Perspective*, Palgrave Series in Contemporary Korean Studies, https://doi.org/10.1007/978-981-95-9785-7_6

Audretsch and Feldman in 1996, innovation activities and the external effects of research and development (R&D) exhibit a geographical concentration across various industries.

Despite the ominous implications of these novel growth theories for developing nations, Korea is a notable exemplar of countries that have indeed "caught up" and are now leaders in a number of technological domains, including electronics and semiconductors. Korean firms have intensified their endeavors to fortify innovation foundations and pursue technological advancement, transitioning from initial technology imitation strategies to emulating advanced firms (Kim, 1997; Lee & Lim, 2001; Song et al., 2001; Mathews & Cho, 2007). As Kim (1997) noted, Korean electronics and semiconductor firms successfully transitioned their resources from imitation to innovation during the technology catch-up process. This strategic shift enabled these firms to surpass leading firms in advanced nations and establish themselves as new industry leaders. Song et al. (2001) similarly argued that the Korean semiconductor industry's success in technology catch-up stemmed from its rapid shift away from technology licensing. This strategic transition entailed the augmentation of in-house R&D capacities, complemented by the proactive engagement in diverse technology sourcing methodologies, including the establishment of overseas research institutes and the acquisition of talent. Lee and Lim (2001) examined the conditions that enabled Korea's technological catch-up, focusing on the technological regime as a critical factor. Building on these extant studies, Chang et al. (2024) demonstrated through simulation models and case studies of Korean firms that latecomers must pursue a balanced allocation of resources between imitation and innovation during their catch-up process. While a considerable amount of resources must be allocated to imitation in the initial stages, over time, a greater share of resources should be directed toward innovation activities.

Additionally, Miao et al. (2021) conducted an in-depth analysis focusing on the technology catch-up processes of Korean, Taiwanese, and Chinese firms. The researchers examined how the external technological environment, the breadth and depth of internal technological capabilities, and learning from the experiences of successful peers influence technology catch-up. Consequently, as Korean companies fortified their internal innovation capacities to expeditiously attain parity with leading firms, their patent filings in advanced economies, such as the United States, exhibited a marked increase in both volume and quality from the late 1980s onward.

The present chapter is an examination of the evolution of technology sourcing strategies among Korean companies in the electronics/semiconductor industry. The study analyzes how Korean electronics firms have utilized various technology sourcing modes—technology licensing, joint ventures, mergers and acquisitions, and in-house research and development—according to their developmental stages. Therefore, the first part of this chapter describes the process by which LCFs in emerging markets achieve technological catch-up, centered on Kim's imitation-to-innovation model. It specifically details the technology sourcing modes utilized during this process. The second part analyzes how Korean electronics companies have employed various technology sourcing modes, focusing on major corporate cases and existing research. The final part focuses on the case of Samsung Electronics, a representative Korean electronics/semiconductor company that successfully pursued technological catch-up and leaped to become a world-class company.

Imitation to Innovation in Technology Sourcing Strategy of Latecomer Firms

Given their frequent absence of strategic assets, such as technology or global market access, LCFs initially engage in imitation of industry leaders' knowledge and technologies (Mathews, 2002). It is evident that, over time, certain LCFs that have developed innovation capabilities endeavor to emulate incumbents, thereby jeopardizing their status as global market leaders or industry innovators (Miao et al., 2021; Min et al., 2024a).

Kim's Imitation to Innovation Model

Kim's research is grounded in Korea's remarkable experience of transforming from a self-sufficient agricultural economy in the 1960s into a highly industrialized global competitor within just over 30 years. During this period, Korean firms successfully transitioned from a "learning-by-doing" stage to a "learning-by-research" stage, accumulating technological capabilities. This unique development path serves as a crucial case study demonstrating how technological latecomers can acquire and advance technology.

Kim's model does not merely address changes in products or technologies when explaining the technological development process of Korean companies. He applied four interrelated analytical frameworks to analyze the dynamics of technological learning at the corporate level. The three stages of technological learning explain its dynamics through the following four key analytical frameworks. The first analytical framework is the technological trajectory. Unlike developed countries, which follow a path from the birth to the maturity of technology, developing latecomers follow the opposite trajectory. That is, they adopt a strategy of first acquiring mature technologies that are easy to enter and inexpensive, then gradually progressing through transitional technologies to the stage of developing new technologies. The second analytical framework is absorptive capacity, composed of two key elements: prior knowledge base and intensity of effort. These are essential conditions for firms to effectively internalize external technologies. The third analytical framework is crisis construction. The most subtle yet crucial feature of Kim's model is the role of crisis. Kim emphasizes that successful firms not only experience external crises but also deliberately set "challenging goals" to foster internal crises. These crises become strategic tools that accelerate the organization's technology learning efforts and force a shift in learning direction from imitation to innovation. While external crises (e.g., refusal of technology licensing by advanced firms) can act as catalysts, actively creating crises leads to more effective learning. The final analytical framework is modes of technology transfer, where the effectiveness of technology transfer depends entirely on the absorptive capacity of the recipient firm. Package licenses where the supplier guarantees performance carry less risk but induce passivity in the recipient. Conversely, acquiring technology from multiple sources and integrating it internally involves greater risk, but paradoxically, this forces the creation of crises that accelerate technological learning.

Kim's model distinguishes the accumulation of technological capabilities into three stages based on these four analytical frameworks. It emphasizes a dynamic process where transitions between stages are accelerated by catalysts like crises, rather than a simple sequential progression over time. Kim's imitation to innovation model proposes that the process of technological catch-up follows a sequential evolutionary path: LCFs first build an initial knowledge base through duplicative imitation of mature technologies developed by industry leaders; next, they gradually accumulate capabilities required for innovation through creative imitation of existing technologies or products; finally, they become innovators (Min et al., 2024a). These stages are not clearly distinct but are interconnected, and imitation sometimes serves as a lever for innovation.

1. Duplicative imitation stage: Dominant in Korea's industrial development during the 1960s and 1970s, this stage involved strategies for mass replication of mature foreign products. Duplicative imitation is defined as the development of copies of original products, in the forms of straightforward knock-offs or clones, based on the reverse engineering of mature technologies whose patents or copyrights have expired (Kim, 1997; Raustiala & Sprigman, 2012). For a considerable number of LCFs from emerging economies, emulating the success formula validated by incumbent firms is imperative for survival in the face of intense competition and subsequent convergence with incumbents that possess robust innovation capabilities (Kim, 1997; Luo et al., 2011; Chang et al., 2024; Min et al., 2024a). The goal during this period was to enter the market by selling products similar to foreign ones at significantly lower prices.
2. Creative imitation stage: This stage, observed in Korea during the 1980s and 1990s, moved beyond simple replication to include activities that added value to technology and improved existing techniques. This was achieved through benchmarking, strategic alliances, and independent research and development (R&D) activities aimed at achieving better performance or lower production costs than the original product (Min et al., 2024b). The mere imitation of the leader will not enable the latecomer to surpass the leader, who is characterized by continuous innovation and the advancement of technological frontiers. As the latecomer endeavors to bridge the technological divide by assimilating the leader's technologies, the leader frequently introduces even more sophisticated technologies, thereby further widening the gap (Song et al., 2001; Min et al., 2024a).

However, during the creative imitation stage, firms do not merely replicate the products or technologies of incumbents. Instead, they attempt to creatively reorganize and recombine existing knowledge (Kim, 1997; Wang et al., 2023). Creative imitation frequently accompanies the acquisition and exploitation of knowledge from external sources, primarily through technology licensing. During the creative imitation stage, LCFs obtain essential information about original technologies, learn the operating principles of products, and internalize effective organizational routines, all of which prepare them for innovation (Li & Kozhikode, 2008). Creative imitation necessitates that LCFs engage in active internal R&D activities to determine how to recombine acquired knowledge to address new customer needs or to enter new markets

(Kim, 1997; Shenkar, 2010; Posen & Martignoni, 2018; Wang et al., 2023; Min et al., 2024a).

3. Innovation stage: This final stage signifies strengthening independent R&D activities to develop new products and systems, reaching a level where they can compete with advanced-country firms in the global market. This stage aims to secure technological leadership and leap to become a technological leader. It also targets gaining an advantage in technological competition with advanced countries.

To successfully transition from imitators to genuine innovators, LCFs must demonstrate the capacity for independent, long-term, large-scale R&D investment, which carries a significant risk of failure (Kim, 1999). LCFs can acquire both tangible and intangible strategic assets by engaging in internal R&D activities. The tangible assets include R&D staff, R&D equipment, and financial resources. The intangible assets include tacit knowledge, innovation capabilities, and organizational routines. These assets help motivate and manage innovation. These strategic assets are critical for LCFs to overcome uncertainty led by trial and error and to cope with inevitable modifications that frequently arise during the process of new technology or product development (Li & Kozhikode, 2008; Min et al., 2024a). While LCFs may augment their absorptive capacity through imitation in the nascent stages of catch-up, the authentic capacity to absorb contemporary technologies and transform them into valuable products cannot be cultivated without a substantial amount of internal R&D activity (Kim, 1997; Sohn et al., 2009; Chang et al., 2024).

Linking these developmental stages from Kim's imitation-to-innovation model to Korea's industrialization stages yields the framework shown in Table 6.1.

A key point in Kim's model is that these three stages do not follow a strictly linear path. For example, attempts to build internal R&D capabilities can provide stronger bargaining power when negotiating foreign technology licenses, and the process of acquiring new foreign technologies can serve as an opportunity to further strengthen internal technical capabilities. In other words, there exists a cyclical relationship where imitation can lead to innovation, and innovation efforts in turn enhance the quality of imitation.

Kim does not explain technological innovation solely through corporate-level efforts. He emphasizes the importance of the national

Table 6.1 Evolutionary stage in Kim's imitation to innovation model

Stage	*Primary Objective*	*Core Activities and Mechanisms*	*Period of Korea's Industrialization*
Duplicative Imitation	Securing foundational technological capabilities and minimizing risk	Maturity phase foreign product replication, reverse engineering, package licensing	1960s–1970s
Creative Imitation	Improving existing technology and creating added value	Strengthening in-house R&D, design replication, strategic alliances	1980s–1990s
Innovation	Securing technological leadership through in-house R&D	Development of new products and technologies	1990s Onward

innovation system, where macro-level factors like government policy and the sociocultural environment interact complexly. During the early stages of economic development in the 1960s and 70 s, the Korean government played a leading role in achieving ambitious growth targets by fostering large conglomerates (chaebols) and allocating resources selectively. However, since the 1980s, as private firms took the lead in technological advancement, the government's role shifted to that of a facilitator, creating a policy environment enabling firms to pursue innovation autonomously. Additionally, high-quality education and Confucian values, which fostered diligence and educational fervor, are cited as important sociocultural factors that supplied the human resources necessary for technological learning (Kim, 1997).

Chang et al. (2024) examined how latecomers should allocate resources between innovation and imitation to overtake industry leaders across different technological regimes, based on Kim's imitation-to-innovation model. Utilizing computational models, they ascertained that an exclusive emphasis on imitation or innovation hinders leadership transitions. In the initial stages of technological development, when the level of technology is relatively low, latecomers to the field are advised to prioritize imitation by allocating a greater proportion of their resources to this endeavor. However, as these entities progress, it becomes imperative to allocate a greater proportion of their research and development resources to innovation. Their findings suggest that, particularly in instances of a substantial gap between the latecomer and the industry leader, surpassing the leaders necessitates a more balanced approach between imitation and innovation.

When the opportunity for innovation emerges, the latecomer must determine the optimal timing to transition from imitation to innovation in order to "run faster than their target." These findings from the simulation model support the technological catch-up process conceptually presented in Kim (1997, 1999)'s imitation to innovation model.

Technology Sourcing Modes Employed in the Technological Catch-Up Process

As also shown in Kim's imitation to innovation model, emerging economies' LCFs have utilized various technology sourcing modes in their technological catch-up process, ranging from licensing to in-house R&D. The choice of technology sourcing modes in the technological catch-up process varied depending on the LCF's evolutionary stage.

The most commonly used technology sourcing modes in the duplicative imitation stage of Kim's model are reverse engineering and technology licensing (Dunning, 1994; Kim, 1997). Reverse engineering involves disassembling a finished product to understand its basic concepts and applied technologies for replication. It was primarily used by latecomers in the technology catch-up phase to imitate the technologies of leading firms. Unlike reverse engineering, which is an unofficial—conducted without the technology owner's consent or royalty payments—licensing is an official form of technology sourcing where the technology is transferred from the technology-holding company in exchange for a usage fee. While licensing offers the advantage of legally acquiring technology, it often excludes cutting-edge technologies. Moreover, technology providers tend to be reluctant to transfer core know-how, posing a risk of persistent technological dependency (Song et al., 2001; Song, 2016).

Accordingly, LCFs pursuing technological catch-up tend to secure and strengthen in-house R&D capabilities for creative imitation, even if they initially source technology through reverse engineering and technology licensing. While building their own R&D capabilities, LCFs also pursue strategic alliances or mergers and acquisitions (M&As) of foreign companies to accelerate catch-up (Song, 2016). Overseas M&A is the fastest method for acquiring knowledge abroad. Recently, emerging market companies, such as Chinese firms, have actively pursued overseas acquisitions to achieve rapid technological catch-up (Deng, 2010).

Given the significant costs and risks associated with overseas M&A, companies unwilling to bear these burdens may instead attempt technology sourcing through strategic equity investments in overseas ventures, such as startups, rather than acquiring management control via M&A. Shan and Song (1997) found that European pharmaceutical companies tend to make strategic equity investments in US biotech ventures to secure technology. Such strategic equity investments for technology acquisition can promote continuous innovation by maximally ensuring the autonomy of the investee company's R&D activities. Simultaneously, they enable a more accurate valuation of the technology created by the investee, potentially functioning as the first stage of a phased acquisition with real option characteristics.

Another means for global knowledge sourcing and innovation, reducing costs and risks compared to M&A, is strategic alliances, including joint ventures. Kim and Song (2007) demonstrated that strategic alliances promote innovation in the pharmaceutical industry, specifically finding that accumulated partnership experience between strategic alliance partners fosters trust relationships, leading to better innovation outcomes. Recently, more informal forms of global knowledge sourcing and innovation activities have also become active. Representative examples include increased open innovation activities at the global level through industry-academia collaborations with overseas universities, forming consortia with foreign companies, and utilizing collective intelligence communities (Asakawa et al., 2014).

Furthermore, the global sourcing of talent—recruiting engineers working overseas to secure technology and strengthen the innovation base—is also growing in importance (Song, 2016). Song et al. (2001, 2003) empirically demonstrated that the cross-border movement of technical talent is a crucial source of global knowledge sourcing. Song et al. (2001) examined, through case studies, how Korean and Taiwanese firms utilized various technology sourcing and innovation modes and evolved them over time while pursuing advanced firms. Specifically, this study highlighted that recruiting engineers from advanced firms to secure cutting-edge technology was crucial during the early stages of technological catch-up in Korea and Taiwan's high-tech industries. In a similar vein, studies by Alnuaimi et al. (2012) on Indian firms found that engineers recruited from abroad generated higher-impact patents than those recruited domestically. Furthermore, Filatotchev et al. (2011) also demonstrated that talent returning from developed countries served as a crucial pathway for Chinese firms to acquire advanced technologies and disseminate them to local firms. Synthesizing these studies reveals that talent acquisition from abroad constitutes a vital foundation for technology sourcing and innovation, particularly for late-entrant firms in emerging markets. Furthermore, Song et al. (2003) termed learning through talent acquisition as "learning-by-hiring," demonstrating that this approach is particularly effective when talent is deployed into non-core businesses or new technology paths that are technologically distant from the core technology path.

Recently, LCFs in emerging markets have been pursuing more active knowledge sourcing and innovation activities through various means, such as establishing overseas research centers, technology-acquisition M&A, and joint ventures (Luo & Tung, 2007; Song, 2016; Miao et al., 2018). Noting this phenomenon, Shan and Song (1997) argued that while traditional foreign direct investment focused on transferring competitive advantages accumulated by the home country/headquarters overseas to overcome the 'liability of foreignness' in target countries (Hymer, 1976), they argued that a new type of foreign direct investment is evolving into 'knowledge-seeking foreign direct investment' that actively acquires knowledge overseas. Almeida et al. (2002) empirically demonstrated that among the various modes of global knowledge sourcing—such as licensing, joint ventures, and establishing overseas research centers, greenfield investments through overseas research centers is the most suitable mode for knowledge acquisition and innovation. This study argues that greenfield investments hold a relative advantage over licensing or joint ventures in terms of knowledge acquisition and innovation because global firms can best leverage various formal and informal channels, such as human exchanges, within their corporate structures.

Technology Sourcing of Korean Electronic Firms

Korean firms have also accelerated efforts to strengthen innovation foundations, moving beyond technology imitation strategies to catch up with advanced firms (Kim, 1997; Lee & Lim, 2001; Song et al., 2001; Mathews & Cho, 2007). Kim (1997) highlighted how Korean electronics and semiconductor firms effectively shifted resources from imitation to innovation during the technology catch-up process, enabling them to overtake leading firms in advanced nations and emerge as new leaders themselves. Song et al. (2001) similarly revealed that the Korean semiconductor industry's rapid shift away from technology licensing during its catch-up process, coupled with strengthening its own R&D capabilities and actively utilizing various formal and informal technology sourcing modes—such as establishing overseas research institutes and securing talent—proved crucial. Lee and Lim (2001) analyzed the conditions enabling Korea's technological catch-up by focusing on the technological regime. Building on these existing studies, Chang et al. (2024) demonstrated through simulation models and case studies of Korean firms that latecomers must pursue a balanced allocation of resources between imitation and innovation during their technological catch-up process. While significant resources must be allocated to imitation initially, over time, a greater share of resources should be directed toward innovation activities. Furthermore, Miao et al. (2021) conducted an in-depth analysis focusing on the technology catch-up processes of Korean, Taiwanese, and Chinese firms. They examined how the external technological environment, the breadth and depth of internal technological capabilities, and learning from the experiences of successful peers influence technology catch-up. Thus, as Korean firms rapidly strengthened their internal innovation capabilities to catch up with advanced firms, the patents they filed in advanced countries like the US also grew rapidly in both quantity and quality starting in the late 1980s. Song (2006a, 2006b) conducted a time-series analysis of U.S. patents to deeply examine the causes behind the surge in U.S. patents filed by Korean firms. This revealed that corporate R&D investment and innovation capacity building, particularly by large corporations, played the most crucial role, rather than government policy.

Recently, Korean companies' global R&D networks have also become active, leading to a sharp increase in patents filed overseas by their overseas research institutes. Korean companies' global R&D activities began in earnest around the mid-2000s (Samsung Economic Research Institute, 2012). At the center of this is Samsung Electronics, whose case will be detailed later. In the automotive industry, as IT capabilities like software technology grow increasingly vital, Hyundai Motor Company has also recently taken proactive steps to build a global R&D network, such as establishing the Hyundai Cradle research center in Silicon Valley.

How Samsung Electronics and LG Electronics, Korea's leading electronics companies, achieved technology catch-up and ultimately leapfrogged Sony, which represented Japan's electronics industry in the twentieth century, through strengthening their own R&D activities, is clearly evident from the changes in the number of U.S. patent registrations from 1976 to 2021 shown in Fig. 6.1. Until 2004, Sony led in US patent registrations, but starting in 2005, Samsung Electronics began surpassing Sony. By 2021, Samsung's 6502 registrations were more than

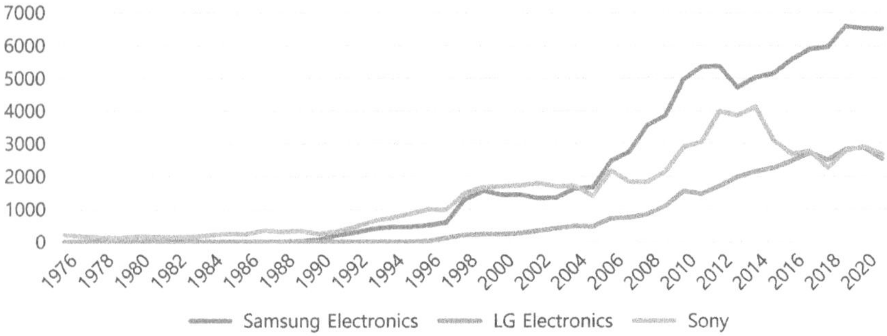

Fig. 6.1 Electronics-related patents registered in the USPTO by Samsung, LG, and Sony

double Sony's 2678. LG Electronics also surpassed Sony in U.S. patent registrations for the first time in 2019 and has been filing nearly the same number of patents as Sony since the 2020s.

The Case of Samsung Electronics

Samsung Electronics is a world-class company representing Korea. In 2024, Samsung Electronics recorded sales of 301 trillion won and an operating profit of 33 trillion won, generating the highest sales and profits among Korean companies. Samsung Electronics has significantly contributed to the Korean economy, accounting for over 20% of Korea's exports. As a global company generating over 90% of its revenue overseas, the Samsung brand ranked 5th for four consecutive years in the prestigious BusinessWeek/Interbrand ranking. Since the top four brands in this ranking were American tech giants—Apple, Microsoft, Amazon, and Google—the Samsung brand surpassed Japanese and German brands to claim the top spot among non-American corporate brands. Furthermore, since 2022, Samsung has demonstrated world-class technological prowess by securing the top spot in the U.S. patent rankings for three consecutive years.

In the electronics and semiconductor industries, where fierce global competition makes technology sourcing and innovation capabilities essential for continuous new product and technology development to become a leader, Samsung Electronics leaped from a latecomer to a global top-tier company. From 1993 to 2024, Samsung Electronics maintained the number one market share position in the global memory semiconductor industry for over 30 years. From 2006 to 2024, Samsung Electronics surpassed Sony to hold the number one position in the global TV industry. Furthermore, Samsung Electronics became the global leader in smartphone sales volume starting in 2012. Although it ceded the top spot to Apple in 2023, it regained the number one position in 2024. Furthermore, Samsung Electronics ranks second globally in the semiconductor foundry and image sensor sectors, following TSMC and Sony, respectively. It has also become a global powerhouse in the home appliance sector, trailing only LG Electronics. Additionally, Samsung Display, a subsidiary of Samsung Electronics, has maintained its position as the world leader in smartphone OLED displays. Samsung Electronics' ability to become a global powerhouse across diverse sectors of the electronics/semiconductor industry stems from its effective implementation of technology sourcing and innovation strategies.

The most crucial driving force behind Samsung's ability to become the world leader in semiconductors, OLED, smartphones, and digital TVs was the establishment of a robust 'learning organization' where continuous learning and innovation within the organization fostered the creation, sharing, and dissemination of knowledge. To maximize the efficiency of R&D investment, Samsung Electronics operates a three-tiered, systematized R&D organization. Business division development teams handle short-term commercialization technologies, Samsung Research and the Semiconductor Research Institute focus on mid-to-long-term future promising technologies, and the Samsung Advanced Institute of Technology (SAIT) is responsible for core elemental technologies for future growth engines, creating synergies. Alongside these internal structures, the global R&D network established through research institutes located worldwide—in the US, Europe, Asia, and beyond—plays a crucial role. It serves not merely as a base for technology development but as a strategic foothold for securing innovative technologies and talent locally overseas.

Throughout this process, Samsung has consistently pursued a technology-first strategy, maintaining long-term, aggressive investment to build its own R&D capabilities. When necessary, it has boldly recruited genius-level engineers at significant cost or adopted cutting-edge technologies, refining and advancing them. Through this approach, Samsung has elevated its dynamic capability to develop innovative products and technologies to the world's highest level by effectively combining knowledge acquired externally through various channels with knowledge secured internally through its own investments (Song & Lee, 2014).

To secure world-class innovation capabilities, Samsung's top management demonstrated learning and innovation-oriented leadership. They continuously instilled a sense of crisis and a challenging spirit within the organization, particularly by setting ambitious goals achievable only through innovation. Furthermore, through massive investments in R&D, they have continuously strengthened internal innovation capabilities. They actively nurtured specialized learning organizations like Samsung Research, positioning them as the driving force for creating more systematic, long-term, and Samsung-specific knowledge.

Samsung's world-class innovation capabilities can be broadly categorized into 'external knowledge absorption capabilities' and 'internal innovation capabilities'. Samsung employed a fast follower strategy during its technological catch-up process. To rapidly pursue leading companies during this phase, Samsung Electronics first developed its external knowledge absorption capability. Through this process, it swiftly absorbed external knowledge using various technology sourcing modes, including technology licensing, reverse engineering, strategic alliances, and scouting experienced engineers.

In the case of memory semiconductors, Samsung initially secured 64 K DRAM technology through technology licensing from Micron Technologies. To better absorb and internalize the technology acquired from Micron Technologies, Samsung established the SSI research institute in Silicon Valley in 1983. Centered around Korean engineers in Silicon Valley, it secured over 200 engineers. This enabled rapid in-house technology development starting from 256 K DRAM (Song & Lee, 2014).

Recently, as Samsung has leaped forward as a global leader, the importance of innovation capabilities has grown relative to its external knowledge absorption capabilities, which utilize various technology sourcing modes. While still actively pursuing external knowledge acquisition through overseas research centers and open innovation, Samsung has developed its innovation capabilities to the point of expanding technological frontiers or creating new product categories based on its world-class internal R&D capabilities. The following sections detail how Samsung Electronics leveraged diverse technology sourcing modes to absorb and internalize external knowledge while strengthening its internal innovation capabilities through large-scale R&D investment.

Utilizing Diverse Technology Sourcing Modes and Strengthening Absorptive Capacity

Samsung emphasized speed and efficiency in technology development. Rather than rigidly insisting on in-house development, it adopted a strategy of introducing technology and then digesting and improving it to suit Samsung's needs. This approach reflected Chairman Lee Kun-Hee's philosophy: "It is far more advantageous to spend 5 or 10 billion won to acquire technology in a month than to invest 1 billion won and develop it over three years." Samsung's independently secured R&D capabilities played a crucial role in this process of absorbing acquired external technologies and refining them into more competitive and differentiated technologies. For example, Samsung Electronics signed a technology licensing agreement with U.S.-based Qualcomm in September 1992. Six years and five months after first mass-producing the core chip for CDMA mobile phones domestically, it succeeded in localizing the core chip through accumulated in-house technological capabilities (Song & Lee, 2014).

Furthermore, when technology licensing proved difficult for cutting-edge technologies, Samsung secured the technology by offering exceptional compensation and recruiting domestic or foreign engineers possessing the know-how for such technologies. When Samsung entered the memory semiconductor industry, leading companies in the US and Japan all refused technology transfers. Only Micron Technologies, a US venture company struggling with funding shortages at the time, transferred design technology. However, even Micron Technologies viewed Samsung with caution, selling the 'fish' but being extremely reluctant to teach the 'fishing method'. Consequently, Samsung focused intensely on building its own technological development capabilities from the very beginning.

The most crucial strategy during this period was recruiting Korean engineers working at leading overseas semiconductor companies. To attract top Korean engineers, Samsung offered salaries more than three times higher than the president of Samsung Electronics at the time. This was unimaginable in 1983. Furthermore, to recruit talented Korean-American engineers and skilled foreign engineers active in Silicon Valley, the epicenter of semiconductor technology, Samsung established a large overseas research institute, SSI, in Silicon Valley in 1983, coinciding with its full-scale entry into the semiconductor industry. At that time, establishing a large overseas research institute to develop technology simultaneously with entering a specific industry was something even advanced companies in Europe, America, or Japan could scarcely imagine (Song et al., 2001; Song & Lee, 2014).

Furthermore, when technical advice was needed, Samsung actively recruited and utilized experienced foreign engineers. For instance, Japanese technical advisors played a particularly significant role during the early days of the semiconductor industry. Recently, hundreds of engineers from countries around the world—including the US, India, China, and Russia—have been recruited to work in Samsung's domestic R&D departments, alongside Korean and Japanese engineers. In this way, Samsung actively secured superior external technologies by licensing them when necessary or recruiting outstanding overseas engineers, while simultaneously investing heavily in building its own independent R&D capabilities. Aggressive investment in internal R&D was also essential to strengthen absorptive capacity—the ability to effectively understand and assimilate advanced external technologies. As a result, Samsung has accumulated dynamic capabilities for innovation by combining imported technologies with its own, rapidly securing more differentiated or efficient technologies.

Large-scale R&D Investment and Strengthening Internal Innovation Capabilities

Without Chairman Lee Kun-hee's technology-centric philosophy and his consequent active investment in R&D, Samsung would not exist as a global top-tier company. Following the Second Founding, Chairman Lee explicitly enshrined technology alongside talent as core management elements in the corporate philosophy, shifting the management paradigm from a management-centric to a technology-centric focus. In line with this technology-focused strategy, Samsung has many CEOs with backgrounds in science and engineering.

Based on Chairman Lee Kun-Hee's strong philosophy of prioritizing technology and R&D, Samsung consistently pursued a technology-first policy. Even during the economic crisis of the late 1990s, when it undertook bold restructuring, Samsung did not reduce its R&D investment; instead, it increased it. Samsung Electronics' R&D investment scale has grown significantly since the declaration of 'Technology Preparedness Management' in 2005. 'Technology Preparedness Management' refers to establishing a comprehensive technological management system that secures future technological leadership through foresight surpassing competitors and constant preparedness, enabling adaptation to any environmental changes. Chairman Lee Kun-hee emphasized, "We must focus the group's management capabilities on developing technologies that can become global standards and expanding intangible assets, looking ten years ahead. Without distinct, proprietary technologies to assert in this era of technological supremacy, we risk becoming perpetually second- or third-rate, dependent on technologically advanced companies." This vision led to the declaration of Technology Preparedness Management (Song & Lee, 2014).

Samsung Electronics has been ranked as one of the world's top spenders on R&D since the 2010s. Furthermore, over 50% of Samsung Electronics' domestic workforce consists of R&D personnel, making it the organization with the most PhDs in Korea. Samsung Electronics' strategic moves are particularly prominent amid the semiconductor R&D investment competition in the AI revolution era. Looking at the 2024 R&D investment status of global semiconductor companies, Intel's R&D investment growth rate was only 3.1%, while Samsung Electronics recorded a 71% increase in R&D investment.

Technology Sourcing Through Open Innovation

Recently, the accelerating pace of external environmental change and the increasing complexity of knowledge development have made internal capability development alone insufficient. Consequently, the importance of open innovation—acquiring external knowledge or jointly developing necessary knowledge with key external entities—has grown significantly. Samsung formally introduced the open innovation concept in the late 2000s and has actively secured external knowledge in various forms both domestically and internationally. As mentioned earlier, Samsung has long incorporated external knowledge through various methods, meaning it had already adopted the open innovation concept unconsciously long ago. However, since the late 2000s, Samsung has strengthened investments in open innovation—such as industry-academia collaboration, strategic equity investments in venture companies, and strategic alliances with major corporations—while reestablishing a culture and systems suitable for open innovation. The reason Samsung has recently emphasized open innovation is that the difficulty of developing technologies required for innovative product development has increased, the convergence of technologies has accelerated, and uncertainties in technology and markets have grown. Consequently, relying solely on internal R&D capabilities has proven insufficient to respond to the rapid changes in technological environments (Song & Lee, 2014).

Samsung has actively pursued strategic alliances for joint technology development with global top-tier companies from an open innovation perspective. This was particularly true in system semiconductors, an area where Samsung's technological capabilities remained relatively weak until recently. In 2004, Samsung entered into a strategic alliance with IBM concerning advanced logic technology, embarking on the path to excellence in its System LSI business. Through this alliance, both companies successfully developed advanced 65-nanometer and 45-nanometer logic processes for 300-millimeter wafers. Global system semiconductor companies such as Infineon, Chartered, and Freescale participated in the joint development of 32-nanometer logic technology. This enabled Samsung to strengthen its global competitiveness in system LSI technology, following its success in memory technology. The System LSI Division signed a next-generation CPU technology agreement with ARM Holdings, UK, which was recognized as the world leader in CPU core technology since 2001. After introducing the latest core technology, applying it to smartphone application processors and other products, Samsung was able to leap forward as a world-class application processor company.

In the TV sector, securing core technologies through strategic alliances significantly contributed to increasing market share and ultimately achieving the top global position. SAIT secured Samsung's core DNIe technology for digital TV image signal processing through joint work with a Russian partner. Although digital TVs were not yet available at the time, preventing immediate commercialization, developing DNIe technology laid the decisive groundwork for Samsung to become the global leader in the digital TV sector starting in 2006. This success story of innovative products based on open innovation is being repeated in the mobile phone sector. The Galaxy Note, developed through a strategic alliance with global electronic pen manufacturer Wacom, is a prime example. Samsung Electronics worked closely with Wacom to develop a pen solution applying Wacom's digitizer pen to the capacitive panels of smart devices. The jointly developed technology was adopted in the Galaxy Note, achieving tremendous success (Song & Lee, 2014).

Samsung has also actively pursued industry-academia collaborations with leading domestic and international universities from an open innovation perspective. For instance, the DMC Research Institute, which oversees technology development of set products such as TVs, alliances, and smartphones, has conducted joint research with Korea's leading research-focused universities, such as Seoul National University and KAIST, as strategic industry-academia partners for solution technology development. Furthermore, it has run open-call industry-academia programs with major universities in the Americas, Europe, Asia, and Russia to discover and validate innovative ideas. Furthermore, Samsung has implemented the Industrial Affiliate Program (IAP) and visiting researcher programs, dispatching company researchers to top universities in specific fields, with leading U.S. engineering institutions such as MIT, UC Berkeley, Stanford, Carnegie Mellon, and the University of Maryland. Recently, it also established an innovation research institute at the Indian Institute of Technology, a world-class engineering university in India.

Furthermore, since the 2010s, Samsung has actively pursued strategic equity investments and M&A in venture companies to secure core technologies, utilizing corporate venture capital entities such as the Samsung Catalyst Fund, Samsung Next, and the Strategic Innovation Center, established in Silicon Valley and elsewhere. Acquiring Loop Pay to secure the foundational technology for Samsung Pay and acquiring SmartThings to secure Internet of Things (IoT) technology are prime examples of Samsung securing innovative technologies through acquisitions of U.S. venture companies. More recently, Samsung strengthened its technological response to the AI revolution by acquiring Oxford Semantic Technologies, a UK company possessing AI-based knowledge graph technology, and Sonio, a French company possessing medical AI technology.

The acquisition of Harman International Industries, a global leader in automotive electronics and audio, for $8 billion in 2017 stands as Samsung's flagship overseas M&A case. This acquisition, executed to enter the automotive electronics sector in earnest while responding to the smart car trend, successfully secured a new growth engine for Samsung Electronics in automotive electronics. By combining Harman's world-class expertise in automotive software and audio systems with Samsung's world-leading capabilities in semiconductors, displays, and 5G, synergies were created. As a result, Harman has been generating profits in the trillions of won annually since 2023, contributing to Samsung Electronics' performance. Notably, through collaboration with its subsidiary Harman, Samsung developed 'Harman Ignite,' a future platform for connected cars.

Recently, Samsung has actively established overseas research institutes to expand its global R&D network, further strengthening its innovation capabilities by securing cutting-edge technologies and top talent abroad. In 2013, Samsung Electronics operated 29 research institutes across 16 countries worldwide, employing 21,000 researchers (Song & Lee, 2014). Some research centers in developed countries also conducted exploratory research to secure future technologies. For example, the center in Austin, USA, has been researching next-generation CPU cores.

Recently, as the importance of software technology has grown, Samsung has also established research centers in Silicon Valley, Bangalore, India, Russia, and Ukraine to strengthen its relatively weaker software capabilities. A representative software-focused institute is Samsung Research America (SRA). As a flagship example of Samsung Electronics' global R&D network, SRA is located in Silicon Valley, USA, and focuses on creating future competitive advantages by "proactively securing technologies that don't exist in the world yet, technologies that can change the world." SRA has grown into a large-scale research institute with over 1000 employees by intensively recruiting software engineers holding master's and doctoral degrees from leading U.S. universities such as MIT, Stanford, and UC Berkeley, focusing on developing next-generation software technologies. SRA has concentrated on pioneering research to develop future technologies applicable to Samsung's key products, including next-generation communication technologies, AI and platform technologies, mobile processor innovation technologies, and digital health-related technologies. Notably, SRA established a core research organization called the Think Tank Team. It gained attention by recruiting an Indian engineer in his early 30 s, who earned his Ph.D. from the MIT Media Lab, as an executive to lead the team.

By the 2020s, India had emerged as one of Samsung Electronics' most important overseas R&D hubs. The Bangalore R&D center surpassed SRA to become the largest overseas R&D facility. In 2024, to strengthen semiconductor design capabilities, Samsung opened its second research institute in Bangalore, the SSIR. This institute conducts practical research addressing short-term market demands through its Solution Product Development Group, which focuses on solid-state drive (SSD) research. It also collaborates with the Indian Institute of Science (IISc) on next-generation quantum technology research.

Since the late 2010s, Samsung Electronics has recognized the importance of artificial intelligence (AI) and worked to build a global AI research

Table 6.2 Status of Samsung's Global AI Center Network

Location	*Establishment year*	*Key research areas*	*Key features and personnel*
South Korea (Seoul)	2017	AI Oversight Hub	Center of the global AI research network
United States (Mountain View)	2018	Language AI, On-Device AI, etc.	AI Centers within SRA
United Kingdom (Cambridge)	2018	AI Leading-Edge Technology	Recruitment of Dr. Andrew Blake
Canada (Toronto)	2018	AI Core Technology	Establishment of Strategic Partnerships with Local Universities
Russia (Moscow)	2018	AI Algorithms	Research on foundational technologies based on mathematics and physics
United States (New York)	2018	AI Research	AI research related to robotics in collaboration with Professor Sebastian Seung of Princeton University
Canada (Montreal)	2018	AI Research	Industry-academia collaborative research with Professor Yoshua Bengio of the University of Montreal

network. To this end, as shown in Table 6.2, it established research centers near leading global universities driving AI advancement, including SRA in Silicon Valley, as well as AI research centers in New York, Montreal, Toronto, Cambridge, and Moscow. Each center has conducted specialized research tailored to its regional characteristics. For example, the Cambridge, UK center recruited Dr. Andrew Blake, formerly of Microsoft, as its leader and focused on pioneering AI technology research. The Toronto, Canada center collaborated with local top universities to research core AI technologies. Furthermore, the Moscow, Russia center specialized in handling AI algorithms based on its strengths in fundamental sciences like mathematics and physics.

Conclusion

This chapter examined how Korean companies, particularly Korean electronics companies, as LCFs in emerging economies, successfully caught up with advanced-country companies and enabled firms like Samsung Electronics to leap to world-class status by appropriately mixing various technology sourcing modes during diverse rapid technological catch-up processes. This analysis drew on existing research and a case study of Samsung Electronics. As Kim (1997) insightfully analyzed in the imitation-to-innovation model, Korean electronics firms like Samsung Electronics were able to rapidly absorb and internalize external knowledge even during the duplicative imitation stage through reverse engineering and technology licensing. This was achieved by actively investing in strengthening their own R&D capabilities. Through large-scale investment in internal R&D and the active recruitment of engineers possessing advanced technology to facilitate learning-by-hiring, they were able to rapidly modify externally introduced technologies and enter the creative imitation stage. Furthermore, to leap forward as a global leader through innovation, Korean electronics companies like Samsung Electronics have actively pursued the establishment of global R&D networks through overseas research centers, open innovation, and industry-academic collaborations with world-renowned universities. In this way, by appropriately shifting the mix of technology sourcing modes—at each stage of the technological catch-up process and effectively balancing externally acquired technologies with those developed through internal R&D, Korean electronics/semiconductor companies like Samsung Electronics, LG Electronics, and SK Hynix were able to rise to become world-class companies.

The evolution of technology sourcing modes during the rapid technological catch-up process of these Korean companies is now being replicated by Chinese firms. Chinese companies, similarly to Korean firms during their catch-up process, have also appropriately mixed various technology sourcing modes according to evolutionary stages while making large-scale investments to strengthen internal R&D capabilities. As a result, they have rapidly emerged as global leaders in emerging sectors such as AI, robotics, rechargeable batteries for electric vehicles, and drones. These success stories from Korea and China represent counterexamples to Romer's endogenous growth theory. In his endogenous growth theory, Romer argued that major technological and industrial fields have long been dominated by firms from a few advanced countries due to increasing returns to scale of physical and human resources, the cumulativeness/path dependence of knowledge accumulation, and the localization of knowledge spillovers. He contended that catch-up by latecomer firms (LCFs) from emerging economies is difficult. However, these cases demonstrate that even in technology-intensive industries, LCFs from emerging economies can achieve catch-up. This is possible by actively securing external knowledge through diverse technology sourcing modes while simultaneously strengthening internal R&D capabilities from the early stages. Korea's economic miracle, the most notable success case in the twentieth-century global economy, was made possible precisely by the successful technology sourcing strategies of these firms.

References

Almeida, P., Song, J., & Grant, R. M.-A. (2002). Cross-Border Knowledge Building by Firms, Alliances, and Markets. *Organization Science, 13*, 147–161.

Alnuaimi, T., Opsahl, T., & George, G. (2012). Innovating in the Periphery: The Impact of Local and Foreign Inventor Mobility on the Value of Indian Patents. *Research Policy, 41*(9), 1534–1543.

Asakawa, K., Song, J., & Kim, S. (2014). Open Innovation in Multinational Corporations: New Insights from the Global R&D Research Stream. In H. Chesbrough (Ed.), *New Frontiers in Open Innovation*. Oxford University Press.

Chang, S., Kim, H., Song, J., & Lee, K. (2024). Dynamics of Imitation versus Innovation in Technological Leadership Change: Latecomers' Catch-Up Strategies in Diverse Technological Regimes. *Research Policy, 53*(9), 105056.

Deng, P. (2010). What Determines Performance of Cross-Border M&As by Chinese Companies? An Absorptive Capacity Perspective. *Thunderbird International Business Review, 52*(6), 509–524.

Dunning, J. (1994). Multinational Enterprises and the Globalization of Innovatory Capacity. *Research Policy, 23*(1), 67–88.

Filatotchev, I., Liu, X., Lu, J., & Wright, M. (2011). Knowledge Spillovers Through Human Mobility Across National Borders: Evidence from Zhongguancun Science Park in China. *Research Policy, 40*(3), 453–462.

Hymer, S. (1976). *The International Operations of National Firms: A Study of Direct Foreign Investment* (Vol. 14, pp. 139–155). MIT press.

Jaffe, A., Trajtenberg, M., & Henderson, R. (1991). Geographical Localisation of Knowledge Spillovers as Evidenced by Patent Citations. *Quarterly Journal of Economics, 108*, 577–599.

Kim, L. (1997). *Imitation to Innovation: The Dynamics of Korea's Technological Learning*. Harvard Business School Press.

Kim, L. (1999). Building Technological Capability for Industrialization: Analytical Frameworks and Korea's Experience. *Industrial and Corporate Change, 8*(1), 111–136.

Kim, C., & Song, J. (2007). Creating New Technology Through Alliances: An Empirical Investigation of Joint Patents. *Technovation, 27*(8), 461–470.

Lee, K., & Lim, C. (2001). Technological Regimes, Catching-Up and Leapfrogging: Findings from the Korean Industries. *Research Policy, 30*(3), 459–483.

Li, J., & Kozhikode, R. (2008). Knowledge Management and Innovation Strategy: The Challenge for Latecomers in Emerging Economies. *Asia Pacific Journal of Management, 25*, 429–450.

Luo, Y., & Tung, R. L. (2007). International Expansion of Emerging Market Enterprises: A Springboard Perspective. *Journal of International Business Studies, 38*(4), 481–498.

Luo, Y., Sun, J., & Wang, S. L. (2011). Emerging Economy Copycats: Capability, Environment, and Strategy. *Academy of Management Perspectives, 25*(2), 37–56.

Mathews, J. (2002). Competitive Advantages of the Latecomer Firm: A Resource-Based Account of Industrial Catch-Up Strategies. *Asia Pacific Journal of Management, 19*(4), 467–488.

Mathews, J., & Cho, D. (2007). *Tiger Technology: The Creation of a Semiconductor Industry in East Asia*. Cambridge University Press.

Miao, Y., Song, J., Lee, K., & Jin, C. (2018). Technological Catch-Up by East Asian Firms: Trends, Issues, and Future Research Agenda. *Asia Pacific Journal of Management, 35*, 639–669.

Miao, Y., Salomon, R., & Song, J. (2021). Learning from Technologically Successful Peers: The Convergence of Asian Laggards to the Technological Frontier. *Organization Science, 32*(1), 210–232.

Min, B., Kim, Y., & Song, J. (2024a). How Does Technology Catch-Up Experience Affect Innovation Performance of Latecomer Firms?: Evidence from the Korea Pharmaceutical Industry. *Asian Journal of Technology Innovation, 32*(3), 652–671.

Min, B., Song, J., & Jin, C. (2024b). Latecomer Firms' Technological Learning Strategies for Creative Imitation: Evidence from the Korean Pharmaceutical Industry. *Technology Analysis & Strategic Management , 36(11), 3524–3536.*

Posen, H., & Martignoni, D. (2018). Revisiting the Imitation Assumption: Why Imitation May Increase, Rather Than Decrease, Performance Heterogeneity. *Strategic Management Journal, 39*(5), 1350–1369.

Raustiala, K., & Sprigman, C. (2012). *The Knockoff Economy: How Imitation Sparks Innovation*. Oxford University Press.

Romer, P. (1990). Endogenous Technological Change. *Journal of Political Economy., 98*(5), S71–S102.

Samsung Economic Research Institute. (2012). Analysis of Cases and Current Status of Open & Global R&D of Korean Companies. (in Korean).

Shan, W., & Song, J. (1997). Foreign Direct Investment and the Sourcing of Technological Advantage: Evidence from the Biotechnology Industry. *Journal of International Business Studies, 8*(2), 267–284.

Shenkar, O. (2010). Copycats: How Smart Companies Use Imitation to Gain a Strategic Edge. *Strategic Direction, 26*(10), 3–5.

Sohn, E., Chang, S., & Song, J. (2009). Technological Catching-up and Latecomer Strategy: A Case Study of the Asian Shipbuilding Industry. *Seoul Journal of Business, 15*(2), 25–58.

Song, J. (2006a). What Is Behind the Surge in Korean Patenting? *International Business Journal, 16*(4), 51–79. (in Korean).

Song, J. (2006b). Intellectual Property Regimes, Innovative Capabilities, and Patenting in Korea. *Seoul Journal of Business, 12*(2), 57–75.

Song, J. (2016). Evolution of Knowledge Sourcing and Creation Modes in the Global Network. *Korean Management Review, 45*(4), 1069–1088. (in Korean).

Song, J., & Lee, K. (2014). *The Samsung Way: Transformational Management Strategies from the World Leader in Innovation and Design*. McGraw Hill Professional.

Song, J., Almeida, P., & Wu, G. (2001). Mobility of Engineers and Cross-Border Knowledge Building: The Technological Catching-Up Case of Korean and Taiwanese Semiconductor Firms. In R. Buggelman & H. Chesbrough (Eds.), *Comparative Studies of Technological Evolution: Research in Technological Innovation, Management and Policy* (Vol. 7, pp. 59–84). Elsevier.

Song, J., Almeida, P., & Wu, G. (2003). Learning-by-Hiring: When is Mobility More Likely to Facilitate Inter-firm Knowledge Transfer? *Management Science, 49*(4), 351–365.

Wang, L., Wu, B., Pechmann, C., & Wang, Y. (2023). The Performance Effects of Creative Imitation on Original Products: Evidence from Lab and Field Experiments. *Strategic Management Journal, 44*(1), 171–196.

CHAPTER 7

Post-crisis Restructuring of Chaebols

Sea-Jin Chang

Korean business groups, commonly referred to as chaebols, are collections of legally independent companies that operate under shared family ownership (Chang, 2003; Chang & Hong, 2000). Technically, any firm with at least two affiliates can be classified as a business group. However, the popular press often references the official definition set by the Korea Fair Trade Commission (KFTC). Since 1987, the KFTC had been announcing a list of the top 30 largest business groups. In 2002, following the Asian Financial Crisis, the KFTC replaced the top 30 list with a two-tier system. Under this new structure, groups with 10 trillion won or more in assets were restricted to allocating no more than 40% of their combined equity capital to their affiliates. Meanwhile, groups with 2 trillion won in assets were prohibited from issuing new equity or providing debt guarantees to other affiliates. As the Korean economy and its companies grew, the threshold for this second group was raised to 5 trillion won in 2008 and to 10 trillion won in 2016, and the threshold for the first group was adjusted to 0.5% of GDP in 2022. Additionally, business groups with 5

S.-J. Chang (✉)
National University of Singapore, Business School, Singapore, Singapore
e-mail: schang@nus.edu.sg

H.-k. Kwon (ed.), *Korean Political Economy from a Comparative-Historical Perspective*, Palgrave Series in Contemporary Korean Studies, https://doi.org/10.1007/978-981-95-9785-7_7

trillion won in assets were required to adhere to governance structure disclosure regulations.

Due to the frequent changes in the KFTC's official definition of chaebols, it is challenging to present consistent statistics over the years. In this chapter, we have selected 37 groups that have appeared on the KFTC list for most years between 2000 and 2024. We have excluded older groups that no longer meet KFTC listing requirements, such as Daesung, Samchunli, and Daehan, as well as newer business groups like Kakao, Naver, Netmarble, and Celtrion, which operate in the internet, gaming, and biotech industries. Additionally, groups specializing in financial services, such as Mirae Asset and Kyobo Life Insurance, have been excluded, as they are regulated by the Korea Financial Supervisory Service.

The list of 37 chaebols, along with their number of affiliates as of 2024, is shown in Table 7.1. These chaebols are quite large; for example, Samsung Group has combined assets of 946 trillion won and combined revenue of 359 trillion won, with 63 affiliates as of 2024. In contrast, Hansol is the smallest group included in the table, with assets of 5.4 trillion won and revenue of 5 trillion won. Figure 7.1 illustrates the aggregated assets of chaebols and their return on assets (ROAs) over the 2000–2024 period. The aggregated assets of chaebols display steady growth throughout this time frame. A similar upward trend would be observed if we plotted the average number of affiliates or sales.

The ROA, which measures profitability, fluctuates in response to global economic conditions. It rose sharply after the Korean economy rebounded from the Asian Financial Crisis, during which chaebols restructured their debt and divested from loss-making businesses. However, the ROA experienced dips during significant global downturns, such as the Global Financial Crisis in 2009, the economic slowdown in 2015, and the Covid-19 pandemic. Despite these fluctuations, chaebols have generally been more profitable in the post-crisis period compared to the pre-crisis period.

During 2000 and 2024, chaebols underwent several structural changes. In this chapter, we will review the post-crisis restructuring activities and more recent changes in the operation of chaebols, including holding company structure.

Table 7.1 List of the largest chaebols

Group	*No of affiliate*	*Assets (aggregated)*	*Revenue (aggregated)*	*Spinoff (year)*	*Governance structure*
Samsung	63	945,843	358,916		Cross shareholdings
Hyundai Motors	70	354,852	285,234	Hyundai (1999)	Cross shareholdings
SK	219	334,360	200,962		Holding Company (2015)
Hanhwa	108	243,326	72,664		Operational holding company
LG	60	177,903	135,401		Holding Company (2001)
Lotte	96	137,974	67,651		Holding Company (2017)
HD Hyundai	29	84,792	70,764	Hyundai (2000)	Holding Company (2017)
GS	99	80,824	84,338	LG (2004)	Holding Company (2004)
DB	25	72,984	22,931		Operational holding company
Shinsegae	53	62,052	36,609	Samsung (1991)	Operational holding company
Hyundai Marine & Fire Insurance	13	44,315	16,462	Hyundai (1999)	Operational holding company
CJ	73	39,856	31,174	Samsung (1993)	Holding Company (2007)
Hanjin	34	39,092	19,722		Holding Company (2013)
LS	67	38,811	34,568	LG (2002)	Holding Company (2008)
Doosan	22	26,960	10,370		Holding Company (2021)
Hyundai	5	25,508	8308		Cross shareholdings
Hyundai Department Store	27	22,184	12,892	Hyundai (1999)	Cross shareholdings
Harim	45	17,557	12,485		Holding Company (2011)
Kumho Asiana	24	17,393	10,863		Holding Company (2023)

(*continued*)

Table 7.1 (continued)

Group	*No of affiliate*	*Assets (aggregated)*	*Revenue (aggregated)*	*Spinoff (year)*	*Governance structure*
HDC	35	16,997	6706	Hyundai (1999)	Holding Company (2018)
Hyosung	57	16,720	16,424		Operational holding company
KCC	14	14,201	7091	Hyundai (1958)	Operational holding company
Eugene	60	14,103	4372		Operational holding company
Kolon	48	13,059	11,199		Holding Company (2010)
Taeyong	82	12,315	6600		Holding Company (2023)
Seah	26	11,810	9420		Holding Company (2018)
Eland	31	10,910	4592		Operational holding company
Hankook Tire	24	10,383	4224		Holding Company (2013)
Kumho Petrochemical	14	9596	7773	Kumho Asiana (2010)	Operational holding company
Dongwon	26	9383	9038		Holding Company (2022)
Halla	13	8842	6594	Hyundai (1962)	Holding Company (2014)
Amore Pacific	13	8350	3325		Holding Company (2007)
Aekyoung	31	7125	4683		Holding Company (2023)
Samyang	13	6927	4641		Holding Company (2011)
Nongshim	23	5688	4462		Holding Company (2023)
Hite Jinro	11	5530	2798		Holding Company (2008)
Hansol	21	5369	5058	Samsung (1991)	Holding Company (2015)

Source: Korea Fair Trade Commission, May 2025

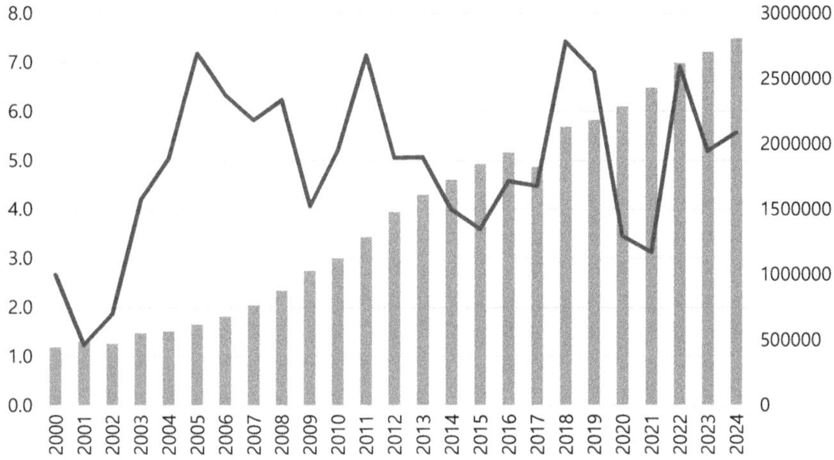

Fig. 7.1 Aggregated assets and ROA

The Post-Crisis Restructuring of Chaebols

When the Asian financial crisis hit Korea in 1997, thirteen of the top thirty business groups, known as chaebols, were pushed into technical bankruptcy along with the country itself. The International Monetary Fund (IMF) stepped in with relief funds but required the Korean government to adopt strict restructuring measures in exchange. In response, the Korean government injected public funds to rescue insolvent banks and initiated efforts to restructure the chaebols (Chang, 2003).

Efforts to restructure chaebol finances focused on three key areas: significantly reducing debt-equity ratios, eliminating debt guarantees, and conducting corporate workouts for weaker chaebols. A large portion of the decrease in chaebols' debt-equity ratios during this period was achieved through the revaluation of securities and real estate, as well as affiliate firms issuing new equity to one another. In 1997, the top 30 chaebols' total cross-debt guarantees amounted to 63.5 trillion won. By 2000, this figure had been drastically reduced to just 1.3 trillion won. Additionally, the Korean government implemented the "Big Deal" plan, which aimed to consolidate industries and refocus chaebols on their core competencies. Under this plan, weaker firms were absorbed by healthier ones, either through mergers or acquisitions, as part of the broader restructuring effort.

The Korean government also made significant efforts to reform the corporate governance structure of chaebols and enhance transparency and accountability. Measures were introduced to strengthen the roles of outside directors and independent auditors, with listed companies initially required to appoint at least one outside director. By 1999, these firms had to ensure that outside investors made up at least 25% of their Boards of Directors. Additionally, an electronic reporting system was implemented, and regulations concerning inadequate reporting of contingent liabilities, such as cross-debt guarantees among affiliates, were tightened. To further promote corporate transparency, commercial laws were amended to simplify M&A procedures, facilitating both friendly and hostile takeovers. The requirements for filing class action lawsuits against listed companies were relaxed, and access to a firm's accounting data became easier, as the representation requirements for such actions were significantly reduced. These reforms were part of a broader effort to improve the corporate governance of chaebols and curb practices that contributed to their vulnerabilities.

In addition, the Korean government mandated that chaebols abolish their group-level staff organizations, which played a central role in coordinating the activities of various affiliates. However, chaebols resisted this directive by simply shifting the functions of these staff organizations to their flagship companies. Given the ongoing need for coordination among group affiliates, the government's demand was somewhat unrealistic. To further increase accountability, the government encouraged chaebol "chairmen" to take on the role of Chief Executive Officer in individual affiliates, making them directly liable for any wrongdoing.

While Korea rebounded swiftly from the Asian Financial Crisis, the improvements in regulatory frameworks and corporate governance reforms have had enduring effects on the country's chaebols. The KFTC significantly tightened regulations around cross-shareholding practices, which had previously allowed chaebols to consolidate control over vast conglomerates with minimal actual ownership. Simultaneously, the enhancement of the corporate governance system led to heightened demands for transparency, accountability, and stronger performance from firms.

While most chaebols remained intact after the Asian Financial Crisis, some spun off groups of affiliates into separate entities, primarily driven by succession planning. The largest chaebols, including Samsung, Hyundai, and LG, divided some of their businesses among second-generation family members as a way to distribute inheritance while maintaining family control even before the Financial Crisis.

For instance, in the 1990s, Shinsegae, CJ, and Hansol were spun off from the Samsung Group to second-generation family members. Similarly, in the late 1990s, Hyundai Motors, Hyundai Department Store, Halla, HDC, and Hyundai Heavy Industries were spun off from the Hyundai Group and handed over to founders' brothers and second-generation family members. Likewise, the LG Group spun off GS and LS groups to business partners and founders' brothers in the early 2000s. Another example is Kumho Petrochemical, which was spun off from Kumho Asiana Group by a second-generation family member. These spinoffs helped manage succession while ensuring the original family's continued influence over the businesses.

Despite these frequent spinoffs, the core businesses of chaebols have largely remained under the control of their de facto successors, typically the eldest sons. For example, both LG and Doosan passed group chairmanship to their eldest sons, continuing the tradition of primogeniture in Korean family-owned conglomerates. However, there are notable exceptions where second or third sons were chosen as successors, such as in the case of Samsung. In Samsung's case, while elder brothers were spun off with groups of affiliates, the third son, Lee Kunhee, was ultimately chosen to lead the group. This practice demonstrates that while the eldest son is often the preferred successor, other family members may inherit leadership in certain circumstances.

Despite spinning off several subgroups, conglomerates like Samsung, LG, and Hyundai have remained the largest chaebols as of 2024, demonstrating the resilience of their core businesses and the continued consolidation of power within their family lines.

The Emerging Holding Company Structure

Table 7.1 illustrates the governance structures of large chaebols, which can generally be classified into three types: cross-shareholding structure, holding company structure, and operating holding company structure.

Cross-Shareholding Structure: In this type of governance, families maintain control over the entire business group through cross-shareholdings among major affiliates. Essentially, if Firm A owns shares in Firm B, Firm B owns shares in Firm C, and Firm C owns shares in Firm A, this creates a loop where the controlling family can effectively amplify their control over the group beyond their actual ownership stakes, creating a significant "wedge" between ownership and control. The KFTC has long regulated this practice, recognizing that it allows family owners to consolidate control while holding only a small percentage of equity directly.

This structure was particularly dominant among chaebols before the 1997 Asian Financial Crisis. During Korea's period of rapid economic development up until the 1990s, family wealth often failed to keep pace with the rapid growth of these conglomerates. Consequently, family equity shares were diluted over time. To maintain control, core affiliates increased their ownership stakes in other affiliates, creating a loop of cross-shareholding that effectively amplified family control. For instance, prior to the financial crisis, families in the top 30 chaebols held, on average, only 9% of equity stakes, but cross-shareholding accounted for 35% of control (Chang, 2003). This structure allowed families to extend their influence over vast assets and affiliates without the need for significant direct investment.

In the aftermath of the 1997 financial crisis, when the Korean government forced chaebols to reduce their debt-to-equity ratios to 200%, chaebols issued new shares, which were frequently purchased by other affiliates, leading to a substantial increase in cross-shareholding after the crisis. This practice, while initially helping chaebols meet debt restructuring targets, further entangled ownership structures and perpetuated the very governance issues the government sought to address. The KFTC actively sought to limit the expansion of cross-shareholdings by imposing ceilings based on the size of combined assets within business groups, and thereby curbing the reliance on circular ownership structures that artificially inflated control without corresponding equity. Over time, these concerns led to increased regulatory pressures and corporate governance reforms, pushing many chaebols to transition to more transparent structures, such as the holding company model. These reforms aimed to simplify ownership structures and reduce the complexities created by cross-shareholding.

Holding Company Structure: In response to these heightened regulations in the post-crisis era, many Korean business groups began simplifying their ownership structures by transitioning to the holding company model. This shift was seen as a way to increase transparency and accountability, as the holding company structure allowed for more direct control of affiliates while reducing the complexities associated with cross-shareholdings. By consolidating ownership under a central holding company, chaebols aimed to comply with regulatory requirements while maintaining strategic control over their subsidiaries. This trend has since become a defining characteristic of the modern governance structure within many of Korea's largest conglomerates.

A holding company structure involves a group-level holding company that holds shares of major affiliates, with families concentrating their ownership in these holding companies. There are two main types of holding companies:

1. **Pure Holding Company**: Its primary role is to own and control other firms without engaging in any direct business operations.
2. **Operating Holding Company**: This type not only acts as a holding company but also conducts its own business operations while holding shares of key affiliates.

In Korea, the holding company structure was prohibited until 1999. The country's legal system, which was largely inherited from Japan following the end of the colonial period, initially banned holding companies. After World War II, the Occupation Forces in Japan specifically prohibited holding company structures and dissolved *zaibatsus*—large family-controlled conglomerates that relied on holding company models. Korea adopted a similar legal framework, following Japan's lead in banning holding companies.

However, in 1999, Korea reversed this policy and allowed the holding company structure as part of broader efforts to facilitate corporate restructuring. Incidentally, Japan began allowing the formation of holding companies in 1998 (Shimotani, 2012). The adoption of the holding company model has since played a key role in restructuring many of Korea's largest conglomerates. Both cross-shareholding and the holding company structure allow families to exert greater control over business groups than their actual ownership might suggest, creating what is commonly referred to as a "wedge" between ownership and control. This occurs because holding companies can raise capital by borrowing from banks and listing on stock exchanges, enabling families to control the holding company without necessarily owning a majority of shares. In turn, the affiliates owned by the holding company can also be listed or secure loans, further reducing the need for the holding company to maintain a majority stake in them. Nonetheless, the KFTC favors the holding company structure over cross-shareholding.[1] This preference arises because the holding company model avoids circular ownership, which is common in cross-shareholding, and minimizes incentives for "tunneling," where resources are transferred among affiliates in ways that benefit controlling families but may not align with the interests of minority shareholders.

Since their legalization in 1999, the number of holding companies has shown a steady increase over time. This growth trajectory reflects the increasing use of the holding company structure as a preferred governance model in Korean business groups, especially as a way to simplify ownership structures and comply with evolving regulations. However, a notable dip in this growth began in 2017, when the capital requirement for holding companies was raised from 100 billion won to 500 billion won. By 2024, there are 172 holding companies managing 2373 affiliates. Table 7.1 outlines the governance structures of major Korean business groups, highlighting those that transitioned to a holding company structure and indicating the year of transition where applicable.

In general, smaller-sized chaebols and those with relatively higher levels of family ownership have been more successful in resolving cross-shareholding issues and transitioning to a holding company structure. A prime example is LG Group, one of Korea's top 5 chaebols, which transitioned to a holding company structure in 2004. LG created LG Corporation, a pure financial holding company responsible for managing shares in key affiliates such as LG Electronics and LG Chemical. The fourth-generation family owner, Koo Kwangmo, along with his extended family members, holds controlling shares in this financial holding company, which is listed on the Korean stock market. Similarly, spinoffs from LG Group, such as GS Group and LS Group, also adopted the holding company structure around the same time. Likewise, CJ Group and Hansol Group, both spinoffs from Samsung Group, transitioned to the holding company structure. Another prominent example is SK Corporation, where the Choi family concentrates its family ownership. SK Corporation holds shares in key affiliates like SK Telecom and SK Innovation.

It, however, remains fundamentally challenging for large groups, particularly those with limited family wealth, to fully resolve cross-shareholding arrangements and transition to a holding company model. For instance, over the past two decades, Samsung has made significant efforts to

[1] For a policy report on the effectiveness of the holding company regulation in Korea, see Lee (2014).

simplify its ownership structure and reduce cross-shareholding. These efforts included merging affiliates and consolidating family ownership into key affiliates that control other entities. A notable example is the 2014 merger between Samsung Everland, a privately held affiliate in leisure and amusement, and Cheil Industries, a publicly listed textile company. Cheil Industries held stakes in several other affiliates, including Samsung Engineering and Samsung Petrochemical. Additionally, Samsung Everland held significant shares in Samsung Life Insurance, further entangling the ownership structure. In 2015, this combined entity merged with Samsung Corporation, which itself held substantial shares in Samsung Electronics. As a result of these mergers, Samsung's ownership hierarchy became somewhat more streamlined, with Samsung Corporation now owning key affiliates like Samsung Life Insurance, Samsung Electronics, Samsung Engineering, Samsung SDS, and Samsung Biologics. However, the cross-shareholding issue persists, as Samsung Life Insurance still holds shares in Samsung Electronics and several other Samsung affiliates. This demonstrates the enduring complexity of fully resolving cross-shareholding structures, even with concerted efforts toward simplification.

Hyundai Motors, a spinoff from the Hyundai Group, has grown to become the largest among the former Hyundai subgroups but continues to operate under a cross-shareholding structure. As of 2023, Jung Yuisun, a third-generation family member, directly owns 2% of Hyundai Motors, 1.7% of Kia Motors (an acquired automobile assembly company), and 0.3% of Hyundai Mobis, which is responsible for supplying parts. The cross-shareholding among these entities is circular: Hyundai Mobis owns 16.7% of Hyundai Motors, Hyundai Motors holds a 33.9% stake in Kia Motors, and Kia Motors owns 17.4% of Hyundai Mobis. This circular ownership structure enables the Jung family to retain control of the entire Hyundai group despite holding relatively small direct equity stakes. Hyundai Motors has yet been able to transition to a holding company structure due to the limited ownership by Jung family.

On the other hand, the operating holding company structure is a hybrid model where the firm not only holds shares in key affiliates but also conducts its own business operations. This structure is typically adopted by groups that are able to reduce some cross-shareholding but are unable to fully transition due to constraints in family wealth or other factors. For example, Hanwha Corporation, part of the Hanwha Group, acts as an operating holding company. It holds shares in key affiliates while simultaneously running its own business operations in sectors like chemicals and energy. This dual function allows Hanwha Corporation to maintain control over its affiliates while continuing its core operations. Similarly, other conglomerates such as Shinsegae, Kumho Express, Hyosung, Eugene, KCC, Kumho Petrochemical, and Dongwon are largely governed by operating holding companies. These groups balance the control of their affiliates through shareholding while still being actively involved in business activities, a common strategy for chaebols that face challenges in fully transitioning to a pure holding company model due to limited family resources or other strategic considerations. This structure provides a level of flexibility, allowing families to retain control and influence while mitigating some of the complexities associated with cross-shareholding.

As these cases demonstrate, the holding company structure has become the standard ownership and governance model for smaller chaebols, where family wealth is often sufficient to control a relatively smaller group of affiliates. This structure offers a simplified and more transparent governance model compared to the complexities of cross-shareholding, making it easier to maintain family control while complying with modern corporate governance standards.

Figure 7.2 depicts the shifting trends in family and affiliate ownership over time, with some notable changes. Overall, the ownership stake held

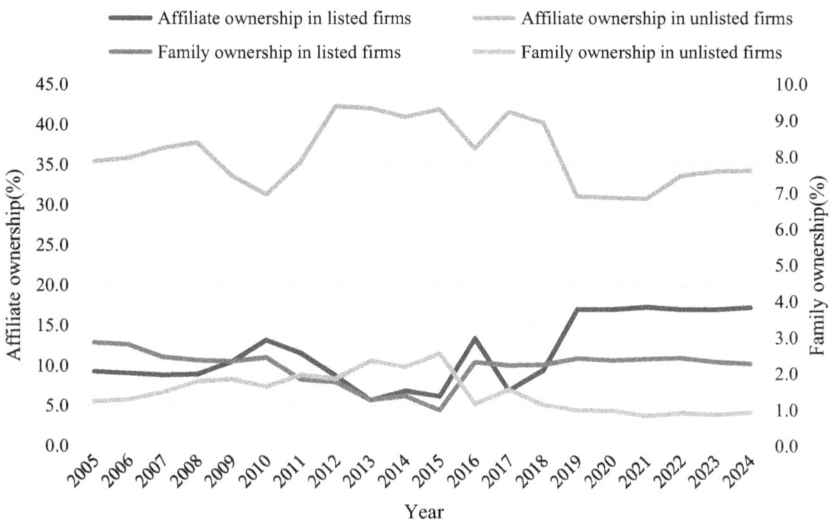

Fig. 7.2 Family versus affiliate ownership in chaebol-affiliates

by extended family members has declined, while affiliate ownership has increased. By 2024, affiliate ownership exceeds 50%, whereas family ownership has dwindled to around 3%. When breaking this down between listed and unlisted affiliates, family ownership saw a sharp rise within listed firms but declined in unlisted affiliates. Similarly, affiliate ownership within listed firms has increased over time, while it has fallen in unlisted affiliates. This trend highlights a broader strategic shift, wherein families are concentrating their wealth and influence in listed affiliates, particularly in listed holding companies, both pure and operating. This move aligns with a strategy to consolidate family control through holding companies. By securing controlling shares in listed holding companies, families are able to maintain governance over a wide range of affiliates, even with reduced direct ownership stakes.

Since 1999, however, the KFTC tightened regulations on holding companies by raising the capital requirement. For example, as in Fig. 7.3, a notable slowdown in trend began in 2017, when the capital requirement for holding companies was raised from 100 billion won to 500 billion won. This move was aimed at preventing the abuse of the holding company structure as a tool for maintaining family control without sufficient financial backing. By increasing the minimum capital threshold, the KFTC sought to ensure that holding companies had the necessary financial capacity to manage their subsidiaries effectively, rather than merely serving as a mechanism for consolidating family influence. This regulatory change made it more challenging for chaebols to adopt the holding company model, as they now need to meet higher financial requirements. By 2024, there are 172 holding companies managing 2373 affiliates.

These holding companies in Korea, originally devised to simplify chaebols' ownership structures and curb tunneling, are now facing increasing scrutiny. A key issue is that most of these holding companies—many of which are publicly listed—are significantly undervalued. As of March 20, 2025, their price-to-book ratios (PBRs) remain well below 1, with LG at 0.42, SK at 0.37, Lotte at 0.28, and CJ at 0.83.[2] In other words, the market values the shares of these holding companies at far less than the value of their underlying assets, which are largely composed of equity stakes in their subordinate operating companies that themselves are traded on stock exchanges.

[2] Chosun Ilbo, "Shares of holding companies are depressed due to dual listing," March 20, 2025.

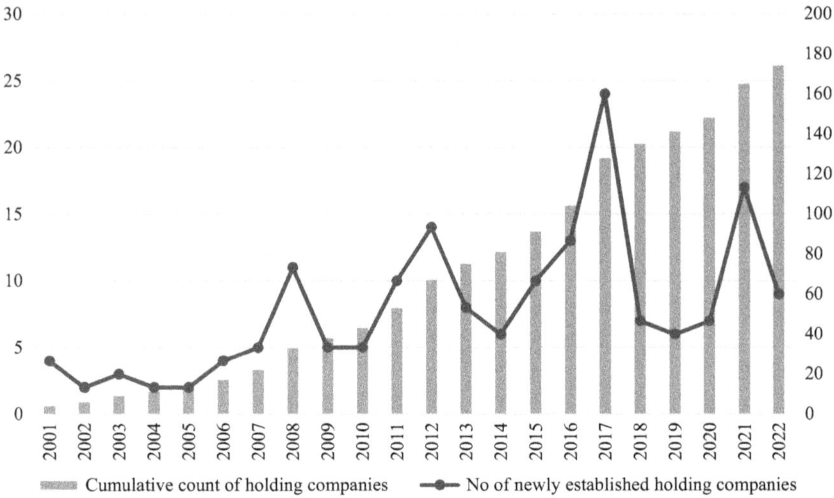

Fig. 7.3 Trend of holding companies

Under the Lee Jae-Myung administration, which began in 2025, the government pledged to boost the stock market valuation of Korean firms by advancing corporate governance reforms. A key milestone was the amendment of the Commercial Act in 2025, which significantly enhanced shareholder rights. In response, the stock prices of holding companies rose substantially, amid growing expectations that their price-to-book (P/B) ratios would improve in line with these governance reforms.

Chaebols have long been considered as the multidivisional structure, which separates strategic oversight from operational management: divisional managers are responsible for the day-to-day operations of individual business units, while corporate-level executives, supported by centralized staff functions, oversee strategic decisions such as resource allocation, new business entry, and divestitures across the entire group (Chang & Choi, 1988). Building on Chandler's foundational work, Williamson (1975, 1985) applied transaction cost economics to interpret the multidivisional structure as a governance mechanism designed to address bounded rationality and opportunism. According to this view, the structure decentralizes operational decisions to the divisional level—where managers possess local knowledge—while centralizing strategic control at the corporate headquarters.

However, the holding company structure might weaken the operation of the multidivisional structure that has been the basis for creating synergies among affiliates. As mentioned earlier, the holding company primarily relies on dividends from its operating companies for revenue. It cannot easily access cash directly from these companies, as they are often publicly listed and governed by their own boards of directors, who may oppose inter-affiliate loans. Although the holding company can charge affiliates for the use of group-level brand names, it cannot freely extend such benefits to newly established or financially distressed affiliates facing cash shortages.

The shift toward more decentralized management structures has led to increased autonomy for individual affiliates, which are now more focused on their own business performance rather than group-wide synergies. This change aligns with broader corporate governance reforms that emphasize transparency, shareholder rights, and financial independence of affiliates. However, it has also made it more difficult for chaebols to mobilize resources across the group, particularly in times of crisis or when pursuing large-scale investments that require coordination among multiple affiliates (Khanna & Palepu, 1997). As a consequence, the holding company structure may struggle to create synergies among affiliates as effectively as it did prior to the transition.Conclusion

In this chapter, we examine how the transition to the holding company structure, following its legalization in 1999, was a response to the dilution of family ownership and the increasing complexity of cross-shareholding. The Korean government favored the holding company model over cross-shareholding because it simplifies ownership structures and reduces incentives for tunneling. However, this structure does not fundamentally resolve the limitations inherent in the chaebol system, where control often exceeds actual ownership. In effect, the holding company structure has enabled chaebol families to retain control despite holding relatively small ownership stakes, thereby perpetuating their dominance. However, the Korean government has initiated reforms to strengthen corporate governance codes and enhance the protection of shareholder rights. It is also worth noting that the holding company structure may limit the ability to create synergies through resource pooling among affiliates.

References

Chang, S. J. (2003). *Financial Crisis and Transformation of Korean Business Groups: The Rise and Fall of Chaebols*. Cambridge University Press.

Chang, S. J., & Choi, U. (1988). Strategy, Structure and Performance of Korean Business Groups: A Transactions Cost Approach. *Journal of Industrial Economics, 37*, 141–158.
Chang, S. J., & Hong, J. B. (2000). Economic Performance of Group-Affiliated Companies in Korea: Intragroup Resource Sharing and Internal Business Transactions. *Academy of Management Journal, 43*(3), 429–448.
Khanna, T., & Palepu, K. (1997). Why Focused Strategies May Be Wrong for Emerging Markets. *Harvard Business Review, 75*(4), 41–51.
Lee, S. (2014). *Effectiveness Analysis and Improvement Measures of the Holding Company System*. KDI Research Report 2014–09.
Shimotani, M. (2012). Japanese Holding Companies: Past and Present. *Japanese Research in Business History, 29*, 11–28.
Williamson, O. E. (1975). *Markets and Hierarchies*. Free Press.
Williamson, O. E. (1985). *The Economic Institutions of Capitalism*. Free Press.

CHAPTER 8

Tradition as a Bridge between Political Economy and Sociology: In Search of the Distinctiveness of South Korea's Modernization

Yong-Chool Ha

Bringing the State Back In: And the Rise of the Gap Between Political Economy and Sociology of Late Industrialization

Interest in the sociology of late industrialization has been limited for several intellectual reasons: there has been insufficient differentiation among various patterns of industrialization; the state's role in driving social change has not been properly addressed; scholars have often assumed that

This chapter is an adapted version of chapters 1, 2, 3, and 4 of the author's *Late Industrialization, Tradition and Social Change in South Korea* (University of Washington Press, 2024).

Y.-C. Ha (✉)
Henry Jackson School of International Studies, University of Washington, Seattle, WA, USA
e-mail: yongha5@uw.edu

H.-k. Kwon (ed.), *Korean Political Economy from a Comparative-Historical Perspective*, Palgrave Series in Contemporary Korean Studies, https://doi.org/10.1007/978-981-95-9785-7_8

industrialization universally leads to class-based social outcomes; and the concept of tradition within industrialization remains conceptually unclear.

It was not until the 1970s, when the political economy approach became the leading research paradigm, that the contextualization or differentiation of industrialization began to receive meaningful academic attention from the perspective of social change. The prevailing lack of interest in the diverse and contingent social consequences of industrialization stems from the fact that both the dominant Marxian and structural-functionalist frameworks largely overlooked these issues, primarily because they took market-based industrialization and economic processes as given. Consequently, these perspectives do not distinguish between different patterns of industrialization, and this absence of differentiation effectively prevents consideration of multiple possible paths to industrialization and social transformation.

The lack of adequate attention to the differentiation of industrialization stems from the assertion that both paradigms possess universal applicability, as well as from the presumption that industrialization produces universal social consequences. This presumption is itself rooted in Western experiences.

Interest in alternative trajectories to capitalism emerged with the political economy perspective on late industrialization during the late 1970s and early 1980s. At that time, several scholars revised the Marxist understanding of the state, demonstrating that the state's bureaucratic structure was distinct and partially independent from the interests of the capitalist ruling class. They contended that the state's relative autonomy and administrative capacity were crucial factors in achieving societal stability and economic growth.

The transition to examining late industrialization marked a significant break from previous approaches, particularly in terms of contextualizing industrialization. The most notable theoretical advancement of the political economy approach was its shift in analytical emphasis from society to the state. The state was reintroduced as a central explanatory factor for economic development, especially in newly industrializing nations such as South Korea and Taiwan. The core argument is that the state's relative autonomy and administrative capacity are essential components in realizing economic development.

From the standpoint of social change during late industrialization, the political economy approach made it possible to anticipate diverse patterns of social transformation by acknowledging the existence of different industrialization trajectories, particularly through its emphasis on the state's role as opposed to the market. The prevailing political economic perspective—from the developmental state model to more recent discussions on varieties of capitalism—has tended to concentrate almost exclusively on the state as a comprehensive institution, focusing on government policy incentives and the relationships between the state and business.

Nevertheless, in most political economy studies, society is considered primarily in terms of its impact on economic developments. As a result, the political economy approach has inadvertently left the social and cultural dimensions of industrialization largely unexplored. Institutionalism has yet to fully address how the state's significant involvement in economic development influences society. In fact, society, tradition, and institutions are frequently referenced to explain economic institutions and development, but there is little attention paid to broader macro-social implications (Smelser & Swedberg, 1994).

The critique of universal patterns of industrialization was not paralleled by a similar movement within sociology. This gap within sociology has led to an unclear conceptual status for the sociology of the non-Western world, including cases of late industrialization. This situation may be closely related to the renewed interest in political economy and, more importantly, to the general decline in macrosociological inquiry within sociology during the 1980s, as the following statement demonstrates:

> Sociology was the architectonic discipline in America during the heyday of Parsons and Seymour Martin Lipset, but it turned away from big theory and the explanation of macrolevel outcomes during the 1980s, just as new waves of democratization and development sent political science and economics in search of such theories. Somehow, Europe avoided this divorce between sociology, politics, and economics, but social theory has become a European preserve, without the influence over American social science that Europeans achieved in cultural studies. (Hall, 2007, p. 137)

More specifically, although the state's role in driving economic development is widely acknowledged, there has been little focus on the broader social consequences of state actions. The concept of embeddedness, as discussed in the literature (e.g., Evans, 1995), exemplifies this tendency. Embedded autonomy describes the state's position as being integrated within society through networks such as school ties as Fig. 8.1 shows, while still retaining enough independence to formulate and implement

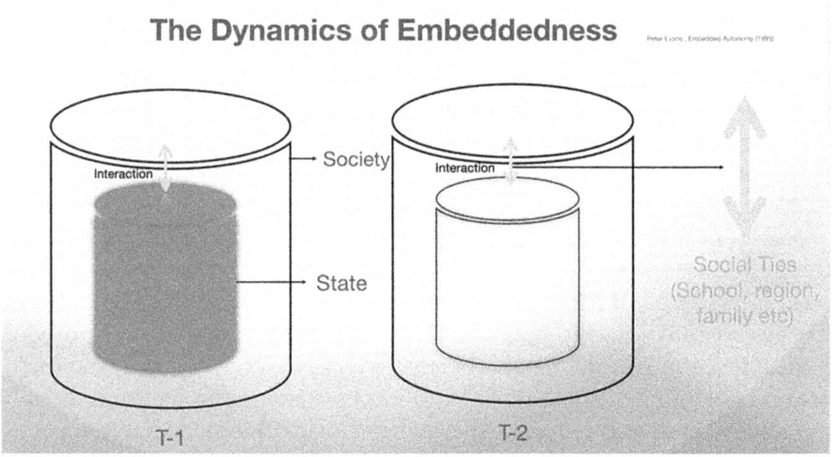

Fig. 8.1 Dynamics of embeddedness

policies even in the face of societal opposition. This embedded autonomy is often credited as a crucial factor for economic achievement. While social and cultural elements are frequently referenced to account for economic success, there has been minimal exploration of how society itself is transformed during industrialization as a result of this embeddedness. Consequently, the intricate nature of society under state-led industrialization has rarely received sufficient scholarly attention. Furthermore, when the state was reintroduced into social science discourse, the analysis remained confined to debates within political economy theory. The effort to bring the state back into focus did not extend to a sociological level (Skocpol, 1985). As a result, the political economy approach has left the social consequences of late industrialization conceptually ambiguous.

Narrowing the Gap: Understanding Social and Institutional Ironies of Late Industrialization

This paper introduces a new perspective for analyzing the specific social consequences of late industrialization, with a focus on South Korea. The distinctive social and institutional transformations associated with late industrialization arise from the way traditional institutions and values are invoked and reinforced to achieve rapid economic growth. These processes can be described as "social and institutional ironies" of late industrialization. The central irony is that institutions and values typically seen as resistant to change are, in fact, reactivated as essential tools to accelerate industrialization. Therefore, understanding social and institutional change in late industrialization requires an examination of these ironies of economic success, an area that remains insufficiently explored in existing research. This paper argues that uncovering these apparent paradoxes is fundamental to grasping the unique social and institutional changes that occur during late industrialization. The limited attention given to these ironies helps explain the persistent divide between political economy and sociology in studies of late industrialization.

Seeking to identify the unique social consequences of late industrialization means rejecting the expectation or application of universal social outcomes. Each instance of late industrialization is characterized by its own domestic social and economic conditions and international context, resulting in varying degrees of state intervention and policy choices. While late industrializing countries share certain structural features, such as economic backwardness and a prominent role for the state, the specific content of these features differs from case to case. As a result, it is not possible to predict similar social consequences across different contexts. This characteristic of late industrialization highlights the importance of historical specificity and contextual analysis over generalization (Johnson & Keehn, 1994; Johnson, 1997). Only by adopting this approach can we identify and explain alternative dimensions of social change that go beyond class or stratum.

Neofamilism: Social Consequences of the Tradition–Late Industrialization Nexus

The social and institutional ironies of late industrialization emerge from the necessity to accelerate the process itself. The onset of late industrialization is often driven by a sense of backwardness, insecurity, and inferiority among the elite, which generates a heightened sense of urgency. In response, traditional institutions and values are reintroduced as mechanisms to speed up industrialization. These traditions serve beneficial functions by offering familiarity in communication and institutional practices during this period. As such, traditional institutions and values become institutional imperatives of late industrialization, taking on various forms depending on the specific domestic social and historical context (Murakami, 1984; Dahrendorf, 1967).

In South Korea's case, familial, school, and regional ties were strengthened and integrated through state recruitment and its interactions with business, a phenomenon described as neofamilism. Neofamilism refers to the dynamic reinforcement of social ethos and relationships based on primary ties that developed throughout Korea's industrialization. These processes addressed questions of identity, provided survival strategies, and influenced institutional operations. The prefix "neo" highlights that these traditional relationships have been revived and transformed within an industrial context, distinguishing neofamilism from the familism typical of agrarian societies. Neofamilism is outward-looking and oriented toward mobility, aligning with Korea's export-driven strategy. It also represents a more narrowly defined structural arrangement than broader concepts like traditionalism (Jowitt, 1983; Walder, 1986). Familism here extends beyond the conventional family, encompassing a wide range of primary ties based on kinship, region, and school. These overlapping ties are utilized individually or collectively to access state incentives (Kulp, 1925; Ok, 1989).

It is important to highlight that the persistence of traditional elements during and after industrialization, or their universality across time and space, is not the central point. Rather, what matters is that specific traditional primary ties were actively reinforced and strengthened throughout the process of state-led industrialization. Neofamilism differs from clientelism in that it encompasses a variety of relational forms, with clientelism being just one possible manifestation. For example, school ties can be activated almost anywhere and at any time, often without deliberate management, and may take on contractual, noncontractual, or clientelistic forms.

While neofamilism can be analyzed within the framework of network analysis, the term itself is used to capture the unique social ethos and structural characteristics found in Korea, such as the concept of the corporate family, regional solidarity, and the interconnectedness of family, school ties, social mobility, and status. Since status in this context is collective and familial rather than individual, conventional ego-centered network analysis cannot fully account for the essence of neofamilism. The term also serves to clarify the dynamic process by which these ties are reinforced during industrialization, a process often overlooked in standard network analyses.

Therefore, neofamilism should be understood as the social outcome of the state's reintroduction and strengthening of pre-industrial social patterns during late industrialization. It has become a deeply institutionalized source of identity, a crucial survival strategy, and the foundation for organizational practices in South Korea. Additionally, neofamilism has developed into a distinct social structure that both coexists with and moderates class relations. These neofamilial phenomena warrant thorough and systematic investigation within the context of Korea's late industrialization.

Park's Industrialization Drive and the Emergence of Neofamilism: The Dynamics of Late Development

The initial point to note is that late industrialization is triggered by the realization among elites of their nation's backwardness (Nettl & Robertson, 1968). Understanding when, why, and how elites come to recognize their country's lateness is crucial for analyzing the patterns of social change associated with late industrialization.

A common thread in elites' perception of backwardness is a sense of relative underdevelopment compared to neighboring countries, regions, and the broader world. Simultaneously, elites often find themselves in a fragile position regarding legitimacy, both in relation to other elite groups and to society at large.

This feeling of inferiority subsequently generates a sense of urgency, prompting leaders of late industrialization to set ambitious industrialization goals and to focus intensely on the speed of progress. It is typical for such leaders to push for rapid achievement of industrialization targets and high rates of economic growth.

An ironic aspect of late industrialization is that the stronger the feelings of backwardness, inferiority, and urgency, the more likely it is that traditional institutions and values are reintroduced. This is paradoxical because, under normal circumstances, rapid industrialization would be expected to bring about swift social changes that fundamentally alter traditional institutions and values.

The reason for this irony lies in the following logic: the greater the drive for rapid economic growth, the more leaders tend to rely on familiar institutions and values. In other words, to achieve high growth rates under intense urgency, it is rational to utilize familiar institutions and values, as people undergoing this transition are more comfortable within a familiar environment. This sense of comfort helps explain the paradox of late industrialization: the faster the process, the greater the reliance on traditional institutions and values.

This leads to a related question: to what extent are leaders of late industrialization aware of their use of traditional institutions and values, and do they consciously view these as positive tools for facilitating industrialization? In other words, a key factor in understanding social change during late industrialization is the degree to which traditional values and institutions are deliberately invented (Hoffmann, 1994).

On one hand, leaders may employ a "harnessing" strategy, using tradition to advance industrialization, often without consciously considering the invention of tradition. Even if leaders are unaware of traditional practices or view them negatively, these institutions and values may still operate and influence social and institutional changes during late industrialization. This phenomenon can be described as "the introduction of tradition through the back door" (Janelli & Janelli, 1982; Kim, 1997).

The second approach involves the explicit "invention" of tradition, where leaders intentionally prepare for a comprehensive creation of tradition. This invention can affect social change at two levels: the recruitment methods for officials involved in implementing industrialization, and the social institutions responsible for managing social conflicts (Murakami, 1984; Vlastos, 1998).

Mechanisms for the Emergence of Neofamilism: Park Chung Hee's Sense of Backwardness, Inferiority, Urgency, and Ambitiousness

Park's perception of backwardness was shaped and preceded by his broadly negative assessment of Korean history, which encompassed a wide-ranging view of the nation's past. Drawing from his general overview of Korea's historical trajectory, he expresses regret that, despite favorable natural and human resources, Korea was unable to establish a significant international presence—a situation he attributes primarily to internal challenges.

> ...It is five thousand years since our founding father founded the fatherland. Our nation is based on one of the few purest races in the world, but our history has been one of internal division, mutual hatred, and conflict in the

> midst of poverty and idleness. With sharing pure blood, God-given land, and unique culture, we have not been able to establish a nation worthy of name. Reflecting upon our past our history has been a history of insult and bloody tears. How could such a nation have dared to look outside when inside was as such... (Park, 2017, pp. 22–23)

> Our history beginning with the twentieth century had been one of hostile external environments and currents, the colonization for the forty years, the import of decadent culture since the end of WWII, Korean War and consequent confusion, poverty and the two revolutions... This disgraceful half century of our history witnessed offenses against our good customs and ideological and political confrontation, lavish spending and waste, idleness, vanity, mutual hatred, and jealousy, which all gave rise to a society of instability and harshness in emotion. (Park, 1968, p. 271)

Park's negative assessment of Korean history contributed to his profound sense of backwardness. This perception of backwardness originates from his general observations of the domestic situation.

> Our five thousand years of Korean history from the Old Koguryo period through the Three Kingdom Period, the Unified Shilla, the post-Three Kingdom, the unified Koryo to the Yi dynasty of the five hundred years were one of retreat, unsophistication, and stagnation. When did we ever dominate others by crossing the border, seek reforms and change by bringing in ideas and materials from abroad, demonstrate and extend our unified power to the outside and exalt our autonomy through special industries and culture? We have been pushed and purposelessly assimilated into foreign cultures and could not make any inch of progress from the primitive economy. We spent most of our time on fratricidal infighting. It was a history of microcosm of the feudal society which was characterized by idleness, remissness, and stagnation. (Park, 1971, p. 252)

Park's sense of backwardness in turn led to his strong sense of urgency to overcome backwardness. He frequently expressed the need for the economic transformation of the country to overcome backwardness:

> There is no progress and prosperity in human life which can be achieved without blood and sweat shedding effort. At a historical turning point clouds of retreat which are covering our fatherland and history of our nation will not clear up unless we who are living today make life and death effort to

free ourselves from the bridle of disgrace and backwardness. (Park, 1968, p. 269)

We cannot continue to live like this, and if we do so, we are bound to starve to death or to face the collapse of the country. We do not possess anything, and we did not attempt to do so. … our industries were in shambles and in retreat without making progress forward. What was augmenting was debts and burdens. (Park, 1969, vol. 3, p. 72)

Priority of Economy and Ambitious Goal Setting

Park's awareness of Korea's backwardness led him to deliberately emphasize the significance of economic development as the primary means to overcome this condition. His sense of urgency was reflected in the establishment of exceptionally ambitious economic targets, as demonstrated by the following remarks.

Without a full stomach, there is no politics or society or culture. Also, without hope for economic development there is no reform for other areas. Not to repeat without economic rehabilitation no victory from communists and no independence. Economy is hard to deal with and cannot be managed only with knowledge and eagerness. We cannot afford to leave our economy as it is. We should fight for victory, and if we succeed, we will survive; if we lose, we will permanently die. (Park, 1965, p. 58)

In this context, Park's urgency and ambition were reflected in the establishment of exceptionally high economic targets and a strong emphasis on rapid progress. These ambitious goals were evident at both macro and micro levels. Park criticized the annual GNP growth rates of the early 1950s as being only 4 to 5%, and 6% in the latter half of the decade, which he considered insufficient. He subsequently set much higher targets. For the first five-year economic plan (1962–1966), the planned annual growth rate was 7.1%, but the actual growth surpassed this, reaching 8.3%. This trend continued with the second and third five-year plans: the actual growth rate for the second plan was 11.4%, exceeding the planned 7.0%, and for the third plan, the actual rate was 11.2%, compared to the planned 8.6% (Jones & Sakong, 1980, pp. 94–97).

Neofamilism and Social and Institutional Distinctiveness

This section analyzes the emergence of neofamilism which starts at the state level. First, it starts with the recruitment patterns of Park. The state recruitment patterns were emulated by the business sectors, and through interactions between the state and business was formed the structure of neofamilism. The final section demonstrates the process of diffusion of neofamilism throughout Korean society.

Park's Recruitment Patterns: Combination of Merit and Regionalism

As the following data illustrates, Park implemented a distinctive recruitment strategy by selecting individuals who had succeeded in passing rigorous civil service examinations (merit) and who also shared his regional background.

Career Bureaucrats Distribution

Regional Distribution of Career Bureaucrats(MCI)

		1948-1955	1956-1960	1961-1965	1966-1970	1971-1975	1976-1979	Total	
Category	Region	*n*	*n*	*n*	*n*	*n*	*n*	*n*	%
Civil Service Exams	Southeastern	-	-	5	6	23	14	48	35.6
	Southwestem	1a	2	4	2	5	5	19	14.1
	Seoul/ Kyonggi	-	1	8	11	13	12	45	33.3

Merits and Regionalism

	1948-1955	1956-1960	1961-1965	1966-1970	1971-1975	1976-1979	Total
	n %	*n* %	*n* %	*n* %	*n* %	*n* %	*n* %
Total Recruits	69	14	90	48	89	69	378
SNU Graduates	3 4.3%	5 35.7%	43 47.8%	28 58.3%	50 56.2%	28 40.6%	157 41.5%
SNU + Southeastern	1 33.3%	2 40.0%	12 27.9%	8 28.6%	21 42.0%	10 35.7%	54 34.4%
SNU + Southwestern	1 33.3%	1 20.0%	7 16.3%	2 7.1%	3 6.0%	3 10.7%	17 10.8%
SNU + Seoul/Kyonggi	1 33.3%	-	18 41.9%	14 50.0%	13 26.0%	12 42.9%	58 36.9%
SNU + Choong-Chung	-	2 40.0%	3 6.8%	4 14.3%	10 20.8%	2 7.4%	21 13.5%
SNU + Otheer Regions	-	-	3 25.0%	-	3 14.3%	1 10.0%	7 13.0%

15

Mimesis in Recruitment and the Formation of Neofamilial Nexus

Park's sense of urgency for economic development, combined with his belief that Korean businesses were not adequately prepared for export promotion, resulted in the creation of a wide array of incentives designed to support businesses in achieving economic and export growth. In this environment, companies were highly motivated to seek out state support to strengthen their competitive positions. The company-specific allocation of state incentives further encouraged individual firms to actively pursue these benefits, leading each business to exhaust every possible avenue to secure access to state resources.

This heightened sense of urgency and the constantly shifting landscape fostered deep and frequent interactions between the state and individual companies. Under these conditions, it was entirely rational for businesses to adopt recruitment practices that mirrored those of the state, and these mimetic patterns between the state and the private sector had significant social and institutional repercussions.

In essence, the recruitment strategies used by the Ministry of Commerce and Industry (MCI), for example, were replicated by the business sector as a means of gaining entry into the ministry, which controlled various incentives critical to business interests. Strong personal connections based on regional and school affiliations formed the basis for close relationships—and at times, collusion—between government and business, resulting in a phenomenon of government–business "mingling."

The structural features of neofamilism became evident. Park's recruitment of administrative officials was grounded in a combination of regionalism and educational ties, such as high school and college connections. The internal organization of Korean chaebŏls, as described in Figure, is essentially three-tiered: at the top, family members oversee ownership and management; non-family members occupy various managerial roles, typically based on school ties and regional proximity to the owner group; and at the base, the solidarity among average workers is rooted in regional ties (Janelli, 1993, p. 136; Kim, 1997).

Interactions Between the State and Business: Neofamilism In Action

The following interview materials illustrate the mutual perceptions between bureaucrats and business, as well as the motivations and patterns behind the mobilization of neofamilial ties. To begin with, businesses were fully aware that bureaucrats were under significant pressure to achieve the export goals set by President Park, and that they were therefore committed to supporting business interests.

Q: How were bureaucrats at that time, especially those of the Ministry of Commerce and Industry?

A: They thought without export the country would collapse and thus thought export as an issue where life or death is at stake. Successful implementation of export targets was regarded as a way to demonstrate patriotism. Bureaucrats' determination to fulfill export targets was much stronger than now.

In these circumstances, businesses aligned themselves with bureaucrats, fully recognizing the latter's commitment to achieving export goals and seeking to maximize their own interests as a result:

Q: How did the business community view the government's support for export?
A: As the government lent every possible support to business, had to follow decisions on support for business precisely, without making any changes. As President Park was so occupied with export, we could not but actively support it. However, bureaucrats dipped their hands in policy support to products for domestic market, let us say, 0.5% for personal gains while 5% for political slush funds.

A businessperson described the uncertainty of the period as follows:

Q: Was the situation during industrialization so uncertain that businesspeople felt that everything was possible and, at the same time, that nothing was possible?
A: This was due to ambiguity in laws and regulations. The interpretation of laws and regulations varied, depending upon the situation. As such, officials tended to decide in favor of business. However, there were also situations that could not be subject to arbitrary decisions of officials.

According to the testimony of a former MCI official, efforts to gain access to the ministry were clearly felt within the bureaucracy:

Q: There was a saying that companies locate and maintain various personal ties within the ministry to contact them whenever problems arise.
A: It was quite natural. Most companies could not survive without them. They carefully cultivate the ties.

Q: From when did you notice it?
A: In the past, companies could not do this, due to the lack of systematic management, but since the latter part of the 1970s, companies did it quite strategically. Prior to the 1970s it was done not in a systematic way but on a case-by-case basis.

Q: Were school ties and regional ties mobilized?
A: If they decide to do so, they use school and regional ties as a way to open communication channels. In my case I have a lot of people who are connected through school and regional ties, and managerial peo-

ple in companies mobilize whatever they have, and that was the normal practice of the time.

In this context, businesses made use of every possible connection as a means of communication to secure a favorable environment for their operations, as illustrated by the following example:

Q: Whom did you contact at the ministry?
A: Of course, those whom I know, alumni, school ties, previous coworkers, high school and college classmates and alumni.

Q: Were they able to take care of difficult problems?
A: They tried to do their best to solve the problems.

This means that businesses judiciously and strategically mobilized school, blood, and regional ties to obtain information and financial support from the government. These comprehensive efforts to establish channels within the state extended beyond the ministry level, reaching as far as the national assembly and the highest levels of power:

Q: How did you contact the government?
A: Is it not true that there was no person in the presidential house and secretariat who could not be connected, not only through my own ties but also through school and regional ties of my friends and the friends of my friends? Companies systematically use these ties. When you become a high-level manager of a company you are requested to submit a list of people in major institutions that you know, including all the people in political, administrative, and financial fields. When problems occur, a total mobilization of human contact is launched with the MCI. The CEO calls for an executive meeting, identifies target officials in the ministry, and entrusts a certain executive to take charge in fulfilling the mission. The designated person discusses the scale of money to be spent for the mission, and mobilizes every possible tie, sometimes succeeding in influencing more favorable regulations. From a business perspective it is a sort of investment. There are cases where a long-term investment is done through travel support and sending them abroad for training.

Q: There is a rumor that those who can have a better connection with the government received more rapid promotion. What do you think of this?

A: It depends on the area. Public relations, general administration and dealings with the government are important in private companies. Therefore, the extent of external connection is considered at the time of hiring new entrants. For this reason, Seoul National University is important.

Q: Then, did you use school ties when you contacted officials?

A: In my case, yes, I used school ties extensively. In Korea, nothing can be done without acquaintances. Lobbying is needed as a way to realize changes in regulations for new factories, permission for trade, etc. For this reason, companies need a superman. Companies tell their employees to mobilize every means, even if they have to violate laws. Companies tell them that companies will try their best to release them when they get caught due to legal violation.

As such, companies tried to mobilize all possible ties to set up a "bridge" with the government. On this phenomenon, one former high-ranking bureaucrat stated the following:

Q: How did companies try to set up a communication channel with the ministry?

A: It would not be far-fetched to say that they tried to hang on to every possible "string" (tie).

Such practices of contacting the government were widely recognized. In particular, companies considered lobbying through various personal ties as a standard approach, largely because the state was viewed as the primary source of support for business needs:

Q: How important was the connection with the state in doing business?

A: The connection with the government was most important in building new factories and doing business. State-business collusion started from this. There is nothing that exists without reason. Since the state held all the financial sources, the connection with the government was quite essential for business.

Q: How about a specific example?
A: When companies tried to secure special access to low-interest loans, each company tried their best in lobbying … naturally regional and school ties become important. For me I am a graduate of college of business and of a vocational high school. Since the number of graduates was not large, we knew each other well among the graduates of the college, and seniors and juniors knew each other well.

Diffusion of Core Neofamilism and Social Consequences

The foundational neofamilial relationships established between business and the state were subsequently replicated and extended throughout society via two main mechanisms. The first, within the economic sphere, involved the structural connections between chaebŏls and small and medium-sized enterprises (SMEs). By 1975, 46 chaebŏls accounted for 13.4% of GDP and 36.7% of manufacturing GDP (Jones & Sakong, 1980, p. 266). In 1982, SMEs with 5 to 299 employees represented 97.3% of all industries, yet their share of value-added GNP was only 36.2%. This significant concentration of economic power in large conglomerates resulted in SMEs becoming highly dependent on chaebŏls. In 1982, 38% of SME business involved subcontracting with chaebŏls, a figure that rose to 74% by 1991.

This high degree of dependency compelled SMEs to tolerate various exploitative practices from larger firms, such as delayed payments and enforced price reductions (Hong, 1993, p. 111). Each chaebŏl maintained numerous subcontracting relationships with SMEs, and one consequence was the transfer of the neofamilial ethos from chaebŏls to SMEs (Hong, W., personal communication, November 24, Hong, 1999). The following interview with a small enterprise CEO is quite revealing:

Ha: What do you think about the impact of chaebŏls on small-medium industry in terms of business practices?
Han: Chaebol had a great deal of impact on small-medium industries. The latter tried to learn from the former in mobilizing various connections to approach chaebols to obtain contracts. Small-medium industries envied chaebols' access to the state through the mobilization capacity of chaebols through school, blood, and regional ties. Small-medium industries learned from big business the need

> to mobilize various ties as chaebols set the tone for business practices for the entire economy. Small-medium industries during the 1970s also relied on blood ties and other ties in securing personnel and financial resources.

A second avenue for the spread of neofamilism was the distinctive political and economic position occupied by white-collar workers within chaebols. As the Fig. 8.2 shows, the white-collar employees of chaebols formed the backbone of the middle class. As of April 1975, there were 1,404,399 workers nationwide, and 29.3% of them were employed by enterprises with more than five hundred staff members (Office of Labor of Republic of Korea, 1977, pp. 52–59). The ramifications of this are significant for both social and institutional structures. Although white-collar workers are classified as middle class based on their economic status, their identities were narrowly defined and shaped by the three neofamilial ties, making

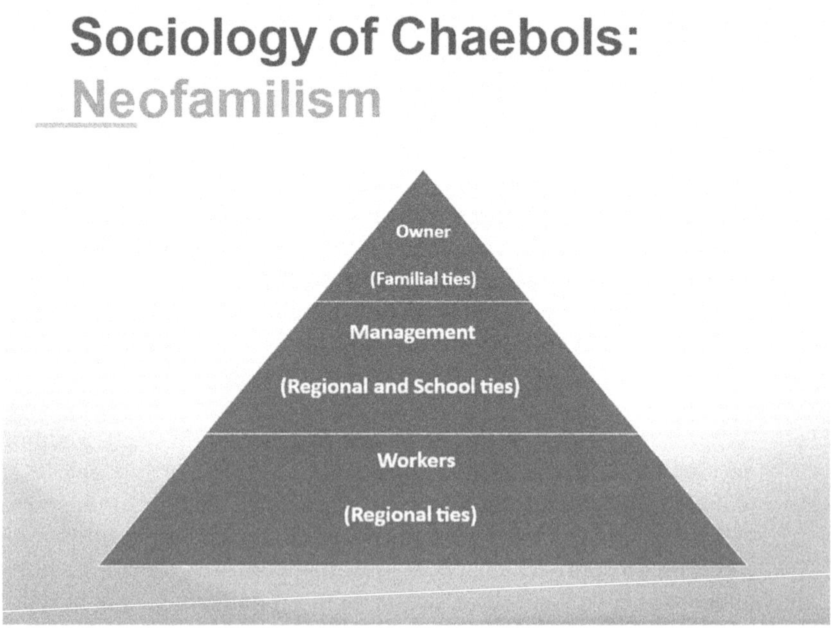

Fig. 8.2 Sociology of Chaebol

them the principal agents responsible for disseminating neofamilism throughout Korean society.

Distinct Social and Institutional Consequences of South Korea's Late Industrialization

In addition to the rise of neofamilism resulting from South Korea's state-led late industrialization, several institutional outcomes also appeared, each carrying significant consequences for the country's modernization and modernity.

De-bureaucratization and Hollowed-Out Bureaucracy

One of the distinct institutional consequences which defies Weberian industrialization-bureaucratization thesis is that South Korea's late industrialization resulted in de-bureaucratization and hollowed-out bureaucracy.

The primary factor driving debureaucratization was the top leader's acute awareness of national backwardness and the resulting sense of urgency. This urgency decisively influenced the establishment of goals, as well as the style and substance of decision-making and policy implementation. Consequently, these pressures altered the ministry's operational methods and ultimately affected bureaucratic integrity.

The president's perception of backwardness and urgency was reflected in policy and implementation through an emphasis on speed. The leader's ambitious approach placed considerable pressure on bureaucrats. Excessive initiatives and interventions from the top dampened bureaucratic autonomy and rendered bottom-up decision-making virtually impossible. This reliance on the top leader for decision-making and policy initiation led to intense competition among bureaucrats to gain the president's trust and support, and fostered the so-called "wild horse" phenomenon, where outsiders sought direct access to the top leader, bypassing bureaucratic channels. Collectively, these dynamics contributed to the politicization of the public bureaucracy.

Additionally, decision-making driven by urgency increased the demand for information from outside the bureaucracy. More significantly, the president's export-oriented agenda compelled bureaucrats to forge closer relationships with business. This intermingling resulted in arbitrary decisions and situational responses, as company-specific policies were often not grounded in institutionalized procedures. Export-oriented policies produced double-edged outcomes: on one hand, export volume served as an objective metric for evaluating bureaucrats and acted as a constraint on corruption, since exports depended on the international market. On the other hand, an obsessive focus on export promotion led to relaxed standards in the application of rules and regulations, resulting in greater arbitrariness in decision-making and implementation.

Finally, the urgency-driven, president-centered approach to decision-making frequently transcended the boundaries of administrative agencies, disrupting established interactions between different units. The MCI's capacity to coordinate among its various divisions deteriorated. President Park's regional origins and his pressing drive for industrialization fostered an organizational culture that blended regionalism with merit-based personnel policies. By leveraging both the merit system and regionalism, the top leader was able to secure loyalty and improve the effectiveness and efficiency of economic development initiatives. As a result, the concentration of MCI officials from Korea's southeastern region led to the formation of informal groups based on regional ties.

This phenomenon was not confined to the MCI but extended into the business sector and broader society as well (Ha, 2005). The imitation of state practices by society increased the vulnerability of the bureaucracy to external influences, particularly from business interests. Alongside these structural dynamics, the president's frequent admonishments and personnel changes in response to unmet export targets further destabilized organizational cohesion.

With respect to decision-making, the rapid pace of economic development necessitated frequent changes, fostering a pragmatic approach in which all available means were employed to achieve objectives. During policy implementation, particularism became prevalent, as government actions increasingly targeted specific companies, thereby deepening the entanglement between bureaucrats and business in the decision-making process. The widespread presence of particularism in policy execution highlights the high degree of uncertainty and volatility, resulting in significant ambiguity in everyday decision-making and implementation.

In summary, the effectiveness of the merit system was undermined when combined with regionalism, and the pursuit of overly ambitious goals through hasty implementation blurred the lines between internal and external boundaries. Consequently, the MCI did not become more bureaucratic; instead, its bureaucratic character was gradually eroded by persistent external influences.

Differentiation of State-Society Relations

The examination of the state's role in Korea's late industrialization offers a unique perspective for distinguishing patterns of state-society relations. To properly contextualize these relations, it is essential to consider both the scope and intensity of state intervention in the industrialization process. Analysis of the interactions between the state and business (society) in Korea reveals that the conventional state vs. society framework does not adequately capture the South Korean experience. Instead, four distinct patterns of interaction can be identified: state vs. society; state in society; state over society; and state with (or and) society.

State vs. Society Model

Great Britain serves as a prime example of this model. It is widely recognized that Britain underwent spontaneous industrialization, with the market assuming a dominant role and the state's involvement remaining minimal. Social class emerged as a new foundation for identity, while individualism became the prevailing mode of personal existence. Insofar as British civil society stood in implicit opposition to the state (unlike the more active opposition of the French bourgeoisie), the state's functions were largely confined to providing legal frameworks for charity, encouraging workers to establish self-help savings banks, supporting fraternal societies, retail and industrial cooperatives, and ensuring legal protections for labor unions (Garrad, 2002, p. 101).

This understanding of state and society among the bourgeoisie led to the widespread formation of voluntary organizations at both rural and urban levels. The nationwide proliferation of such organizations distinguishes the British case from that of late-developing countries, where civil organizations are typically concentrated at the central or urban level. In Britain, voluntary organizations operated according to democratic principles, fostering a strong affinity with the political democratization process that followed.

State in Society Model

The state in society model depicts a scenario where the state remains detached from social organizations; as a result, these organizations operate independently, without engagement from or accessibility to the state. In the African context, colonial boundaries often failed to align with traditional tribal territories, making it difficult for the state to extend its influence into village life. Consequently, traditional villages retained their autonomy and resisted state intervention. Migdal describes this as a strong society versus a weak state, characterizing it as a "web-like society" in which, once the state enters the villages, it becomes unable to maneuver or withdraw (Migdal, 1988, Chapters 1 and 2; Lewis, 1992, p. 46).

State over Society Model

This model draws on the political, economic, social, and international experiences of former socialist countries, including the Soviet Union and Eastern Europe. Its most distinguishing characteristic is that the state absorbed political, economic, and social functions. From the outset, this highly centralized system was dysfunctional. One institutional outcome of the flawed socialist system was a widening gap between formal and informal institutions. Faced with severe shortages of goods in the formal sector, socialist societies increasingly depended on informal social relations for survival. These informal practices involved subverting official goals, widespread false reporting, and dishonesty, all of which further deepened the divide between official and private spheres.

Opposition to the communist system was forced underground or subjected to intense surveillance. When the communist system abruptly collapsed, opposition groups that had formed under strict state control resurfaced, only to confront the significant challenge of overcoming entrenched legacies. These groups became entangled in a strong sense of elitism and hierarchical status. Gaining entry into these opposition groups—which evolved into pro-democratic forces—became a formidable task, requiring the right connections. This monopolistic tendency fostered unity within the groups but undermined effective conflict management. Over time, opposition groups fragmented, leading to political divisions as different factions competed for resources and members.

State-Leading Society Model

This model is grounded in examples of late capitalist industrialization, primarily from Germany and to some extent Japan, with comparative reference to the Korean case. As such, it is especially pertinent for understanding the development of civil society in Korea.

A consistent feature across cases of late industrialization is the prominent—often decisive—role played by the state in driving industrialization; the specific nature and extent of state involvement differ by case, shaping the patterns of social change that result. Nevertheless, in all instances, the state supported business, which retained ownership and responsibility for economic outcomes. The impact of the state on social transformation during late industrialization is determined by the prevailing social-structural conditions and the extent to which the state manipulates traditional values, behaviors, and institutions.

Although the social-structural outcomes of late industrialization are not uniform, Germany, Japan, and Korea share a strong statist or elitist tradition, in which the state stands above individuals or society and is seen as a leading force. This perception of the state is reflected in the ethos and evolution of civil society in Germany and Japan.

Neofamilism and Its Implications for Korean Civil Society

The three central dimensions of neofamilism—identity, individual survival strategies, and institutional consequences—carry significant implications for civil society. Neofamilial identity refers to how these ties shape an individual's sense of self and play a crucial role in determining strategies for survival. The strength and nature of one's neofamilial connections directly influence access to state power.

As a strategy, neofamilism involves leveraging these ties to advance socioeconomic interests; rather than adhering to universal norms, individuals utilize neofamilial relationships to pursue personal advantage. This practice undermines the consistent application of universal standards and predictability in administrative and legal processes.

At the institutional level, neofamilism is the outcome of its identity and strategic aspects. It encompasses the impact that neofamilial identities and survival strategies have on institutions. The proliferation of small, neofamilial units leads to a fragmentation of society's structural coherence, leaving institutions increasingly susceptible to external influence through these ties.

Neofamilism operates on both macro and micro scales. On the macro level, it inhibits the formation of class-based groupings, as evidenced by the prevalence of regionalism in Korean elections at all levels (legislative and presidential) (Kim, 1995, pp. 225–29). On the micro level, transfers and promotions within public bureaucracies are largely determined by school and regional affiliations, a pattern also seen in the business sector, where blood, school, and regional ties are prominent in management structures. These features call for a reassessment of other institutional outcomes of Korea's industrialization; widely held assumptions about a unified middle class, the rise of civil society, and bureaucratization must be critically reconsidered.

The Korean middle class is unified only by income, while its members remain divided by their varying degrees of access to state power. In reality, the entire society is stratified according to how accessible state power is to different groups. Regarding bureaucratization, contrary to common belief, the Korean bureaucracy has been hollowed out, with its bureaucratic characteristics significantly diminished.

The widespread presence of neofamilism in Korean society is evident through its structural and practical manifestations, permeating political, administrative, social, and cultural spheres. Neofamilism has become a defining element of personal identity and a crucial strategy for survival. Its prevalence carries significant consequences for civil society, regardless of how that term is defined. For example, neofamilial practices reveal that social trust is confined to small groups formed around school, blood, and regional ties. As a result, genuine communication and the flow of information are restricted, circulating only within these groups. Individuals seek "real" information, which is validated exclusively through neofamilial connections; trust is determined by the perceived reliability of the person sharing the information. Consequently, information is not widely disseminated, and the circle of contacts is limited to those with shared neofamilial ties, with differential treatment for those inside and outside these groups. Boundaries between different neofamilial groups are highly rigid. This situation poses serious challenges for legal universalism, as laws are not applied consistently or equally. In such a context, the concept of a modular personality is virtually unimaginable.

Equally important is the use of neofamilial ties primarily as a means to access state power and secure state-provided incentives. This behavior reflects a dependency on the state, which stands in stark contrast to the autonomy found in state-versus-society or state-in-society models. In fact, neofamilial practices in Korea contributed to a form of state-leading-society model, where both the state and society were weakened during industrialization: the state became "hollowed out" due to continual penetration by neofamilial groups, while society lacked a broader, abstract sense of collective identity beyond these small group affiliations.

This analysis demonstrates how neofamilism interacted with ruling opposition groups (elites) engaged in democratization, social movements, and political parties, helping to clarify the relationship between democratic transition and civil society.

The complexity of this relationship is rooted in the dual political orientations of the Korean masses, who both supported and participated in democratization while simultaneously maintaining anti-democratic tendencies as described. Rather than presuming alignment between the perspectives of the masses and those of opposition groups, it is necessary to account for the nuanced nature of their interactions.

A particularly important factor is the pronounced cognitive dissonance experienced between college life and post-college life. During their university years, most students felt a strong collective guilt for not actively joining student movements (Kim, 2011, p. 90). This psychological burden intensified after graduation, as individuals entered the business world and were compelled to adopt neofamilial practices for survival. In these circumstances, cognitive dissonance arose between lived experience and personal conscience, forming a psychological and emotional bridge between salaried white-collar workers and opposition groups, especially student organizations.

Political parties continued to exploit regionalism as a means of securing electoral support (Ha, 2024, pp. 154–55). Similar to the hollowing-out of the developmental state caused by 'dysfunctional' personalistic, tribal, or neofamilial allegiances, this same pattern is evident here, impeding the development of a more rational and mature policy and political system. Political parties failed to offer alternative policy choices or new frameworks for understanding politics, society, and international relations. Instead, they maintained an elitist approach, treating elections primarily as a formal mechanism for acquiring power.

In fact, Korean neofamilial practices contributed to a particular form of state-leading-society model, in which both state and society were weakened during industrialization: the state became "hollowed out" due to continual penetration by neofamilial groups, while society lacked a broader, abstract sense of collective identity beyond small group affiliations.

Concluding Remarks

This paper offered a new perspective for understanding the social and institutional consequences of late industrialization, using South Korea as a case study. It highlighted the institutional ironies of late industrialization, emphasizing how tradition was reintroduced to facilitate rapid development. The analysis demonstrated that traditional elements—such as blood ties, school ties, and regional ties—were incorporated through Park Chung Hee's distinctive recruitment patterns, which were subsequently adopted by the business sector and ultimately led to the emergence of neofamilism. Furthermore, the paper showed how neofamilism influenced state dynamics, civil society, and democratization, suggesting a more concrete approach to studying modernization. Finally, this work challenged universalist approaches to the social consequences of industrialization, underscoring the importance of contextualizing industrialization patterns to identify the distinct and unique social and institutional outcomes that result.

References

Dahrendorf, R. (1967). *Society and Democracy in Germany.* Doubleday.

Evans, P. (1995). *Embedded Autonomy: States and Industrial Transformation.* Princeton University Press.

Garrad, J. (2002). *Democratisation in Britain: Elites, Civil Society and Reform since 1800.* Palgrave.

Ha, Y. (2005). Pogŏn chŏngch'aek kyŏljŏng kwajŏng esŏ kukka ŭi yŏkhal: 1993nyŏn hanyak chojegwŏn punjaeng ŭl chungsimŭro [The Role of the State in Health Policy-Making: The Case of the 1993 Korean Herbal Pharmacy Disputes]. *Han'guk chŏngch'i yŏn'gu* [Journal of Korean Politics], 14(2), 33–68.

Ha, Y. (2024). *Late Industrialization, Tradition and Social Change.* University of Washington Press.

Hoffmann, D. L. (1994). *Peasant Metropolis: Social Identities in Moscow, 1929–1941.* Cornell University Press.

Hong, C. (1993). Han'guk esŏ ŭi hach'ŏng yeyŏrhwae kwanhan yŏn'gu [*A Study on the Subcontract System in Korea*] (Doctoral dissertation). Seoul National University.

Hong, W. (1999). Personal Communication, November 24.

Janelli, R. L. (1993). *Making Capitalism: The Social and Cultural Construction of a South Korean Conglomerate.* Stanford University Press.

Janelli, R. L., & Janelli, D. Y. (1982). *Ancestor Worship and Korean Society.* Stanford University Press.

Johnson, C. (1997). Preconception vs. Observation, or the Contributions of Rational Choice Theory and Area Studies to Contemporary Political Science. *PS: Political Science & Politics, 30*(2), 170–174.
Johnson, C., & Keehn, E. B. (1994). A Disaster in the Making: Rational Choice and Asian Studies. *National Interest, 36*(Summer), 14–22.
Jones, L. P., & Sakong, I. (1980). *Government, Business, and Entrepreneurship in Economic Development: The Korean Case*. Council on East Asian Studies, Harvard University.
Jowitt, K. (1983). Soviet Neotraditionalism: The Political Corruption of a Leninist Regime. *Soviet Studies, 35* (3), 275–297. https://doi.org/10.1080/09668138308411481
Kim, M. (1995). Chŏngch'i kyunyŏl, chŏngdang chŏngch'i kŭrigo chiyŏkchuŭi [Political Cleavages, Party Politics, and Regionalism]. *Han'guk chŏngch'i hakpo [Korean Political Science Review], 28*(2), 215–237.
Kim, S.-K. (1997). *Class Struggle or Family Struggle? The Lives of Women Factory Workers in South Korea*. Cambridge University Press.
Kim, W. (2011). *Ich'yŏjin kŏt e taehayŏ [Memories of Things Lost]*. Imaejin.
Kulp, D. H., II. (1925). *Country Life in South China: The Sociology of Familism*. Teachers College, Columbia University.
Lewis, P. M. (1992). Political Transition and the Dilemma of Civil Society in Africa. *Journal of International Affairs, 46*(1), 31–54.
Migdal, J. S. (1988). *Strong Societies and Weak States: State-Society Relations and State Capabilities in the Third World*. Princeton University Press.
Murakami, Y. (1984). *Ie* Society as a Pattern of Civilization. *Journal of Japanese Studies, 10*(2), 279–363.
Nettl, J. P., & Robertson, R. (1968). *International Systems and the Modernization of Societies: The Formation of National Goals and Attitudes*. Basic Books.
Nodongch'ŏng [Office of Labor Affairs]. (1977). *Han'guk nodong t'onggye yŏn'gam* [Yearbook of Labor Statistics of South Korea]. Sŏul Nodongch'ŏng. Office of Labor of Republic of Korea.
Ok, S. (1989). *Hyŏndae Han'gugin ŭi kajokchuŭi kach'igwan e taehan yŏn'gu* [A Study of Korean Perceptions of Familism] (Master's thesis). Seoul National University.
Park, C. (1965). *Choguk ŭi kŭndaehwa [Modernization of Fatherland]*. Tong A Ch'ulp'ansa.
Park, C. (1968). *Chungdan hanŭn cha nŭn sŭngnihaji mothanda [He Who Stops Does Not Win]* (S. Pŏmsik, Ed.). Hollym.
Park, C. (1969). *Pak Chŏnghŭi Taet'ongnyŏng yŏnsŏl munjip [Collection of President Park Chung Hee's Speeches]* (Vol. 3). Chimungak.
Park, C. (1971). *Minjok ŭi chŏryŏk [The Nation's Potential]*. Kwangmyŏng Ch'ulp'ansa.
Pak, C. (2017). *Kukka wa hyŏngmyŏng kwa na*. Seoul. Kiparang.

Skocpol, T. (1985). Bringing the State Back In: Strategies of Analysis and Current Research. In T. Skocpol et al. (Eds.), *Bringing the State Back In* (pp. 3–37). Cambridge University Press.

Smelser, N. J., & Swedberg, R. (1994). The Sociological Perspective on the Economy. In N. J. Smelser & R. Swedberg (Eds.), *The Handbook of Economic Sociology* (pp. 3–26). Princeton University Press; Russell Sage Foundation.

Vlastos, S. (Ed.). (1998). *Mirror of Modernity: Invented Traditions of Modern Japan*. University of California Press.

Walder, A. G. (1986). *Communist Neo-traditionalism: Work and Authority in Chinese Industry*. University of California Press.

CHAPTER 9

What Advanced Economies Can Learn from Korea: A View from Australia

Elizabeth Thurbon

Introduction

For decades, South Korea has been admired as a textbook case of successful late development. From the ashes of the Korean War, it became one of the world's most technologically advanced and globally competitive economies in just two generations. Scholars and policymakers have long studied Korea's catch-up strategy, highlighting the transformative role of its 'developmental state', its export-oriented industrialisation, and its mix of 'leapfrogging' and 'detouring' approaches to technological upgrading.[1] Yet while Korea is often hailed as a model for developing countries (e.g.

[1] Foundational accounts include: Johnson (1987), Cumings (1987), Amsden (1989), Haggard (1990), Wade (1990), Woo-Cumings (1991), Weiss and Hobson (1995), Mathews and Cho (2000).

E. Thurbon (✉)
University of New South Wales, Sydney, Sydney, NSW, Australia
e-mail: e.thurbon@unsw.edu.au

H.-k. Kwon (ed.), *Korean Political Economy from a Comparative-Historical Perspective*, Palgrave Series in Contemporary Korean Studies, https://doi.org/10.1007/978-981-95-9785-7_9

Lee, 2024), its approach to techno-industrial transformation holds at least as many lessons—perhaps more—for developed ones.

This article takes up that neglected task: to ask what Korea's story of techno-industrial transformation can teach policymakers in advanced economies. Specifically, it identifies ten lessons from Korea's past two decades that are highly relevant for policymakers in advanced liberal market economies like Australia. These lessons are drawn from Korea's strategic management of its transition from fast follower to innovation leader, all while navigating shifting geopolitics and the demands of the green transition.

This analysis is personal and political as well as scholarly. This point demands some elaboration. My deep interest in Korea's economic, social and political transformation began more than thirty years ago in the early 1990s when I was an undergraduate at the University of Sydney. I arrived there a wide-eyed teenager with no knowledge of—let alone interest in—questions of East Asian development. In fact, I had my sights set on a career in the performing arts, a dream shaped by my rather unconventional childhood.

I was born in the 1970s to parents who had both been professional actors before swapping the city stage for an isolated existence on Australia's pristine South Coast. I had the privilege of a childhood immersed in nature and my parents widely creative energy, hosting holidaymakers in the summer months and commuting each day by boat with my brother to our tiny primary school in the upper reaches of the estuary. It was a wonder-filled existence, but also an insulated one. My parents cared deeply about politics and social justice, their commitment to the latter—and our splendid isolation—informing their decision to send me, aged 12, to boarding school in Sydney with the Loreto nuns. But while Australian politics was often discussed at our dinner table, I knew little of international affairs. With overseas travel beyond our means and no exposure through schooling, I remained ignorant of the remarkable economic, political and social transformation taking place on Australia's doorstep in East Asia.

This all changed in my second year of university when I enrolled—almost by accident—in a course called *States and Economic Development*, taught by globally renowned scholar of state capacity, Linda Weiss. For the first time I encountered East Asia's extraordinary postwar economic story. I was also introduced to the idea that 'states' and 'markets' are constructed very differently across contexts, producing remarkably divergent outcomes. This might seem obvious to anyone reading this chapter today. But to my 19-year-old self it was a revelation. And that revelation sparked an interest, and that interest a passion to learn more, and more, and more—until I had not just taken every course available on the topic but also, under Professor Weiss' supervision, written an honours and doctoral thesis on the state's strategic role in Korea's remarkable development and, in 2003, secured a permanent position in the School of Politics and International Relations at UNSW Sydney, tasked with teaching and researching East Asian political economy.

Suffice to say that at some point in that journey, the dream of acting gave way to a drive to understand East Asia's development experience and the strategic role of the state in it. And the more I learned about Korea's highly strategic approach to governing its economy, the more striking the contrast with Australia's became, and the more concerned I grew about Australia's future prosperity and security. For by the early 2000s, Australia's policymakers had fervently embraced neoliberal ideas about the primacy of the 'free market' and the perils of government intervention in the economy. This market fundamentalism manifest most obviously in policymakers' disinterest in the structural composition of the national economy, their disregard for national manufacturing capability, and their deep aversion of anything approximating 'industrial policy'—by then one of the most derided terms in Australian political discourse.

At the time, this stance seemed at least partly—if superficially—defensible. After all, had Korea's disastrous performance in the 1997 Financial Crisis not proved the perils of interventionism?[2] And had Australia's booming resource economy not vindicated its commitment to 'comparative advantage' and hands-off economic management?[3] In this context, the idea of lesson learning from Korea may have appeared irrelevant at best and dangerous at worst.

How times have changed. Like many liberal market economies, Australia now faces a host of complex and interrelated vulnerabilities arising from its stagnant productivity, depleted manufacturing base, and exposure to the dramatic reshaping of global supply chains.[4] Decades of

[2] Spoiler alert: no. The East Asian economies that fared worst had in fact engaged in a process of rapid, reckless and ill-designed financial liberalisation in the lead up to 1997, exposing them to crisis. Those that had retained a significant degree of strategic interventionism, like Taiwan, fared much better. See Thurbon (2001, 2003).

[3] Again, no, and more on this below.

[4] These vulnerabilities have been well documented across a range of government, industry and NGO inquiries, investigations and reports, as reflected in extensive commentary through

deindustrialisation and state retreat from techno-industrial governance have left advanced economies deeply exposed to shocks arising from pandemics, climate change and geopolitical conflict. It has also left them ill-prepared to seize the massive national security- and prosperity-enhancing opportunities associated with the green transition (Thurbon et al., 2024).

Against this backdrop, Korea's ongoing efforts to strategically guide its economy and reorient and revitalise its techno-industrial base offer a striking contrast. Rather than clinging to past advantages, since the late 1990s Korea has deliberately positioned itself in new, frontier technology industries from smart grids to intelligent robotics and digital health. It has achieved this through neither market fundamentalism nor protectionism, but rather through a dynamic partnership between public institutions and private actors, animated by a shared national vision and a commitment to economic openness and market discipline. Now more than ever, the time is ripe to ask: what can we learn from Korea?

This chapter takes a small step toward answering that question. It draws on more than two decades of my own research into Korea's political economy—both individual and collaborative—which has involved extensive fieldwork and detailed historical analysis of the country's ever-evolving financial, industrial, and energy strategies.[5] It also builds on the insights of many scholars whose work has inspired and informed my own. Australia serves as a central point of comparison throughout, not because Korea's institutions and policies can or should be transplanted here (or elsewhere), but because the two countries share important features, face strikingly similar challenges, and express increasingly similar goals. To elaborate, both are open, mid-sized, export-dependent economies; both are deeply integrated with China while also anchored in the US alliance system; both are striving to build and strengthen sovereign capabilities and competitiveness in strategic industries; and both seek to exercise middle-power leadership in the region (and beyond), positioning themselves as development partners of choice in Southeast Asia and the Pacific in particular (Thurbon & Lee, 2022; Hynd, 2024).

organisations including the Asia-Pacific Development, Diplomacy, and Defence Dialogue (AP4D), the Lowy Institute, and the Australian Strategic Policy Institute (ASPI).

[5] In this context, I beg readers' patience if this chapter at some points feels self-referential – a risk associated with my embrace of an explicitly reflexive methodological approach for this piece of writing.

At the same time, Australia and Korea are closely bound together in economic and energy security terms. Their economies are deeply integrated, especially in energy trade. Both confront the existential threat of climate change and the parallel risk to their fossil-fuelled, export-oriented growth models. Each has much to gain—in terms of energy security, economic resilience, and regional influence—from pursuing a rapid and collaborative path to decarbonisation. For me, these are not just abstract parallels; I care deeply about the futures of both countries and see their trajectories as intertwined, with each having much to learn from, and contribute to, the other (although for reasons explained earlier I am concerned here with Korea's lessons for Australia).[6]

It is also important to emphasise that while Australia has much to learn from Korea, Korea—like Australia—faces many of its own pressing economic and social challenges, and its chaebol-dominated 'economic model' and approach to techno-industrial governance more generally are not without their limitations and indeed potential risks and perversions.[7] This much is clear from the extensive scholarly literature on Korea, and I have discussed these limitations, risks and perversions in my own work. Indeed, Korea's economic and social problems are now the subject of extensive commentary globally, thanks to the popularity of films and TV shows like Parasite and Squid Game that highlight the problem of economic inequality in particular. The aim of this chapter is not to reify Korea, or to suggest that Australia somehow tries to replicate the Korean economic model or adopt its approach to economic management holus-bolus. Rather it is to make the simple point that Korea has done some things very well, and that Australia and other advanced economies have much to gain from engaging more closely with—and thinking more carefully about—Korea's highly ambitious and strategic approach to governing the economy.

To this end, the chapter proceeds in four parts. First, it distils ten lessons from Korea's recent experience for advanced liberal market economies, illustrating each with Korean practice and Australian contrast. Second, it explores the barriers to lesson-learning in advanced economies, focusing on ideational, institutional, and political obstacles. Third, it

[6] I also acknowledge the excellent work of established and emerging Australian scholars including David Hundt, Alexander M. Hynd, Christopher Khatouki, Sung-Young Kim, Peter Lee and Lauren Richardson (and others) who, through both their research and engagement activities, also seek to strengthen relations between Australia and Korea.

[7] On the negative social consequences of Korea's 'compressed modernity' under developmentalism, see Chang (2022).

proposes five strategies to help overcome these barriers, drawing on both Korea's experience and emerging Australian experiments. Finally, it concludes by framing Korea not as a blueprint but as a mirror—inviting policymakers in advanced economies to question longstanding assumptions and revive their strategic imagination.

While the analysis focuses on Korea and Australia, its insights speak more broadly to developed countries grappling with the limits of market-led strategies and searching for more active, ambitious, and strategic approaches to promoting techno-industrial transformation for national prosperity and security.

1. A Developmental Mindset Makes the Difference

The most foundational lesson from Korea's economic success lies in the enduring importance of a developmental mindset among political and bureaucratic leaders. This shared outlook has driven successive generations of Korean policymakers to prioritise the goal of continual national techno-industrial transformation and competitiveness and to pursue that goal with such extraordinary ambition, discipline, and persistence.[8]

This mindset—which is characteristic not only of Korea but of Northeast Asia's capitalist 'developmental states' more broadly—is not reducible to ideology or party affiliation. Rather, it is a way of thinking shared widely among policy leaders born originally of Korea's turbulent history and struggle to build a strong, independent nation after decades of Japanese colonialism (1901–1945) and the devastation of the Korean War (1950–1953). Over the decades and since the early 2000s in particular, this mindset has been reinforced by a host of new challenges, from China's unexpectedly rapid rise as a major techno-economic competitor, to the energy, environmental and economic insecurities associated with the climate crisis, to intensifying US–China rivalry that places Korea's most vital economic and security relationships in tension.

At its core, the developmental mindset reflects a distinctive understanding of the purpose of the economy: to strengthen and secure the nation in

[8] On the origins, emergence and evolution of the Developmental Mindset in Korea from the early 1900s to the mid 2020s see Thurbon (2014a, 2016a). On the evolution of that mindset in the context of the energy transition from the mid-2010s to the present see Kim and Thurbon (2015); Thurbon et al. (2023a). This section draws on ideas developed in these publications.

a strategically uncertain world. A 'strong economy' is thus defined not merely by size or growth rate, as is common in the West, but by specific attributes, namely national manufacturing capability, technological autonomy, and export competitiveness. The developmental mindset also entails a distinctive way of thinking about the state and its economic role: because a strong economy is key to national security, the state can and should intervene strategically to advance economic goals. Crucially, interventions should not displace the market but help catalyse it. The developmental mindset views markets as indispensable engines of innovation and efficiency, but recognises that they often need direction, coordination, and risk-sharing to deliver nationally strategic outcomes. State action therefore works to crowd in private investment, create new opportunities, and accelerate learning, rather than substitute for entrepreneurial activity. In this way, the developmental mindset is entirely compatible with capitalism: it does not seek to override markets, but to harness them in pursuit of national resilience and prosperity.

While Korea's developmental mindset emerged in the 1960s from a unique blend of postcolonial nationalism, post-war urgency, and exposure to Japanese industrial strategy, it was institutionalised under successive regimes and has persisted across both conservative and progressive governments. Crucially, it has endured democratisation and remains prevalent to this day.[9] From the 1960s to the present, Korean leaders from across the political spectrum have broadly agreed that promoting long-term techno-industrial transformation and competitiveness is a core responsibility of the state.

This mindset manifests in several ways: the ongoing prioritisation of advanced manufacturing; sustained public investment in mission-critical technologies; and the principle that finance should serve production rather than speculation (as discussed further below). It also legitimises economic instruments often dismissed in liberal economies including development banks, strategic procurement, and conditional subsidies which are viewed not as 'market distortions' but as catalysts for *new market creation* and tools of national strategy.

Australia, by contrast, has long been guided by a liberal economic mindset and a related commitment to horizontal supports, 'market neutrality', and arms-length governance. Its brief experiment with manufacturing-focused industry policy in the postwar decades was

[9] See Thurbon (2014a, 2016a), Kim and Thurbon (2015)), Thurbon et al. (2023a).

systematically dismantled from the 1980s onward, replaced by a commitment to Australia's comparative advantage in raw commodities and, more recently, services.[10] The result has been a kind of institutional amnesia: Australian policymakers have largely forgotten how to value manufacturing as a national asset or to imagine a more strategic role for the state in helping to (re)build local techno-industrial capabilities, especially in industries deemed nationally significant. Alternative economic policy ideas are often simplistically and erroneously characterised by political leaders and the mainstream economists who advise them as 'soviet-style planning', a 'command economy' or 'picking winners'—labels that fundamentally misrepresent the Korean experience (more on this below). The lack of more sophisticated and nuanced thinking makes it difficult to have a sensible national debate about whether we need a more strategic approach to governing the economy in Australia, and what that approach might look like (Thurbon, Hynd, & Tan, 2023b).

To be sure, recent shocks have begun to challenge longstanding neoliberal assumptions in Australia and across the developed world. The COVID-19 pandemic exposed the fragility of global supply chains, while the climate crisis highlights the risks of dependence on fossil exports. These pressures have opened space for new language—'sovereign capability', 'economic security' and 'resilience'—to enter mainstream debate. The Albanese government's 'Future Made in Australia' agenda signals a tentative return to strategic thinking, though it remains deeply contested and currently under specified.

The Korean experience demonstrates that the policymaking mindset matters not just in moments of crisis but as a long-term foundation for ambitious, sustained, and disciplined strategy. The lesson is not simply to invest more in industry, but to do so with clarity of purpose, sustained commitment, and market-conforming modes of intervention aimed at establishing and maintaining global competitiveness. For developed countries like Australia, the challenge is to cultivate a new generation of

[10] Importantly, the developmental mindset is not foreign to Australia; on the contest between developmental and neoliberal ideas in the Australian context during the 1980s and 1990s and the eventual triumph of neoliberalism, see Thurbon (2012a, 2012b, 2016c). Many excellent Australian scholars have traced the emergence and analysed the impact of neoliberalism in Australia across a host of policy spheres, including Stephen Bell, Damien Cahill, Lynne Chester, Lindy Edwards, Elizabeth Humphrys, John Mikler, Michael Pusey, John Quiggin, Frank Stillwell, Dick Bryan, Phillip Toner and Michael Rafferty, among others.

policymakers who recognise that a more strategic approach to governing the economy is not about ideology but about meeting real-world security and development challenges with practical, goal-oriented, and market-compatible responses.

2. The Energy Transition is a Massive National Security Multiplier

Perhaps the most urgent and transformational lesson Korea offers advanced economies is its approach to the green energy transition. Where many countries still frame decarbonisation as a compliance burden or an economic trade-off, Korea has increasingly treated it as a national security multiplier. For Korean policymakers, the shift to clean energy is not just about cutting emissions, it is about strengthening industrial competitiveness, reducing dependence on imported fossil fuels, and enhancing resilience in a turbulent geostrategic environment.[11]

Korea's green industrial turn began in earnest in 2008 as a response to the Global Financial Crisis. Conservative President Lee Myung-bak launched Korea's 'Green Growth' agenda, one of the first national strategies in the world to link climate action directly to economic and security priorities. The logic was clear: Korea, which imports over 90% of its primary energy, is acutely vulnerable to external supply shocks and volatile global prices. By investing in renewables, efficiency, and smart grids, the government sought not only to decarbonise but also to reduce this strategic vulnerability, whilst laying the foundations for a new era of industrial transformation and economic growth.

Progressive President Moon Jae-in's New Deal of 2020—especially its 'green' aspects—built on this foundation, in the context of the COVID-19 pandemic. Far from a narrow environmental plan, it embedded climate targets in a wider techno-industrial strategy, coupling emissions reduction with investments in hydrogen, digital infrastructure, and clean transport. Korea's hydrogen roadmap is particularly revealing. By setting ambitious targets for hydrogen power and fuel-cell vehicles, the government aimed to cut dependence on imported oil while securing a leadership position in the emerging global hydrogen economy. State-backed R&D, market guarantees, and international partnerships supported this dual mission of

[11] See Kim and Thurbon (2015), Thurbon et al. (2023b, 2024); the following four paragraphs draw on these publications.

climate resilience and energy security, an exemplary case of what is best described as 'green energy statecraft' (Thurbon et al., 2024).

Just as significant, however, is Korea's distinctive sequencing strategy for the energy transition (Thurbon et al., 2021, Thurbon, Kim, et al., 2023a). Korea has tended to focus first on creating new clean industries and markets before moving aggressively to wind back the old.[12] The emphasis has been on building credible pathways for green growth, through investment, technology, and demand creation, before confronting the entrenched interests of fossil-fuel incumbents. This 'creation before destruction' approach has sought to make the transition more politically viable, while ensuring that jobs and industrial capacity are ready to absorb the shift away from carbon-intensive sectors.

In sum, from Lee Myung-bak's 'Green Growth' agenda in 2008 to Moon Jae-in's 'Green New Deal' in 2020, successive governments framed decarbonisation as integral to security—reducing reliance on imported fuels while positioning Korea to compete in emerging green industries. Environmental goals have functioned as directional signals, aligning public and private actors around missions that simultaneously advance economic, environmental, and security objectives.

By contrast, countries like Australia have often treated climate action as a zero-sum game: jobs versus the environment, growth versus regulation. This framing has narrowed debate to the costs of action, while obscuring the far greater costs of inaction—including heightened exposure to global fuel price swings and geostrategic risks from dependence on fossil-fuel trade. It has also meant Australia has been slow to capture value-added opportunities in clean commodities, advanced manufacturing, and low-emissions exports, despite world-class renewable resources.[13] Equally crucially, Australia has been slow to capture the enormous social security and justice benefits associated with the energy transition, including the benefits of both community and indigenous ownership of renewable energy (IORE), the latter holding incredible transformative potential for Australia

[12] China has pursued a very similar approach. On the similarities between the Korean and Chinese approaches to economic greening see Thurbon et al. (2023a). On China's approach to greening, see the foundational accounts by Mathews and Tan (2014), Mathews (2017) and Tan (2025).

[13] On the remarkable scope and scale of these opportunities see Garnaut (2019)

grappling with questions of justice for, and reconciliation with, First Nations people.[14]

The Korean lesson is clear: when the energy transition is understood as a security dividend, and sequenced through creation before destruction, public debate starts to shift. Instead of asking what climate action will cost, policymakers and citizens can ask what it will deliver: greater resilience against external shocks, enhanced social and economic security, justice and prosperity, and stronger geostrategic positioning. For Australia, adopting this mindset would reframe the transition from a defensive exercise in emissions management into an affirmative strategy for securing prosperity, sovereignty, and stability in a volatile world. Some of these insights are now beginning to surface in the Future Made in Australia agenda and the First National Clean Energy Strategy, which signal a welcome shift toward treating the green transition as a nation-building, justice-promoting, and security and prosperity-enhancing opportunity. But unless this framing takes deeper root across policy and politics, Australia risks treating the transition as an obligation to be endured rather than a strategic opening to be seized.

3. Competing at the Technological Frontier Demands a Strong State

A common assumption in liberal market economies is that the state's role in the economy should shrink as an economy develops, matures and globalises.[15] Once industrialisation has been achieved and institutions are in place, the market is presumed capable of allocating resources efficiently, with government intervention confined to correcting occasional 'market failures'. Korea's experience directly challenges this assumption. As it has approached and now competes at the technological frontier, the state's strategic role has not diminished—it has become more important.

At earlier stages of development, Korea's state intervention was often framed in terms of nurturing 'infant industries', providing targeted protection, or directing credit. These policies were crucial to Korea's

[14] On these vital opportunities especially in the IORE space see the work of the Australian First Nations Clean Energy Network and the foundational First Nations Clean Energy Strategy: https://www.firstnationscleanenergy.org.au/first_nations_clean_energy_strategy. For scholarly accounts see, for example, Norman et.al. (2025), Goodman et al. (2025) and Fish and Thurbon (2025).

[15] For a foundational examination and critique of this widely held assumption see Weiss (1998, 2005). For a more recent critique see Thurbon and Weiss (2020).

techno-economic catch-up, but they represent only one dimension of development strategy. Once Korea reached the upper middle-income stage in the 1990s, new challenges emerged. The country could no longer rely on imitation, licensing, or reverse engineering to climb the technological ladder (Kim, 1997; Mathews & Cho, 2000; Lee & Lim, 2001). Instead, it needed to generate its own innovations, often in areas where markets were not yet formed, demand was uncertain, and risks were too high for private actors to bear alone.

In this context, the Korean government's role shifted from *catching-up in existing markets* to *catalysing* and *pioneering* new ones. This meant creating the conditions under which entirely new industries and technologies could emerge and shaping incentives so that firms would invest in uncertain but strategically important directions. The government's catalytic role in bringing forth new technologies and industries—from green hydrogen, to smart grids, intelligent robotics and digital health—illustrates this principle.[16] In each case, policymakers have acted not because markets were failing in the conventional sense, but because the market for these future industries did not yet exist.

Korea's experience also highlights how 'market making' involves more than subsidies or R&D spending. It requires long-term strategic vision, institutional coordination, and close collaboration between public agencies, research institutes, and firms to share risks, knowledge and capital—more on this below.[17] For instance, the government's role in setting technology roadmaps, aligning standards, and anchoring demand through procurement has been as important as funding itself. This approach reflects an understanding that innovation ecosystems do not spontaneously organise; they must be deliberately structured and nurtured.

For liberal economies like Australia, this lesson is particularly salient. Policy debates still tend to portray intervention as a 'market distortion' at worst or 'correction' at best, and tolerable only in times of crisis. Yet Korea shows that when competing at the technological frontier, strategic state action is not a deviation from sound policy—it is the very condition for success.[18] Market creation is inherently uncertain, but government can

[16] See for example Kim (2012a, 2012b); Thurbon (2014b, 2016b), Thurbon and Weiss (2019), Thurbon et al. (2023a).

[17] See for example Lee and Lim (2001)), Kwon (2021), Lee (2019, 2024).

[18] The same argument has been made regarding the United States, see for example Mazzucato (2013) and Weiss (2014). For a comparison of US and Korean approaches to economic statecraft at the technological frontier see Weiss and Thurbon (2020)

reduce that uncertainty by signalling long-term commitment, coordinating investment, and absorbing early risks.

The broader implication is that a state's strategic activism—its economic statecraft—must evolve alongside the economy. As countries transition from catch-up to frontier innovation, the role of the state becomes more—not less—important. To succeed, governments must see themselves not simply as regulators or correctors, but as midwives of markets that do not yet exist. Korea's ability to sustain its technological edge rests on this insight. For advanced economies now struggling with deindustrialisation, climate crisis, and geopolitical rivalry, the message is clear: cultivating the industries of the future will require embracing the state's responsibility to make markets, not retreating from it.

4. Planning and Coordination Aren't 'Communist', They are Catalytic for Capitalism

In many advanced economies, the words 'planning' and 'coordination' carry (first) Cold War baggage, conjuring images of centralised command and communist inefficiency. Korea's experience shows this view is profoundly mistaken. Planning, when done well, is not about replacing markets but about catalysing them: setting direction, guiding investment, and creating the institutional conditions for private enterprise to flourish.

From the 1960s, Korea's leaders understood that building a strong and prosperous national economy could not be left to the 'free market'. In the wake of the Korean war, American advisors strongly encouraged Korea to focus on its 'comparative advantage' in agriculture and low-wage manufacturing, warning that attempts to build heavy industries would be wasteful and unrealistic. Korean policymakers strongly disagreed (Amsden, 1989). They recognised that path would lock the nation into perpetual under-development and strategic vulnerability. Instead, through planning and coordination, the state deliberately nurtured heavy and chemical industries, laying the foundations for global strength in steel, shipbuilding, and petrochemicals (Amsden, 1989; Woo-Cumings, 1991). This task was led by Korea's world-renown Economic Planning Board. But Korea's Five-Year Plans served as indicative frameworks rather than rigid blueprints. They set national priorities, mobilised finance, and signalled long-term direction, while leaving firms flexibility in execution. This was not communist dirigisme, but capitalist statecraft designed to break free of dependency and build long-term resilience.

To elaborate, the effectiveness of Korea's planning rested on three principles. Participation: strategies were shaped through structured dialogue with key ministries, firms, financiers, and researchers, ensuring diverse expertise and buy-in. Conditionality: access to state support was tied to strict performance benchmarks, reinforcing discipline and preventing state capture (more on this below). And adaptability: plans were living frameworks, revised in light of outcomes, technological advances, and global shocks. These principles transformed planning from rigid blueprinting into a dynamic process of learning and adjustment.

Korean policymakers also recognised that bureaucrats alone could not foresee technological trajectories or market opportunities. Effective planning thus relied on structured dialogue with corporate actors, who brought critical insights into technological bottlenecks and market dynamics, while the state provided coordination, finance, and discipline. This relationship of 'governed interdependence' between state and business (Weiss, 1995) ensured that planning was neither technocratic guesswork nor corporate capture, but a collaborative process that reinforced competitiveness both during that catch-up phase and later at the technological frontier.[19]

But vision without coordination invites failure. Korea's success also rested on robust institutions of coordination, which brought together ministries, firms, financiers, and researchers around shared goals. The Ministry of Information and Communication (MIC) in the early 2000s, for example, played a pivotal role in planning and coordinating Korea's transition into the knowledge economy (Kim, 2012a, 2012b). It synchronised infrastructure rollout, regulatory reform, and industry support, ensuring that the broadband revolution and semiconductor leap occurred in lockstep. By the early 2000s, Korea had become the world's most connected country, with near-universal high-speed internet access and globally competitive ICT firms like Samsung and Hynix.

A similar model guided Korea's Green Growth strategy. The Presidential Committee on Green Growth, created in 2009, was chaired by the

[19] A vast literature in the corporatist theory tradition explores the question of institutional design to maximise the benefits of public-private collaboration (such as information sharing) while minimising risks of capture. Australia has the opportunity to learn from these insights when deciding when and how to engage industry more closely for industry planning purposes. The burgeoning literature on the notion of 'discipline' in industrial policy, drawing inspiration from Alice Amsden's foundational work, is also instructive in this regard. See for example Pipkin (2026).

President (and later the Prime Minister reporting directly to the President). It convened senior officials from across government, alongside business, academia, and civil society, with authority to shape budgets and regulatory frameworks (Kim & Thurbon, 2015). Unlike many Western climate taskforces that remain siloed or symbolic, the PCGG acted as a genuine centre of orchestration: compelling ministries with narrow mandates—energy, environment, industry, finance, trade and foreign affairs—to work together, and embedding structured channels for firms to signal opportunities and constraints. This ensured that climate and industrial goals were treated not as trade-offs, but as mutually reinforcing national priorities.

For countries like Australia now experimenting with a more planned approach to techno-industrial transformation, the lesson is clear. Too often, policy design is fragmented across agencies, subject to electoral cycles, or dominated by ad hoc business lobbying. Business engagement is either superficial consultation or opaque influence, eroding trust and coherence. Korea shows that planning and coordination done well are not communist relics but catalytic instruments for capitalist renewal. They enable governments to set long-term missions, crowd in private investment, and build resilience through disciplined collaboration with firms. Without such mechanisms, strategies like *Future Made in Australia* risk drifting into incoherence or capture. With them, governments can steer markets toward transformative goals—from decarbonisation to technological sovereignty—and secure prosperity in an age of climate disruption and geopolitical uncertainty.

5. Always Ask "What's Next?": Avoiding the Incumbent Trap

One of the most distinctive features of Korea's developmental trajectory is its relentless orientation toward the future. At each stage of its industrialisation, Korea has asked: *what is next?*[20] Which sectors and technologies are emerging that will shape the global economy— and how can Korea position itself at the frontier? This forward-looking mindset has been crucial to avoiding the 'incumbent trap': the tendency of nations to cling to today's winners, protecting incumbent industries long after their

[20] My gratitude to Keun Lee for helping to articulate this insight.

dynamism has waned, and in the process missing the next wave of opportunity.[21]

The incumbent trap is a familiar story in many advanced economies. Governments double down on legacy industries because they employ many people, carry political weight, or generate short-term revenues. Incumbents often lobby to preserve their advantages, warning of dire consequences if subsidies are withdrawn or regulations tightened. Yet this defensive posture can breed stagnation: resources are tied up in declining sectors, innovation slows, and global competitors surge ahead in emerging industries. Coalitions of vested interests turn yesterday's strengths into tomorrow's liabilities.

Korea worked hard to avoid this trap. Its leading industries have rarely remained static. In the 1960s, textiles and light manufacturing formed the basis of export growth. By the 1970s, Korea had deliberately shifted into heavy and chemical industries, investing in steel, shipbuilding, and petrochemicals. In the 1980s and 1990s, consumer electronics, automobiles, and telecommunications equipment became the next growth engines. In the 2000s, Korea decisively entered semiconductors, mobile phones, and broadband infrastructure, becoming a global leader in ICT. More recently, Korea has expanded into biotechnology, advanced defense industries, and platform-based big tech. At each stage, the question of *"what's next?"* guided state planning, industrial coordination, and corporate strategy.

To be sure, this orientation was not about abandoning existing industries overnight. Korea continued to support steel or shipbuilding even as it invested in ICT and semiconductors. But policymakers and firms always kept an eye on the horizon, cultivating new capabilities before old ones began to plateau. Sequencing mattered: Korea entered new industries while its existing champions were still competitive, allowing time for skills, technologies, and ecosystems to take root.

Avoiding the incumbent trap also required institutional imagination. Ministries, planning agencies, and presidential committees convened not just to manage current sectors but to scan the horizon for emergent opportunities. Government–business forums, research institutes, and public R&D programs played a central role in identifying technological trajectories. And state support was often deliberately experimental, with funding

[21] For an insightful discussion of how the US fell into the 'incumbent trap' in the 1970s, ceding leadership in shipbuilding to Japan (who was then trumped by Korea), see Lee and Ki (2017).

spread across promising but uncertain sectors—from biosciences to digital platforms—and later narrowed to those with real global potential.

For advanced economies like Australia, the lesson is stark. Too often, industrial debates are dominated by defending incumbents: fossil fuel exports, legacy energy systems, or politically powerful sectors. This risks locking the nation into yesterday's strengths while others surge ahead in tomorrow's technologies. Korea's experience shows that effective economic statecraft must continually ask *what is next?*—not only in response to global shocks but in anticipation of them.

This does not mean chasing every technological fad. Korea's choices were disciplined by national strategy: sectors were selected not just for profitability but for their contribution to national resilience through advanced manufacturing capability, technological autonomy, and global competitiveness. By cultivating the capacity to identify and invest in emerging industries, Korea avoided stagnation and maintained its reputation as an adaptive, forward-looking economy.

Australia now faces its own version of the incumbent trap. Reliance on fossil fuel exports and a narrow set of commodities risks crowding out investment in clean energy, green commodities, and advanced manufacturing. To escape this dynamic, Australia must embed horizon-scanning and strategic foresight into its institutions, ensuring that new growth engines are fostered before old ones falter. Today, a great deal of strategic foresighting is going on in Australia—but it is largely being conducted by highly skilled and dedicated non-government organisations which have collectively done so much to demonstrate what Australia could gain from promoting the new green industries of the future, not least green iron.[22] Such organisations are now effectively 'plugging the gaps' in Australian state capacity for horizon scanning and related techno-industrial capability planning, the result of decades of hollowing out under neoliberally inspired reforms. Korea's example demonstrates that the ability to continually ask *what's next?*—and to act on the answer—is essential to long-term prosperity in an era of rapid technological change.

6. Make Finance Serve the 'Real' Economy

Another foundational lesson from Korea relates to the strategic way in which policymakers think about and govern finance. In the developmental

[22] See for example Finighan (2024) Pollard and Buckley (2025); WWF (2025).

mindset, finance has a primary purpose: to serve the 'real' (read: innovation- and production-related economy) and the government's nation-building agenda more broadly (Thurbon, 2016a). This mindset has long informed a strategic approach to governing finance, which includes aligning financial flows with long-term techno-industrial priorities, disciplining speculative behaviour, and ensuring that credit supports productive activity. Korea offers several powerful examples of how this strategic approach to governing finance has helped deliver transformative national outcomes.

First, Korea's Heavy and Chemical Industry (HCI) drive of the 1970s shows the potential power of strategic financial governance. The Korean state used its almost complete control over the banking sector to channel subsidised credit into steel, shipbuilding, and chemicals—industries deemed essential for strategic autonomy. These targeted flows of finance underpinned Korea's rapid industrial deepening, enabling it to shift from light manufacturing to complex, high-value sectors in less than a generation (Amsden, 1989; Woo-Cumings, 1991).

Second, Korea's disastrous experience in the 1997 financial crisis shows the perils of abandoning strategic financial governance. From the early 1990s, in the context of intense international pressure and growing divisions amongst domestic policymakers, Korea embraced what I have described as a rapid, reckless, and ill-designed approach to liberalisation, liberalising finance at breakneck speed, opening capital accounts and deregulating banks in ways that left the economy vulnerable to speculation and overcapacity (Thurbon, 2001, 2003). The result was the devastating 1997 Financial Crisis, when Korea had to accept an IMF bailout and painful restructuring. Taiwan, by contrast, pursued a far more strategic approach to financial liberalisation (Thurbon, 2001, 2007, 2020). It integrated far more cautiously with global markets, capitalising on increased access to foreign capital while maintaining its ability to limit speculation and keep finance and production connected, thereby avoiding a full-blown crisis.

Third, Korea's pivot to SME and venture capital financing shows the ongoing relevance of strategic financial governance in an innovation-intensive era (Thurbon, 2016a; Klingler-Vidra, 2018; Klinger-Vidra & Pacheco Pardo, 2025). Recognising the limits of chaebol-led growth, in the early 2000s, Korea expanded financial support for small and medium-sized enterprises (SMEs) and nurtured a vibrant venture ecosystem. The government created KOSDAQ in 1996 as a stock exchange for high-tech and venture firms, while policy institutions like the Korea Development Bank (KDB) and the Korea Technology Finance Corporation (KOTEC) seeded venture capital funds. The Small and Medium Business Administration also played a key role in expanding credit guarantees for smaller firms. These measures diversified the industrial base and supported new sources of innovation in IT, biotech, and green technologies.

Finally, Korea's recent green finance initiatives highlight the importance of strategic financial governance in an era of climate crisis. Through the (Green) New Deal and state-directed lending by KDB, financial governance has been harnessed to accelerate renewable energy, smart grids, and digital infrastructure. Here again, finance is deployed strategically to meet emerging challenges of climate change, along with technological disruption, and geopolitical competition (Kim & Thurbon, 2015; Thurbon, Hynd, & Tan, 2023b).

The broader lesson for developed economies is that strategic financial governance becomes more, not less, important in an interconnected and crisis-plagued world. For countries like Australia, long accustomed to liberal financial governance, this lesson is critical. As the 2008 Global Financial Crisis revealed, left to their own devices, financial markets often favour speculative or legacy (e.g. fossil fuel-related) asset classes and destabilise rather than strengthen national economies. Today in Australia, vast pools of superannuation savings are channelled into property or offshore assets rather than into the nation's clean-energy industries. A more strategic approach would re-align these funds with national transformation priorities—from green commodities (like green iron, ammonia, and aviation fuel) and critical minerals to advanced manufacturing and digital capability.

Recent steps toward building a national development finance architecture in Australia through institutions such as the Clean Energy Finance Corporation (CEFC), the National Reconstruction Fund (NRF), and the Australian Renewable Energy Agency (ARENA) mark an important shift in this direction. The creation of the NRF in particular is a landmark development: national development banks have long been central to the success of economies like Germany, Japan, and Korea, where they channel finance into productive sectors, accumulate deep industry expertise, and operate with a developmental mindset. Yet without equivalent ambition and coordination, Australia's new institutions risk underperforming if starved of the scale, coherence, and mission-driven ethos that makes development banks effective (Thurbon & Yates, 2023). To succeed, they must not only mobilise capital, but also cultivate the expertise, authority, and sense of higher purpose needed to genuinely transform the economy in a strategic direction.

Korea shows that strategic financial governance can make or break a nation's trajectory. A developmental mindset reframes the purpose of finance: not speculation or wealth extraction, but national transformation and adaptation. For countries facing the twin challenges of decarbonisation and de-globalisation, this lesson has never been more urgent.

7. Don't 'Pick Winners', Use Discipline so Winners Pick Themselves

One of the most enduring myths about Korea's approach to strategic techno-industrial governance is that the government simply 'picked winners' by choosing firms to receive subsidies and protection. In reality, Korea's strategy was far more disciplined (*c.f.* Amsden, 1989). The state did not lock in favourites regardless of performance. Instead, in sectors deemed strategic, it set tough performance standards and allowed winning firms to 'self-select' by demonstrating their ability to meet them. Access to government support was typically conditional, temporary, and contestable, a dynamic process that both rewarded proven capacity and disciplined firms to align with national priorities.

This performance-based discipline was most visible in the way Korea linked finance to export success in the 1960s and 70s (Amsden, 1989; Woo-Cumings, 1991). Subsidised loans and scarce foreign exchange were available only to firms that could prove themselves in international markets. Export targets were set annually, and companies that failed to deliver lost access to preferential support. This meant that firms effectively disciplined themselves to meet global standards, or else they were cut off. For example, in the Heavy and Chemical Industry (HCI) drive of the 1970s, the government identified strategic sectors—steel, shipbuilding, machinery, petrochemicals, electronics—but did not guarantee any one firm's dominance. Instead, firms were given ambitious production and export deadlines and those that failed to deliver were disciplined out of contention.

The same logic carried into Korea's technology programs of the 1980s and 1990s, intended to help Korea make the leap from imitator to frontier innovator (see for example Kim, 1997; Mathews & Cho, 2000; Lee, 2019). Initiatives such as the Highly Advanced National Project (HAN

Project) provided R&D subsidies for semiconductors, computers, and telecommunications, but firms had to co-invest and achieve technical milestones. Those unable or unwilling to commit resources were excluded. Here again, government support was used as a disciplinary lever: only those firms willing to invest, innovate, and deliver results were allowed to continue.

Even in the era of venture capital and SME support, the state applied similar principles.[23] Institutions like the Korea Technology Finance Corporation (KOTEC) offered credit guarantees only for firms that could demonstrate technological competence and growth potential. The creation of KOSDAQ in 1996 opened new finance channels for start-ups, but listing required firms to meet transparency and innovation benchmarks. Firms that fell short were denied access, reinforcing discipline in both financial and technological performance. This approach remains visible in Korea's green growth and hydrogen policies. Access to R&D funding, subsidies, and pilot projects has been tied to measurable outcomes such as efficiency improvements, deployment milestones, and export capacity. Firms unable to meet these standards typically lose out, ensuring resources flow toward those most capable of driving national transformation.

For advanced economies like Australia, the lesson is clear. Effective techno-industrial policy is not about governments trying to guess which firms will succeed. It is about disciplining firms through performance-based frameworks, rewarding results while punishing underperformance. Too often in Australia, subsidies, tax breaks, and concessional finance flow to incumbents—especially in fossil fuel industries—without strong conditionality or accountability. This risks entrenching the very actors who hold back transformation. Otherwise supports are offered as 'grants' to firms with no strategic oversight or performance monitoring—which risks wasting taxpayers money and eroding public confidence in and support for the state's strategic activism. Korea shows that discipline, not discretion, is what makes transformative techno-industrial policy effective. By holding firms to ambitious but clear standards, governments can mobilise private initiative, avoid capture, and ensure that public resources accelerate, rather than obstruct, national transformation.

8. Big is Beautiful but Clustering is Crucial

[23] See for example Thurbon (2016c), Klingler-Vidra (2018); Klingler-Vidra and Pacheco Pardo (2025).

Another key lesson Korea offers advanced economies is the importance of building industrial ecosystems that combine the dynamism of clusters with the strength of large firms. Too often in the West, policy debates polarise between celebrating small start-ups or lamenting the dominance of large corporations. Korea shows that real transformation requires both: vibrant local clusters and globally competitive giants (*c.f.* Kim, 2019; Lee, 2024).

The Korean case illustrates the role of what Sung-Young Kim (2019) has called 'hybridised industrial ecosystems' in driving and maintaining national competitiveness. These are systems in which large firms, SMEs, research institutions, and government agencies are interconnected in mutually reinforcing ways. Large firms provide scale, market access, and technological platforms, while clusters of smaller firms supply flexibility, specialised capabilities, and innovation. This hybridisation avoids the weaknesses of relying solely on fragmented SMEs or on monopolistic conglomerates: it creates an environment where different kinds of firms play complementary roles in industrial upgrading.

Korea's ICT revolution provides a vivid example. The rise of Samsung and LG as global champions in semiconductors, displays, and mobile devices was made possible not just by their own scale, but by dense ecosystems of suppliers, subcontractors, and research clusters. Government coordination, through bodies like the Ministry of Trade and Industry and the Ministry of Information and Communication, ensured that SMEs, universities, and large firms were networked together. The result was a national innovation system where breakthroughs could diffuse rapidly across the ecosystem, while large firms pushed Korean products into world markets.

Keun Lee's (2024) work reinforces this point by showing that large firms are not a developmental liability, but a developmental asset when properly governed. In Korea, the chaebol were subject to strict discipline, export targets, and technological upgrading requirements. They became vehicles for rapid catch-up, able to mobilise capital at scale and compete with multinational corporations on global terms. Without them, Korea's ascent in heavy industry, electronics, and shipbuilding would have been far slower and more precarious—if not impossible. At the same time, clusters and SMEs have been critical in diversifying Korea's economy and enhancing resilience. In sectors like automotive and ICT, networks of specialised suppliers co-located with large firms created dense webs of interdependence. These clusters enabled knowledge spillovers, rapid prototyping, and continuous productivity gains. Policies such as support for industrial parks, technology extension services, and SME financing were vital in sustaining these ecosystems.

The lesson for advanced economies is that industrial policy should not fall into the trap of "small is beautiful" or "big is best." Successful transformation depends on hybridised ecosystems where clusters of smaller firms are nurtured alongside large (preferably local) firms that can scale, export, and compete globally. The relationship is not zero-sum but symbiotic.

For Australia, this is particularly salient. Policy has often emphasised start-ups and SMEs while neglecting the need for strong anchor firms in clean energy, critical minerals, and advanced manufacturing. Without globally competitive large firms in the new, high-tech industries of the future, Australia risks being locked into resource extraction rather than capturing value-added opportunities. Australia's opportunity to pioneer clean commodities industries like green iron should be viewed as an opportunity to start building some of these hybridised ecosystems from scratch—while proactively seeking to avoid the pitfalls associated with Korea's chaebol-dominated growth model.[24] Korea's experience suggests that the path forward is to cultivate clusters and anchor firms together, creating hybridised ecosystems capable of driving innovation, scaling production, and competing internationally.

9. Use Demand to Drive Innovation, Production and Productivity

Another crucial lesson from Korea is that demand-side policy—especially strategic public procurement—can be a powerful catalyst for innovation, production and productivity. Korea has long used its purchasing power to stimulate demand for emerging technologies, create lead markets, and scale new sectors.

This has been particularly evident in information and communication (ICT) and green technologies. Korea's government has committed to procuring hydrogen fuel cell and electric vehicles and installing smart grid infrastructure, for example. These actions have provided guaranteed

[24] As noted at the outset and discussed later in this chapter, Korea is also now experiencing the downsides that can arise from the unchecked expansion of large firms. Australia has the opportunity to bake-in discipline from the outset, so as to maximise the social returns to capital associated with any publicly-supported industry building initiatives.

demand that derisks private investment and accelerates commercialisation. Importantly, this has been done within the constraints of international trade rules, such as the WTO's Government Procurement Agreement (GPA).

In fact, Korea has exploited every inch of the policy space available under its trade obligations (Thurbon, 2015, 2016b). It uses broadly conceived 'value for money' criteria, local content provisions, and innovation incentives in procurement law—not as protectionist tools, but as market-making strategies. This contrasts sharply with Australia, where public officials often misinterpret trade rules as prohibiting even modest strategic interventions (Thurbon, 2015, 2016b, 2016c). This ideational constraint is costly. Australia's procurement system represents more than $100 billion in annual spending—yet little of it is strategically deployed to foster domestic capability, stimulate innovation, or accelerate green transition. Compared with other countries across the developed world—especially the United States—Australia has a woeful track record of using the enormous purchasing power of the government strategically, in the national interest.[25]

Indeed unless the Australian government can overcome its entrenched aversion to strategic public purchasing, it risks missing the opportunity to anchor new clean industries at scale and compromising the Future Made in Australia agenda. Long-term government-backed offtake agreements for green iron, green hydrogen and other clean commodities would provide the market certainty investors need to commit to these massive projects. This is the logic behind the proposed Clean Commodities Trading Initiative (CCTI): using government-backed demand to create markets for clean exports, while minimising risks and maximising rewards to the government and taxpayers (Thurbon & Yates, 2025). Without demand-side mechanisms like these, Australia's energy transition risks stalling before its industrial potential is realised.

Korea's lesson is simple but powerful: governments can and should create early markets for strategic technologies and products. Waiting for global demand to emerge is a high-risk, low-return strategy. By contrast, using public procurement and supply contracts to support emerging industries builds domestic capability, accelerates learning, and sets countries up for global leadership. In the context of the green transition especially, demand is not a passive function—it is a strategic lever. Korea has

[25] On the US's highly strategic approach see Weiss and Thurbon (2006) and Weiss (2014). On Australia's poor performance see Thurbon (2014a, 2015, 2016c).

shown that even under liberal trade rules, states can be active market shapers.

10. Progressive Economic Nationalism Sustains Strategic Activism

In Korea, economic nationalism has long been a foundational element of statecraft. But it is not the exclusionary, defensive nationalism associated with populist movements elsewhere. Rather, it is strategic, outward-looking, and oriented toward progressive global leadership (Thurbon, 2016a; Rodrik, 2023).

This nationalism is rooted in Korea's historical experience of colonisation, war, and dependency, where economic weakness equated to national vulnerability. Economic development became central to sovereignty, dignity, and international standing. That imperative justified ambitious industrial policy, targeted investment in strategic sectors, and strong state–firm coordination—even as Korea remained deeply committed to international trade and cooperation.

National purpose continues to shape economic debate. Plans to invest in batteries, AI, or green hydrogen are not framed only in terms of competitiveness, but as contributions to national resilience, climate responsibility, and global problem-solving. This was the precise framing of Korea's National Strategy for Green Growth, and the related establishment of the Korea-based Global Green Growth Institute (GGGI), dedicated to assisting the pursuit of more sustainable industrial transformation across the developing world (while also boosting Korea's international status and prestige). This sense of collective mission legitimises long-term risk-taking, patient capital, and strategic selectivity.

Australia, by contrast, has often treated 'economic nationalism' as a pejorative term, equating it with inefficiency or parochial protectionism. As a result, strategic policies have struggled for narrative legitimacy. Public debate has been dominated by fiscal score-keeping, with little room for national missions or shared purpose and pride in what we can achieve together when we put our minds to it. Yet there are signs of change. Prime Minister Albanese has invoked a language of progressive patriotism, recasting national pride as compatible with openness, social inclusion, and international responsibility. This reframing creates discursive space to legitimise more ambitious forms of statecraft centred on promoting economic prosperity and national resilience at home and abroad. The Albanese government's ambition to host CoP31 in 2026 held much potential in this regard—insofar as it represented the opportunity to link a transformative national economic project with the ambition to become a more responsible and valued development partner for countries in our region, especially our Pacific Island neighbours as they grapple with the imminent existential threat of climate change.

Korea's experience shows that nationalism can be a progressive and productive: a means of aligning economic policy with social goals, environmental stewardship, and democratic accountability. For Australia and other developed countries, the challenge is to reclaim economic nationalism from reactionary forces and rearticulate it as a tool for equitable and sustainable transformation, recognising that building the economy is inseparable from securing the nation.

Barriers to Lesson Learning

Despite Korea's clear relevance, meaningful lesson-learning from its transformative development trajectory remains rare among advanced liberal market economies.[26] This is especially true in countries like Australia, where deep-seated ideological, institutional, and political obstacles inhibit the serious consideration of Korean-style techno-industrial strategies. The following five barriers help explain why even well-evidenced policy successes in Korea remain neglected or misinterpreted in the West.

1. Ideational Path Dependency: Neoliberalism's Enduring Grip

The most deeply entrenched barrier is ideological. For over four decades, neoliberal economic orthodoxy has dominated policymaking in liberal democracies. Under this logic, markets are seen as the most efficient allocators of resources, and the state's role is confined to correcting clearly defined 'market failures' through 'neutral', price-based instruments like carbon taxes or emissions trading schemes. Structural interventions such as direct public investment, industry planning, or procurement-linked industrial development are viewed as inefficient, distortionary, or even dangerous.

[26] With the exception of COVID-19, where Korea's highly effective management (also grounded in its high degree of state capacity) is widely cited as an example for developed and developing countries alike.

In this context, Korea's proactive, goal-oriented statecraft - if acknowledged at all - is viewed as alien or undesirable. Its use of development banks, public R&D institutions, targeted procurement strategies, and performance-based subsidies are regarded with suspicion: outdated at best, dirigiste at worst. Australia's policymakers have tended to internalise these neoliberal logics, often downplaying their own strategic discretion under international trade agreements, and defaulting to passive, horizontal and often unbankable policy instruments even in the face of urgent economic transformation challenges.

As noted at the outset, this ideational path dependency limits the policy imagination. Strategic techno-industrial policy is dismissed as 'soviet-style planning' or 'picking winners.' National capability strategies are erroneously framed as protectionist. As a result, the very tools that underpinned Korea's transition from follower to leader are marginalised before they can be meaningfully debated.

Dismantling this barrier requires more than policy change—it demands intellectual renewal. This is already underway, with a new generation of scholarship making the case for a more strategic and proactive approach to governance centred around the themes of national resilience through sovereign capability, 'mission-driven' innovation, clean energy transformation, and 'abundance'.[27] But these ideas must now be widely socialised and institutionalised if they are to compete with dominant paradigms (more on this below).

2. Institutional Fragmentation and Policy Silos

Even when ideational shifts occur, institutional barriers can stifle reform. As noted earlier, one of Korea's greatest assets is its coordinating

[27] While the valuable work of American and European thinkers has recently become a point of reference among more open-minded policymakers, it is important to acknowledge that Australia has its own tradition of thinkers who have long argued for a more strategic approach to techno-industrial governance, often drawing inspiration from countries our own region that have so much to teach us. Equally important is the need to learn from Australia's First Nations knowledge holders, whose deep expertise in long-term stewardship, place-based environmental management, and the sustainable governance of natural resources offers valuable insights for navigating the energy transition in ways that are both environmentally responsible and socially just. Indeed, to effectively address the challenges now confronting the nation, it is imperative that Australian policymakers overcome the cultural cringe that has long hindered the exploration and adoption of home-grown and regional solutions to our distinctive national challenges.

capability which, while not failsafe, delivers a relatively high degree of institutional coherence. Over the decades, various ministries and para- or supra-ministerial bodies have been charged with coordinating long-term strategy, managing inter-agency collaboration, and anchoring policy continuity across electoral cycles.

Australia's institutional architecture could hardly be more different. Responsibilities for economic transformation are spread across a range of poorly integrated agencies including Industry, Treasury, Climate Change, and others. These departments operate under separate ministers, budget processes, and performance criteria. Coordination is often informal, episodic, or reliant on individual personalities. Frequent ministerial turnover has also made coherent industry strategy difficult—more than ten ministers have cycled through the industry and innovation portfolio in the past decade, while short-term budgetary cycles also discourage long-term planning. At the same time, in recent years Australia has seen a proliferation of state-backed financing vehicles from the Clean Energy Finance Corporation to the National Reconstruction Fund, and ARENA—each with overlapping agendas and lacking the overarching mandate or central authority needed to orchestrate cross-sectoral missions.

Overcoming Australia's institutional fragmentation requires more than creating new agencies. It demands real integration mechanisms: interdepartmental missions, shared performance frameworks, and strategic coordination centres. Korea's experience offers templates for how this can be done—but any solution will need to be carefully tailored to Australia's distinctive set of capabilities and challenges—including the challenge of federalism

3. Misconceptions of East Asian Exceptionalism

A subtler but pervasive barrier to lesson-learning is the belief that Korea's success is exceptional and culturally inimitable. This narrative suggests that Korea's development model is a function of Confucian values, a compliant population, or a history of authoritarian governance—factors foreign to Western liberal democracies.

This 'East Asian exceptionalism' narrative has a dual effect. On one hand, it creates admiration: Korea is praised as a 'miracle' economy. But on the other, it discourages emulation. If Korea's achievements are seen as culturally specific, path-dependent, or 'miraculous', then its policy tools and approaches are viewed as incompatible with Western systems and values.[28]

This framing is intellectually lazy and politically convenient. It absolves policymakers in countries like Australia from seriously engaging with the design features, institutional arrangements, and strategic orientations that underpin Korea's success. It also underestimates Korea's democratic evolution—since the late 1980s, Korea has become one of Asia's most vibrant democracies, with a free press, competitive elections, and an active civil society. Yet it still engages in sophisticated techno-industrial governance, including planning.

But perhaps most importantly, this framing downplays the crucial role of human agency and learning in Korea's transformation. Korea's strategic policymakers are not superhuman; they did not always think and act so strategically or have the capability to do so. Rather, their unwavering commitment to transforming their nation crystalised at a particular moment in time, in response to intensely felt national challenges. And their strategic governance capabilities were not innate but learned through a process of experimentation, trial and error. Their goal-orientation gave them a risk appetite that might feel foreign to policymakers in Australia, but it is certainly not alien to the West. Indeed the risk appetite of American techno-economic policymakers during the (first) Cold War far exceeded anything seen in Korea (Weiss, 2014; Weiss & Thurbon, 2020).

In sum, Korea's development was not the product of inherent cultural traits, but of strategic choice, institutional innovation, and policy learning. Its transformative trajectory is not a relic of authoritarianism, but a case of adaptive statecraft, demonstrating how democracies can build techno-industrial capacity through accountable, responsive, and inclusive mechanisms. At the same time, learning from Korea does not require copying its institutions or policies wholesale. It requires recognising that its success came from strategic coherence, not cultural uniformity; from bold experimentation, not static tradition. It requires moving beyond admiration (or uninformed aversion) to serious analytical engagement.

4. The Power of Vested Interests

[28] Relatedly, it is fair to say that a sense of cultural and/or racial superiority has prevented many Western nations from looking to East Asia for inspiration—to the West‘s great detriment.

A further obstacle to lesson learning from Korea lies in the entrenched power of vested interests. In Australia—as in other liberal democracies—powerful actors in the fossil fuel sector especially have shaped policy in ways that privilege private super-profits profits over long-term national interest. These actors benefit from regulatory inertia, oppose state intervention, and resist any effort to redirect subsidies or impose performance standards. This resistance is not limited to lobbying or media campaigns. It is institutionalised through revolving doors between business and politics, influence over party financing, and deeply embedded policy networks (Wilkinson, 2025; Mikler & Ryan, 2024; Robert et al., 2025). These actors also frame the narrative, positioning industrial policy as a risk to investor confidence or free trade.

Korea, too, has faced vested interests—particularly in the form of chaebol resistance to restructuring. But the state has shown greater (though not absolute) willingness and capacity to discipline, negotiate with, and redirect these actors toward national missions (Thurbon, Kim, et al., 2023a). Australia has yet to develop such strategic leverage. Tackling this barrier requires political will, regulatory reform, and alliance-building. It also requires reframing industrial strategy not as anti-business, but as pro-enterprise—with a clear distinction between rent-seeking incumbents and innovation-oriented challengers.

5. Weak Narrative Infrastructure and Public Imagination

Finally, lesson-learning is limited by narrative weakness. In Korea, economic development has always been tied to a national story—of postcolonial recovery, national security, modernisation, and global prestige. These narratives have helped align elite and popular interests, legitimise risk-taking, and sustain ambitious missions even under economic stress.

In Australia, economic discourse is dominated by 'market forces', 'comparative advantage' and 'efficiency' (rather than 'effectiveness', which barely rates a mention). There is little public language for talking about transformative national agendas or strategic economic renewal. As noted earlier, terms like 'industrial policy' and 'planning' are often met with scepticism or confusion.

Yet narrative power is essential to build support for any transformation. People must be able to see themselves in the future being built. They must understand not only what is being done, but why. Korea's successive national strategies, most recently the National Strategy for Green Growth and the Green New Deal were all anchored in powerful narratives about national survival, collective resilience, dignity, status and prestige. There is a broader lesson here: that 'statecraft' demands 'soulcraft' to be effective (*c.f.* Lefebvre, 2025).

During the 1997–1998 Asian Financial Crisis, the Korean government launched a campaign to help the nation repay its IMF bailout debt. Ordinary citizens responded in remarkable fashion: millions came forward to donate family heirlooms, jewellery, and even wedding bands in a collective effort to bolster the country's foreign reserves. This unprecedented act of solidarity was possible because the crisis was framed not simply as an economic downturn but as a national survival challenge—a test of Korea's sovereignty and dignity. The mobilisation revealed the depth of Korea's narrative infrastructure: decades of developmental statecraft had embedded a story linking economic strength to national security and collective resilience. It was this powerful narrative that enabled such extraordinary civic participation, aligning personal contributions with the larger project of safeguarding Korea's independence and future.

The 'Future Made in Australia' slogan is a start—but it must be filled with substance, backed by shared purpose, and connected to everyday experiences. Narrative infrastructure is not window dressing: it is an essential foundation of state capacity, helping shape expectations, legitimise statecraft, and coordinate actors around shared national goals.

Overcoming Obstacles: Strategies for Lesson Learning

Recognising the barriers to lesson learning is only the first step. The harder task is designing strategies to overcome them, particularly in advanced liberal market democracies where ideological resistance, institutional weakness, and political inertia run deep. This important topic is rightly the focus of a separate analysis. But based on Korea's experience, international research, and my own contributions, the following five strategies are offered as practical pathways to enable strategic statecraft in countries like Australia.

1. A Discursive Shift: From Industrial Policy to Statecraft

One of the most important steps is a discursive shift. In Australia, the language of industry policy has become politically poisonous (Thurbon et al., 2023b). Decades of partisan politics and neoliberal orthodoxy have cast it as synonymous with protectionism, inefficiency, and 'picking winners' (Thurbon, 2016c). The result is that serious proposals for strategic investment or government–business coordination are quickly dismissed, regardless of their merit. Even when adopted, the term conveys a narrow, technocratic exercise in sectoral support, rather than a bold national project. What is needed is a discursive shift: from 'industry policy' to statecraft (Weiss & Thurbon, 2020; Thurbon et al., 2023b, 2024). Statecraft signals something far more ambitious. It frames economic strategy not as tinkering at the margins, but as a purposeful effort to build the productive, technological, and institutional capacities that underpin national security and resilience. Whereas 'industry policy' suggests isolated interventions, 'statecraft' invokes long term vision, coordination, and nation-building. This distinction matters in a time of polycrisis, when climate change, supply chain fragility, and geostrategic rivalry are interlocking and compounding. Addressing these challenges requires integrated missions that mobilise resources across government, business, and society, not piecemeal policies with narrow aims. Statecraft legitimises such ambition, aligning Australia with global peers who are already pursuing nation-building strategies. In a world where resilience is security, and security depends on economic strength, Australia cannot afford to remain trapped in the limiting language of industry policy.

2. Change how we recruit and train bureaucrats

One major obstacle to a more strategic approach to techno-industrial governance in Australia lies in the way we recruit and train our bureaucrats. The Australian Public Service has long been dominated by officials trained in mainstream economics, with its emphasis on market efficiency, fiscal restraint, and comparative advantage. This intellectual homogeneity has fostered a narrow understanding of the state's role in the economy, reinforcing the view that governments should only 'fix' market failures rather than actively shape and create markets. By contrast, East Asian developmental states have deliberately cultivated heterodox traditions. In Korea, for example, the KDI School of Public Policy and Management has long trained civil servants in development economics and innovation policy, embedding comparative and historical perspectives. In Japan, the Ministry of International Trade and Industry (MITI, now METI) ran extensive in-house programs that blended economics with engineering and industry knowledge, ensuring officials could evaluate and coordinate technological upgrading.

To overcome its own constraints, Australia must broaden the intellectual foundations of its bureaucracy. Recruitment should seek out candidates trained in heterodox economics, innovation studies, and economic history, as well as those with deep industry and technological expertise. Training should expose officials to comparative statecraft traditions, preparing them to collaborate with firms, assess strategic potential, and design adaptive, mission-oriented policies. Without this shift in mindset and skillset, Australia will remain ill-equipped to pursue the ambitious economic statecraft required in an era of polycrisis.

3. Build Durable Institutions with Clear Mandates

No strategy can succeed without institutional architecture. Durable, resourced, and strategically empowered institutions are essential to techno-industrial transformation. Ad hoc funding announcements or fragmented pilot programs will not deliver national capability at scale. What is needed are agencies that can withstand electoral cycles, shape private expectations, and provide long-term policy consistency.

Korea's Ministry of Trade, Industry and Energy (MOTIE) plays such a role. It integrates energy, technology, industrial, and trade strategy into a coherent whole. Its development banks (KDB, KEXIM) provide targeted finance. Its R&D institutions are aligned with industrial missions. This ecosystem enables coordination, learning, and the alignment of public and private investment over time. Australia, by contrast, has a patchwork of institutions—ARENA, CEFC, NRF, various research councils—all doing good work, but often without overarching coordination, secure funding, or embedded mandates. At the same time, there is scope to institutionalise and properly resource the requirement that state and federal agencies should investigate and learn from international best practice. Here, we could see DFAT and AUSTRADE play increasingly important roles as facilitators and enablers of knowledge-sharing and 'lesson learning'—between Australia and other countries especially within our region.[29]

Institution-building is not just administrative—it is political. It requires building coalitions to support the new institution's mission, designing structures that balance autonomy and accountability, and embedding long-termism in a political system biased toward short-term wins. Korea's success lies not only in the institutions it built, but in the strategic consensus that sustained them. Australia needs its own equivalent of MOTIE: a central coordination body that links industry, innovation, energy, and trade. Without such institutional glue, policies will remain fragmented, vulnerable, and underpowered.

4. Use Crisis as a Strategic Opening

Crises disrupt routines, shake assumptions, and create windows for institutional innovation. Korea has long understood how to turn crisis into transformation. The 1997 Asian Financial Crisis was used to restructure its financial system, streamline the chaebol, and launch a new wave of tech investment. The 2008 Global Financial Crisis catalysed green stimulus and public R&D investment. COVID-19 accelerated Korea's digital health systems and biotech platforms. In each case, Korea did not merely respond to crisis—it used it to build. This capacity reflects the presence of 'institutional entrepreneurs': reform-minded actors who link short-term emergency measures with long-term strategic visions.

Australia has not historically excelled at seizing such moments. The GFC led to temporary stimulus, but no major institutional legacy. The COVID pandemic exposed supply chain fragilities but did not yield lasting capability strategies—until the belated creation of the NRF. The climate crisis has prompted some action, but largely through regulatory or incentive frameworks, not structural transformation.

To overcome this pattern, Australia must learn to treat crises not as interruptions to be managed, but as strategic openings to reimagine its economic model, build enduring capabilities, and align emergency response with long-term national purpose. With the right strategic vision, Australia's next crisis could become not just a test of resilience, but a catalyst for lasting renewal.

[29] I am very grateful to Caroline Wang for this valuable suggestion.

5. Forge Policy Coalitions Across State, Industry, and Society

Korea's policy success has always depended on coalitions. The state did not act alone. It built strategic alliances with firms, universities, research institutions, and citizens. These coalitions enabled policy continuity, public legitimacy, and coordinated learning. Even during democratic transition, Korea's developmental compact remained resilient because it was embedded across sectors.

In Australia, policymaking has often been adversarial and siloed. Industry policy is debated without industry. Innovation policy is shaped without long-term R&D partners. Climate policy is made without manufacturing stakeholders. But there are signs of change. The Net Zero Economy Agency, emerging clean industry alliances, and new university-led policy platforms suggest growing appetite for cross-sector collaboration.

To move from isolated reforms to systemic transformation, Australia needs coalitions capable of delivering shared missions (e.g. green iron, battery supply chains), joint ventures (e.g. sovereign manufacturing projects), co-investment platforms (e.g. strategic funds with blended finance), and policy learning spaces (e.g. multi-stakeholder road-mapping processes). Such coalitions must include not just policymakers and industry, but researchers, unions, Indigenous leaders, and communities. They must be built on trust, transparency, and shared benefit—not transactional lobbying.

Conclusion: Korea as a Mirror, Not a Blueprint

Korea's experience of rapid techno-industrial transformation is not a blueprint to be copied. It is, rather, a mirror—one that allows developed countries to re-examine their own assumptions about the necessity and desirability of a more strategic approach to governing the economy to meet pressing national challenges and build long-term security and prosperity.

A few qualifiers are in order. First, the ten lessons identified here are not exhaustive. Korea offers many other sources of inspiration: the economic dividends of sustained investment in education and skills, for example, or the role of cultural capital—from K-pop to the broader Korean Wave—in bolstering national identity, pride, and international influence (see for example Cha & Pacheco Pardo, 2023). At the same time, Korea also faces serious challenges of its own, including but not limited to an ageing population, high wealth concentration, rising inequality, youth unemployment, job precarity, and persistent labour repression relative to its democratic peers in Northeast Asia, Japan and Taiwan (see for example Khatouki, 2025). Similarly, while this chapter has emphasised what Australia can learn from Korea, liberal market economies such as Australia also excel in areas from industrial relations to social security, environmental stewardship and multiculturalism, which may hold lessons for Korea in return.

Yet these caveats do not blunt the central point: Australia, like many developed economies, stands at a crossroads. It must decarbonise, rebuild its industrial base, and secure its economic sovereignty in an increasingly volatile world. Korea's experience shows that this is possible—but only if we abandon outdated assumptions and reclaim the strategic imagination. To learn from Korea is to remember that 'economic development' is not a transitional phase but an ongoing process of national transformation. And the success of that transformation depends on a more strategic approach to governing the economy. Unless Australia embraces this lesson, and does so quickly, its security and prosperity will remain fragile—and its immense potential to emerge as a prosperous, equitable cohesive, and sustainable nation will remain unfulfilled.

Acknowledgements My enormous gratitude to the many scholars—especially my collaborators—whose work has helped inspire and shape this chapter; all cited in context herein. My thanks also to the wide circle of Korean and Australian policy, industry and NGO practitioner-experts who I've had the good fortune of engaging with over many years; their probing questions and crucial insights have also shaped my thinking on this topic. Many provided invaluable feedback on this chapter and I can't thank them enough. I also acknowledge my personal AI assistant, Chaz, which I used as a workshop partner to help test my ideas and assist with editing. Drawing solely on my own corpus of scholarly and policy work, Chaz provided feedback on my initial drafts and helped me clarify arguments and identify and reduce repetition. All articulations, arguments, interpretations, conclusions—and any errors—are my own.

Funding This work was supported by the Laboratory Program for Korean Studies through the Ministry of Education of the Republic of Korea and the Korean Studies Promotion Service of the Academy of Korean Studies (AKS-2018-LAB-1250001).

References

Amsden, A. H. (1989). *Asia's Next Giant: South Korea and Late Industrialization.* Oxford University Press.

Cha, V., & Pardo, R. P. (2023). Korea: a new history of South and North. Yale University Press.

Chang, K-S. (2022). The logic of compressed modernity. Cambridge: Polity Press.

Cumings, B. (1987). The Origins and Development of the Northeast Asian Political Economy. In F. C. Deyo (Ed.), *The Political Economy of the New Asian Lndustrialism* (pp. 44–83). Cornell University Press.

Fish, A., & Thurbon, E. (2025). Advancing Energy Sovereignty and Economic Prosperity for First Nations Through Green Energy Statecraft. *Cosmopolitan Civil Societies: An Interdisciplinary Journal, 17*(2), 71–83.

Finighan, R. (2024). *The New Energy Trade: Harnessing Australian Renewables for Global Development.* Melbourne: The Superpower Institute. https://www.superpowerinstitute.com.au/work/the-new-energy-trade

Garnaut, R. (2019). *Superpower: Australia's Low-Carbon Opportunity.* Black Inc.

Goodman, J., Norman, H., & Ghosh, D. (2025). Indigenous Responses to Climate Change: From Climate Colonialism to Indigenous Climate Justice. *Cosmopolitan Civil Societies, 17*, 1–5. https://doi.org/10.5130/ccs.v17.i2.9911

Haggard, S. (1990). *Pathways Font the Periphery.* Cornell University Press.

Hynd, A. M. (2024). *Becoming Middle Powers: Identity, Status, and Order in the Asia Pacific.* PhD Thesis,. UNSW Sydney.

Johnson, C. A. (1987). Political Institutions and Economic Performance: The Government-business Relationship in Japan, South Korea, and Taiwan. In F. C. Deyo (Ed.), *The Political Economy of the New Asian Industrialism* (pp. 136–164). Cornell University Press.

Khatouki, C. (2025). *Embedded Repression and the Political Economy of Labour Contention in South Korea.* PhD Thesis. UNSW Sydney.

Kim, L. (1997). *Imitation to Innovation: The Dynamics of Korea's Technological Learning.* Harvard Business School Press.

Kim, S. Y. (2012a). Transitioning from Fast-Follower to Innovator: The Institutional Foundations of the Korean Telecommunications Sector. *Review of International Political Economy, 19*(1), 140–168.

Kim, S. Y. (2012b). The Politics of Technological Upgrading in South Korea: How Government and Business Challenged The Might of Qualcomm. *New Political Economy, 17*(3), 293–312.

Kim, S. Y. (2019). Hybridized Industrial Ecosystems and the Makings of a New Developmental Infrastructure in East Asia's Green Energy Sector. *Review of International Political Economy, 26*(1), 158–182.

Kim, S. Y., & Thurbon, E. (2015). Developmental Environmentalism: Explaining South Korea's Ambitious Pursuit of Green Growth. *Politics and Society, 43*(2), 213–240. https://doi.org/10.1177/0032329215571287
Klingler-Vidra, R. (2018). *The Venture Capital State: The Silicon Valley Model in East Asia*. Cornell University Press.
Klingler-Vidra, R., & Pardo, R. P. (2025). *Startup capitalism: New approaches to innovation strategies in East Asia*. Cornell University Press.
Kwon, H. K. (2021). *Changes by Competition: The Evolution of the South Korean Developmental State*. Oxford University Press.
Lee, K. (2019). *The Art of Economic Catch-Up: Barriers, Detours and Leapfrogging in Innovation Systems*. Cambridge University Press.
Lee, K. (2024). *Innovation–Development Detours for Latecomers: Managing Global-Local Interfaces in the De-globalization Era*. Cambridge University Press.
Lee, K., & Ki, J. H. (2017). Rise of Latecomers and Catch-Up Cycles in the World Steel Industry. *Research Policy, 46*(2), 365–375.
Lee, K., & Lim, C. (2001). Technological Regimes, Catching-up & Leapfrogging: The Findings from the Korean Industries. *Research Policy, 30*(3), 459–483.
Lefebvre, A. (2025). *From Statecraft to Soulcraft: How the World's Illiberal Powers Like Russia, China and Increasingly the U.S. Rule Through Their Visions of the Good Life*. Noema. 4 March https://www.noemamag.com/from-statecraft-to-soulcraft/
Mathews, J. A. (2017). *Global Green Shift: When CERES Meets Gaia*. Anthem Press.
Mathews, J. A., & Cho, D. S. (2000). *Tiger Technology: The Creation of a Semiconductor Industry in East Asia* (Vol. 389). Cambridge University Press.
Mathews, J., & Tan, H. (2014). Economics: Manufacture Renewables to Build Energy Security. *Nature, 513*, 166–168. https://doi.org/10.1038/513166a
Mazzucato, M. (2013). *The Entreprenurial State*. Penguin.
Mikler, J., & Ryan, I. (2024). Gaslighting Australia: The Instrumental Power of Australia's Mining and Energy Industries. *Australian Journal of Politics & History, 70*(4), 720–740.
Norman, H., Briggs, C., Langham, E., Apolonio, T., Miyake, S., Niklas, S. & Teske, S. (2025). *Local Aboriginal Land Council Powershift: Sharing the benefits of energy transition*. Sydney, Australia Public Policy Institute.
Pipkin, S. (2026). Discipline to flourish: a framework for the political economy of discipline in industrial policy. *Review of International Political Economy*, (firstonline) 1–22.
Pollard, M., & Buckley, T. (2025). *Green Metal Statecraft: Forging Australia's Green Iron Industry*. Climate Energy Finance. https://climateenergyfinance.org/wp-content/uploads/2024/11/CEF_Green-Metal-Statecraft_FINAL.pdf
Robert, J. T., Milani, C., Jacquet, J., & Downie, C. (2025). *Climate Obstruction: A Global Assessment*. Oxford University Press.

Rodrik, D. (2023). Doing Economic Nationalism the Right Way. *Project Syndicate*, 7 November. https://www.project-syndicate.org/commentary/east-asian-model-vindicates-economic-nationalism-by-dani-rodrik-2023-11.

Tan, H. (2025). *China's International Energy Relations: The Impact of Transition from Fossil Fuels to Renewables*. Cambridge University Press.

Thurbon, E. C. (2001). Two Paths to Financial Liberalization: South Korea and Taiwan. *The Pacific Review.*, *14*(2), 241–267.

Thurbon, E. C. (2003). Ideational Inconsistency and Institutional Inertia: Why Financial Liberalisation in South Korea Went Horribly Wrong. *New Political Economy*, *8*(3), 341–361.

Thurbon, E. C. (2007). The Developmental Logic of Financial Liberalisation in Taiwan. In W. Garside (Ed.), *Institutions and Market Economies: The Political Economy of Growth and Development* (1st ed., pp. 87–106). Palgrave Macmillan.

Thurbon, E. C. (2012a). From Developmentalism to Neoliberalism and Back Again? Governing the Market in Australia from the 1980s to the Present. In K.-S. Chang, B. Fine, & L. Weiss (Eds.), *Developmental Politics in Transition: The Neoliberal Era and Beyond* (1st ed., pp. 274–298). Palgrave Macmillan.

Thurbon, E. C. (2012b). Ideas and Industrial Governance: Has the Influence of Neoliberalism been Overstated? In D. Cahill, L. Edwards, & F. Stilwell (Eds.), *Neoliberalism: Beyond the Free Market* (pp. 180–203). Edward Elgar Publishing Limited.

Thurbon, E. (2014a). Australia: Public Purchasing and Innovation: The Australian Case. In *Public Procurement, Innovation and Policy: International Perspectives*, 35–63. https://doi.org/10.1007/978-3-642-40258-6_3.

Thurbon, E. C. (2014b). The Resurgence of the Developmental State: A Conceptual Defence. *Critique Internationale*, *63*(April/May), 59–75. https://doi.org/10.3917/crii.063.0059

Thurbon, E. C. (2015). The Abandonment of Procurement-Linked Strategic Activism in Australia: Standing Still with Room to Move. *Australian Journal of International Affairs*, *69*(5), 577–594. https://doi.org/10.1080/10357718.2015.1048780

Thurbon, E. (2016a). *Developmental Mindset: The Revival of Financial Activism in South Korea*. Cornell University Press.

Thurbon, E. C. (2016b). Trade Agreements and the Myth of Policy Constraint in Australia. *Australian Journal of Political Science.*, *54*(4), 636–651. https://doi.org/10.1080/10361146.2016.1239569

Thurbon, E. C. (2016c). Trade and Industry Policy: The Growing Partisan Divide. In M. Beeson & S. Hameiri (Eds.), *Navigating the New International Disorder: Australia in World Affairs 2011–2015*. Oxford University Press.

Thurbon, E. (2020). The Future of Financial Activism in Taiwan? The Utility of a Mindset-centred Analysis of Developmental States and Their Evolution. *New Political Economy*, *25*(3), 320–336. https://doi.org/10.1080/13563467.2018.1562436

Thurbon, E., & Lee, K. (2022). A New Agenda for Australia-Korea Cooperation: Building a Development-Friendly Trade and Investment Regime. *The Asia Society*. 23 February.

Thurbon, E., & Weiss, L. (2019). Economic Statecraft at the Frontier: Korea's Drive for Intelligent Robotics. *Review of International Political Economy, 28*(1), 103–127. https://doi.org/10.1080/09692290.2019.1655084

Thurbon, E., & Weiss, L. (2020). The State of Development in a Globalized World. In E. Vivares (Ed.), *The Routledge Handbook to Global Political*. Conversations and Inquiries. Routledge. https://doi.org/10.4324/9781351064545

Thurbon, E., & Yates, O. (2023). 'The Immense Power and Importance of Australia's Newest Bank' The Mandarin. 13 December. https://www.themandarin.com.au/236461-the-immense-power-and-importance-of-australiasnewest-bank/

Thurbon, E., & Yates, O. (2025). *The Case for an Australian Clean Commodities Trading Initiative [Studies in Statecraft]*. AsiaPacific Development, Diplomacy & Defence Dialogue. https://asiapacific4d.com/idea/ccti

Thurbon, E., Kim, S. Y., Mathews, J. A., & Tan, H. (2021). More 'Creative' Than 'Destructive'? Synthesizing Schumpeterian and Developmental State Perspectives to Explain Mixed Results in Korea's Clean Energy Shift. *Journal of Environment and Development, 30*(3), 265–290. https://doi.org/10.1177/10704965211013491

Thurbon, E., Kim, S. Y., Tan, H., & Mathews, J. (2023a). *Developmental Environmentalism: State Ambition and Creative Destruction in East Asia's Clean Energy Shift*. Oxford University Press.

Thurbon, E., Hynd, A., & Tan, H. (2023b). We Urgently Need $100bn for Renewable Energy. But Call it Statecraft, Not 'Industry Policy', Opens in a New Window. *The Conversation*. 13 September.

Thurbon, E., Hynd, A., Tan, H., Park, S., & Walter, A. (2024). *Green Energy Statecraft for Comprehensive National Security*. AP4D Studies in Statecraft #2024. Asia-Pacific Development, Diplomacy & Defence Dialogue, Canberra | Reimagining the Economy, Harvard Kennedy School, Boston, M.A.

Wade, R. (1990) Governing the Market: Economic Theory and the Role of Government in East Asian Industrialization, Princeton, Princeton University Press.

Weiss, L., & Hobson J. (1995). States and Economic Development: A Comparative Historical Analysis.

Weiss, L. (1995). Governed interdependence: Rethinking the government-business relationship in East Asia. The Pacific Review, 8(4), 589–616.

Weiss, L. (1998). *The Myth of the Powerless State*. Cornell University Press.

Weiss, L. (2005). Global Governance, National Strategies: How Industrialized States Make Room to Move under the WTO. *Review of International Political Economy, 12*(5), 723–749.

Weiss, L. (2014). America Inc.?: innovation and enterprise in the national security state. Cornell, Cornell University Press.

Weiss, L., & Thurbon, E. C. (2006). The Business of Buying American: Public Procurement as Trade Strategy in the USA. *Review of International Political Economy, 13*, 701–721.

Weiss, L., & Thurbon, E. (2020). Developmental State or Economic Statecraft? Where, Why and How the Difference Matters. *New Political Economy, 26*(3), 472–489. https://doi.org/10.1080/13563467.2020.1766431

Wilkinson, M. (2025). Woodside vs The Planet: How a Company Captured a Country. *Quarterly Essay, 99*, 1–89.

Woo-Cumings, M. (1991) Race to the Swift: State and Finance in Korean Industrialisation. New York: Columbia University Press.

WWF/Deloite. (2025). Forging Futures: Changing the Nature of Iron and Steel Production. Sydney. https://assets.wwf.org.au/image/upload/f_pdf/WWF_Green_Steel_Forging_Futures_Report_2025

www.ingramcontent.com/pod-product-compliance
Ingram Content Group UK Ltd.
Pitfield, Milton Keynes, MK11 3LW, UK
UKHW021615260926
475829UK00011B/95
* 9 7 8 9 8 1 9 5 9 7 8 4 0 *